Studying the

PRESIDENCY

Studying the

PRESIDENCY

EDITED BY

George C. Edwards III

AND

Stephen J. Wayne

The University of Tennessee Press

KNOXVILLE

Library of Congress Cataloging in Publication Data

Main entry under title:

Studying the Presidency.

Includes index.

1. Presidents — United States — Research — Addresses,
essays, lectures. 2. Presidents — United States — History
— Sources — Addresses, essays, lectures. I. Edwards,
George C. II. Wayne, Stephen J.

JK518.S78 1983   353.03'13'072   82-17472

ISBN 0-87049-378-7

ISBN 0-87049-379-5 (pbk.)

To RICHARD E. NEUSTADT

who led the way

CONTENTS

Studying the

PRESIDENCY

An Introduction to
Research on the Presidency

STEPHEN J. WAYNE

Political observers have written excellent interpretations of
the Presidency. Important questions about Presidential
power have been raised. But considering the amount of such
writing in relation to the base of original empirical research
behind it, the field is as shallow as it is luxuriant. To a
great extent, presidential studies have coasted on the
reputations of a few rightfully respected classics on the
Presidency and on secondary literature and anecdotes
produced by former participants.

Hugh Heclo, "Studying the Presidency:
A Report to the Ford Foundation"
(August 1977)

Problems

PAST

Why has the presidency received so much public attention but until recently so little scholarly inquiry? What is the problem? Is it the nature of the office, the requirements of social science methodology, or the goals of political scientists themselves?

Part of the difficulty undoubtedly lies in the phenomenal growth of the presidency: the expansion of its powers, the enlargement of its staffs, the evolution of its processes. Although these developments have captured the imagination and often the adulation of many journalists, jurists, and political scientists, they have not generated a great deal of social science research. On the contrary, concerns about the need for a stronger president (from the 1930s through much of the 1960s), for a more responsible and accountable president (from the late 1960s to the mid-1970s), and for a more effective and politically savvy president (from the late 1970s to the present) may have actually detracted from systematic and rigorous analysis and contributed to the normative, almost evangelic tone of much of the literature. Presidency watchers seem to have fixated on the Promethean character of the office.

The rapidity of developments also helps account for the gap between organizational and operational changes and knowledge about them. Time is often necessary to differentiate permanent from ephemeral adjustments in structure and process. Time may also be needed to produce sufficient data to examine these adjustments within a comparative perspective. That perspective, in turn, is necessary if patterns are to be seen in the data and generalizations drawn from them.

Nevertheless, institutional developments alone are only partially responsible for the dearth of theoretically sophisticated and empirically relevant literature. The perception that such research would be extremely difficult to conduct has contributed to its scarcity and has taken on the aura of a self-fulfilling prophecy.

4

For years, the so-called behavioral revolution in political science seemed to pass the presidency by. Why? It has been alleged that the general unavailability of data, the lack of measurable indicators, particularly quantitative ones, and the absence of theory impede the collection and analysis of data, thereby discouraging empirical research.

Each of these difficulties did and to some extent still does exist. Obtaining current and reliable information about the presidency has frequently not been easy. Some structural and many operational aspects of the institution have been shrouded in secrecy. Political considerations have often dictated that sources remain anonymous and information be sanitized. Although most official words and actions get into the public record quickly and completely, internal memoranda, option papers, and in-house negotiations can remain behind closed doors for years.

The perception that primary source material on the presidency is not generally available has led many students of the office to depend on insiders for information. Interviews with those who have held official positions in the executive branch have furnished much contemporary documentation. Journalistic and personal accounts have also supplemented this record. The difficulty with relying on this type of information is that it is inevitably limited by and to the perspective of the respondent. Insiders not only have a point of view but frequently a need to justify their policies and behavior in office. Political exigencies and personal needs color perceptions, affect memories, and ultimately influence what is said and to whom it is said. Imprecise recall constitutes another hazard with which interviewers have to deal on a more or less regular basis.

In addition, those in high positions with severe constraints on their time frequently must limit their own accessibility to those outside the government. This is usually done on a need-to-know basis. Well-known journalists and correspondents with large audiences tend to qualify much more easily by the use of this criteria than do political scientists. Getting in the door can be quite a problem, particularly for those without the proper pedigree (such as graduate students).

These factors account for the highly subjective, often frag-

5

mentary, and frequently impressionistic nature of much of what is gleaned from participant observers. They make the compilation of a comprehensive, objective record extremely difficult.

These problems, both real and imagined, have limited the scope of inquiry on the presidency. Potentially important subjects such as political and public liaison, symbolic and moral leadership, and transitions into and out of office have been neglected or understudied because of the inability to obtain empirically relevant information. There have been few comparative studies across administrations and of executives of other governments. Psychologically oriented leadership studies have been in relatively short supply, and the economic advisory process has only recently attracted scholarly attention.

Data problems have also constricted modes of inquiry. They have affected concept formulation, hypothesis generation, and theory building. The lack of comprehensive and comparative data within and among administrations has impeded the testing of propositions, as has the inability to identify a broad range of quantitative measures. Other than approval ratings, voting studies, and legislative scorecards, little material on the presidency has lent itself to quantitative analysis. Even more basic and critical has been the failure to agree on operational indicators of key concepts, such as influence (in Congress), prestige (with the general public), and reputation (within the Washington community). If the measures used are not regarded as valid indicators of the concepts, then the validity of the research findings remains in doubt.

Some of the methodological problems are of the political scientist's own choosing. By concentrating on personalities, on dramatic situations, and on controversial decisions and extraordinary events, students of the presidency have reduced the applicability of social science techniques. Though less glamorous, the making of noncrisis decisions, the operation of standardized processes, and the on-going submissions of advice through normal channels are more amenable to the testing of hypotheses and the building of theories. Regularities in behavioral patterns can be established, typologies developed, and generalizations proposed.

Moreover, it is usually easier to reduce the level of analysis and thereby exercise more control over relevant variables. Crisis decisions, on the other hand, are likely to be more complex. Identifying, much less measuring, key variables in such cases is apt to be extremely difficult.

With few aspects of the institution and even personal behavior amenable to hypothesis testing, there has been little theory on the presidency. What has resulted is a largely descriptive literature replete with narrative, case studies, and interpretative essays. The nature of the literature has increased the difficulty of getting articles published in leading political science journals, particularly during the 1960s and early 1970s, when methodological sophistication and theoretical relevance were deemed to be the most important attributes of social science scholarship and criteria for publishing it. Concomitantly, it has magnified the influence of the small number of reputed classics, particularly those of Edward S. Corwin, Clinton Rossiter, and Richard E. Neustadt.[1] For years, their studies set the tone and affected the substance of much of the presidency literature, generating uncritical acclaim and critical commentary but little empirical research in the process. Similarly, James David Barber has provoked a vigorous (even vicious) debate, but one that has centered primarily on his methodology not his principal findings.[2] That only a few works have had such a large impact has led one political scientist to remark with only modest exaggeration: "To read most general studies of the United States presidency . . . is to feel that one is reading not a number of different books but essentially the same book over and over again. The same sources are cited; the same points are made; even the same quotations . . . appear again and again."[3]

PRESENT

MANY of these problems still persist. The president remains a prime focus of attention and concern. His activities continue to influence the research agenda. Pressures to address current issues and to express judgments on the efficacy and morality of presidential responses have not abated, nor are they likely to do so.

The institution of the presidency is less accessible than others in the government, particularly the legislature. Scholars continue to have difficulty interviewing senior presidential aides, and the information on many decisions and actions is often very sketchy. Nor, in the short run, do primary sources usually provide a complete and comprehensive record. Quantifiable data that cover a wide range of presidential activity is extremely limited.

In addition, conceptual problems cloud research objectives, and the paucity of models generates fishing expeditions. Controversy over the meaning of several key terms and their operational referents has often impeded communication and impaired the conclusions of hypothesis-testing studies.

Finally, priorities within the discipline continue to provide a mixed set of incentives. Although the importance of the contemporary presidency obviously attracts students and directs their research toward key decisions, actions, and policies, the difficulty of applying social science methods tends to discourage those who desire to utilize rigorous, analytic procedures and techniques from doing so.

Potentialities

In one sense this book, or at least the motivation for writing it, is testimony to the continued existence of these problems. The difficulties that political scientists have encountered in studying the presidency and the dissatisfaction that has been voiced with some of their efforts have provided the *raison d'être* for this undertaking. In another sense, however, the existence of this methodological guide and commentary indicates that some of the problems can be overcome. Not only do the contributors believe that more social science research is desirable, but their contributions demonstrate that it is possible.

This book is organized into two parts: Approaches and Analyses and Data Sources and Techniques. The selections in each are designed to correct common misperceptions on the availability of data, adequacy of models, and utility of quantitative methods for studying the presidency.

The discussion of approaches, concepts, and analysis indicates a range of analytic potentialities from hypothesis testing to theory building. These not only suggest the theoretical value for adopting a more scientific methodology but point to the practicality of doing so. Models have been fruitfully employed to explain and predict presidential behavior. Quantitative measures have been used to assess presidential influence and evaluate policy formation.

The chapters on sources of information note that more primary material is available than is generally thought to be the case, that it is not solely historical or qualitative in character, and that it is not restricted to scholars based in Washington, D.C. There are a variety of quantitative data and a range of underutilized sources from congressional publications to legal documents to statistical compilations of one type or another. Similarly, the expansion of the presidency and the institutionalization of its processes have actually improved access by creating more insiders, particularly at the second echelon, who have a need to relate their experience to others.

The growing availability of data has produced a miniexplosion of political science studies on the presidency in recent years. They have ranged from accounts of the political process to models of advisory systems and decision-making structures to analyses of presidential effectiveness within various political arenas. In addition to broadening our knowledge of the presidency, this literature has increased our ability to study it.

The surge of research has coincided with a change in emphasis within the discipline, continuing interest in executive behavior, and increasing incentives and opportunities for presidency scholars. Following years of lauding science for its own sake and of

9

using scientific criteria to judge the merits of manuscripts submitted for journal publication, political scientists have altered the emphasis of their subject matter and relaxed their methodological standards. The late 1960s and the 1970s saw a shift to the study of public policy and related matters. The impact of ideology, the expansion of the mass media, the demands of outside groups, all have become issues of major concern. Given the president's central role in the formulation, adoption, and implementation of national policy, this new disciplinary emphasis has refocused scholarly attention on the executive. Moreover, it has placed students of the presidency in a favorable position to examine questions of public policy, and many of them have.[4]

Several of these policy analyses have been predicated on qualitative data. Some discuss significant normative questions. Descriptive accounts and argumentative essays have begun to appear with some regularity in leading journals. A quarterly devoted to the study of the presidency, *The Presidential Studies Quarterly,* has been created as has another new journal, *President and Congress.* The prospects of getting presidency research published have thus been greatly increased by the appearance of these and other scholarly outlets.

Opportunities for presenting professional papers have also increased. In 1978 the Presidency Research Group (PRG) was established. Designed to provide a forum for scholarship on the presidency, the PRG has begun to publish a newsletter on current research, and it has sponsored a series of panels at the annual meetings of the American Political Science Association (APSA). The interest generated by these PRG panels combined with the nudging of several prominent political scientists has persuaded the planners of the official APSA convention program to devote more attention to the study of the presidency. In 1978, only two panels focused directly on that institution. In 1979 there were eight, and each year from 1980 to 1982 there have been an average of ten.

The collective seeds of these incentives have begun to bear fruit. A principal aim of this book is to stimulate them further. The final section of this introduction briefly outlines the selections written for this volume.

A Brief Outline of the Contents

Part I deals with approaches, cases, concepts, and analysis. It begins with a comprehensive overview of the major perspectives that have been employed to study the presidency: legal, institutional, political, and psychological. In Chapter 1, Stephen J. Wayne describes basic assumptions underlying these perspectives and the models, both implicit and explicit, that have been used as explanatory, and in some cases, predictive tools. Criteria for theory building are presented and used to assess the presidency literature.

Norman C. Thomas examines case studies in Chapter 2. Noting their heuristic value and theoretical potential as well as their limitations, Thomas discusses the ways in which case studies have been and can be used to generate propositions about presidential behavior. He uses a wide variety of examples from the literature to support his position.

John H. Kessel looks at conceptualization in Chapter 3. He is primarily concerned with the constraints it imposes on the conduct of research. Illustrating from his own work, *The Domestic Presidency,* Kessel discusses the kinds of decisions he had to make and the influences he felt when reviewing the literature, operationalizing concepts, formulating the design, and collecting and analyzing data.

In the fourth chapter, George C. Edwards III discusses the merits of quantitative research. He notes the types of data that are generally available and the ways in which they can be analyzed. While indicating the limitations of such analyses, he also indicates their potential for overcoming the descriptive character of much of the presidency literature. Edwards concludes with a plea for more quantitatively oriented work.

Part II focuses on the sources and methods of data collection. Documentary material and personal accounts are examined to demonstrate the wide range of diversified information that is generally available on the presidency.

In Chapter 5, Jennifer DeToro identifies and describes traditional and computer indexes as well as collections of other primary data. She explains how to use this material in doing research on the presidency. Particularly noteworthy is her elaboration of the increasing number of information-retrieval systems that can be employed to create bibliographies and generate factual data on the institution.

Chapter 6, by G. Calvin Mackenzie, explores congressional documents. Included are bills and resolutions, committee hearings and reports, the *Congressional Record,* and various codifications of public laws. Research aides such as those published by the *Congressional Quarterly, National Journal,* and Government Printing Office are also described and evaluated on the basis of their payoff for presidential research. In pointing to additional sources of information, he notes trade presses, Public Affairs Information Service, and various scholarly literature. He concludes with examples of strategies that might be employed in conducting research in presidential relations with Congress.

Louis Fisher provides a perspective on the whys and hows of legal research in Chapter 7. He indicates how to locate a law and how to follow its interpretations by the courts. The chapter contains guides to a variety of legal documents and a short section on current legal research on the presidency.

Two chapters on presidential libraries follow. In Chapter 8, Martha Joynt Kumar provides a survey of the kind of data that is generally available in the libraries and its comparability across administrations. Department and agency files, oral histories, and personal diaries are reviewed, and the author discusses the perspectives that can be obtained from such data as well as the pitfalls of using them. The final part of the chapter offers suggestions on the conduct of library research.

In Chapter 9, Larry Berman describes the evolution of the presidential library system and then provides a step-by-step guide to library usage. His principal but not exclusive focus is the Johnson library, in which he has done considerable research and from which he has produced a study of Johnson's decision to get involved in the Vietnam War.

The focus shifts to participant observation in Chapters 10 and 11, which are primarily concerned with how to obtain information from those who have worked in the process. Two perspectives are presented — that of a journalist and a political scientist. In Chapter 10, Dom Bonafede presents a short history of interviewing as a journalistic device, a discussion of presidential aides as primary subjects, and an enumeration of techniques for successful interviews. He provides a list of the most important dos and don'ts for journalists and political scientists alike. In the following chapter, Joseph A. Pika describes his experience interviewing government officials. Looking at various stages of the research process, from designing the schedule and making appointments to conducting the session and reporting the results, Pika provides an in-depth look at the interviewing process. He notes the potential hazards and utility of obtaining data in this manner.

Together, the chapters on data sources and techniques provide a compendium of information. The material is detailed. There is some overlap. Since the research needs of individual students will differ and their uses of this book may also vary, the editors decided that each chapter should be able to stand by itself. This will permit readers to examine individual chapters in section II in any order that seems most pertinent to their interests and needs.

NOTES

1. Edward S. Corwin, *The President: Office and Powers* (New York: New York Univ. Press, 1957); Clinton Rossiter, *The American Presidency* (New York: Harcourt, Brace & World, 1960); Richard E. Neustadt, *Presidential Power: The Politics of Leadership from FDR to Carter* (New York: Wiley, 1980).

2. James David Barber, *The Presidential Character* (Englewood Cliffs, N.J.: Prentice-Hall, 1977); Alexander George, "Assessing Presidential Character," in Aaron Wildavsky, ed. *Perspectives on the Presidency* (Boston: Little, Brown, 1975), 91–134; James H. Qualls, "Barber's Typological Analysis of Political Leaders," *American Political Science Review* 71 (Mar. 1977): 182–211; James David Barber, "Comment: Qualls's Nonsensical Analysis of Nonexistent Works," *American Political Science Review* 71

(March 1977): 212–25; Jeffrey Tulis, "On Presidential Character," in Joseph M. Bessette and Jeffrey Tulis, eds. *The Presidency in the Constitutional Order* (Baton Rouge: Louisiana State Univ. Press, 1981), 283–313.

3. Anthony King, "Executives," in Fred I. Greenstein and Nelson W. Polsby, eds., *Handbook of Political Science,* vol. 5 (Reading, Mass.: Addison-Wesley, 1975), 173.

4. There are many examples. Here are a few: Thomas E. Cronin, Tania Z. Cronin, and Michael Milakovich, *U.S. v. Crime-in-the-States* (Bloomington: Univ. of Indiana Press, 1981; George C. Edwards III, *Implementing Public Policy* (Washington, D.C.: Congressional Quarterly, 1980); Erwin C. Hargrove, *The Missing Link: The Study of the Implementation of Social Policy* (Washington, D.C.: Urban Institute, 1975); Hugh Heclo, *Modern Social Politics in Britain and Sweden* (New Haven, Conn.: Yale Univ. Press, 1974); Richard E. Neustadt and Harvey V. Fineberg, *The Swine Flu Affair* (Washington, D.C.: Department of Health, Education and Welfare, 1978); Norman C. Thomas, *Education in National Politics* (New York: David McKay, 1975); Aaron Wildavsky, *Speaking Truth to Power: The Art and Craft of Policy Analysis* (Boston: Little, Brown, 1979).

I

APPROACHES

AND ANALYSES

1

Approaches

STEPHEN J. WAYNE

THE CONCEPTUAL FRAMEWORK within which research is conducted affects what is studied and how it is studied, what is found and how it is interpreted. Unfortunately, even the few who have made important analytic contributions to the study of the presidency have not, as a general rule, labored to articulate the definitions, assumptions, and relationships on which their research has been predicated. As a consequence, the study of the presidency has not been marked by a great deal of conceptual clarity or even conceptual consciousness.

Uncertain objectives, imprecise language, and unclear meaning have clouded much of the research, partly because of the difficulty of obtaining systematic data on presidential activity and partly because of the idiosyncratic nature of the position itself. Fascination with individual personalities and events has diverted attention from environmental, institutional, and behavioral regularities to unique aspects of the office and its occupant. The persistent complaint is that there are but forty examples, which is the justification of description, not analysis, as the standard fare.

The difficulties of meeting criteria for theory building have discouraged theoretically oriented work on the presidency. There are few agreed-upon measurable indicators to attract the quantitatively sophisticated. With the payoffs less than for other areas of political science, theory builders have neglected the presidency, and presidency scholars have neglected theory building. This has resulted in less behaviorally oriented literature and explains why the study of the presidency has not kept pace with that of the other institutions of the national government. The absence of theory to guide research has impeded research and ultimately our understanding of how the presidency works.

To improve the study of the presidency it is necessary to become conceptually conscious, to *think* about the presidency. Only then will we be able to appreciate what is seen and what is not observed, what is explainable and what is unexplainable, what is predictable and what cannot be anticipated.

Scientific Inquiry

Let us begin with the basics. Scientific knowledge is a type of knowledge. It is characterized by a particular mode of inquiry. A distinctive characteristic of this inquiry is the *verifiability* of its propositions. That is, scientific statements must be structured in a way that permits confirmation by real-world experience. Without the possibility of confirmation, truth and falsity cannot be established. Science accepts only statements that rest on a factual base, not on faith.

Since scientific statements are predicated on the facts, terms within these statements must be empirically grounded. It would be impossible to confirm the political attitudes of angels, for example. Moreover, the terms must be general in character, or the assertions would be limited only to the particulars of the situation at a certain point in time. Here is where conceptualizing comes in.

Concepts define a class of phenomenon on the basis of one or more distinguishing characteristics. What do Richard Nixon, Gerald Ford, Jimmy Carter, and Ronald Reagan have in common? Obviously, they were all presidents. "President" in this case is a concept. The individuals in question are also men, white, and Christian. These too are concepts.

Existing on varying levels of abstraction, concepts relate directly or indirectly to observable phenomena. The more abstract the concept, the less direct that relationship. There is little problem in identifying concepts that are directly observable. For those that relate indirectly, however, the empirical referents must be specified. This is done by providing the concept with an operational definition, which links the concept to empirical reality.

The concept of presidential popularity, for example, cannot be observed directly, but it can be studied provided there is some agreement on what observable phenomena would be a valid indicator of it. Many scholars have accepted the perennial Gallup poll question, "Do you approve or disapprove of the way President _____ is handling his job," as such an indicator. Their consensus allows them to draw inferences about presidential popularity on the basis of variations in approval/disapproval ratings.

Another example of an empirical indicator of a fairly abstract concept, but one that is more controversial, is presidential support scores in Congress. These scores, calculated by Congressional Quarterly, measure the percentage of agreement between members of Congress and the president on recorded votes for issues on which the president has taken a position. Are these scores indicators of presidential success, effectiveness, and/or influence? Obviously, those who answer no to any or all of these questions would not find an analysis of presidential power based on these scores very convincing.

A consensus on operational definitions facilitates research. Were there to be little or no agreement on terminology, then communication would be extremely difficult. Agreement on language permits the possibility of learning from others.

The most elementary form of scientific knowledge is a statement that relates two or more concepts to one another. The statement is conditional; it is of the "if, then" variety. This form is necessary to indicate cause and effect. Because it is extremely difficult to pinpoint all the factors that singularly or in combination cause a particular effect, researchers in political science usually suggest general tendencies rather than specify precise conditions.

Each scientific statement must be subject to empirical testing. It must be capable of being true or false. That is why the concepts within the statement must have empirical referents and cannot be defined in terms of one another.

Educated guesses based on some knowledge about how the concepts relate are often referred to as *hypotheses*. They begin the research process by suggesting which relationships might be profitably examined. If these relationships are confirmed, the hypotheses may be proposed as *generalizations*. There are numerous hypotheses about the presidency but many fewer generalizations.

A single generalization standing alone does not usually explain and/or predict very much. Linked with other generalizations, however, it can convey greater understanding. This is the function of *theory*: systematically to relate generalizations to one another in order to explain and predict patterns in the world around us. To do this, theories have to get beyond the particulars of a given situation; they have to sort out relevant patterns and integrate them into a comprehensive framework, one that responds to a "why" question. In contrast, descriptions answer "what" and "how."

Technically, a theory cannot be judged true or false, although the generalizations within it can be. The relationships among these generalizations, however, are either logical or illogical. Thus, sound theories are those whose content stands the test of empiricism and whose structure stands the test of logic.

Theories tend to be judged on the basis of their utility — how much they explain and how well they explain it. The more comprehensive the theory, the more it will explain. The fewer the generalizations that comprise the theory, the more economical that explanation.

Theories are the highest form of knowledge. Yet, few, if any, comprehensive theories exist on the presidency or executives in general. Why? Identifying the independent and dependent variables, much less measuring their effects, is extremely difficult. Yet, this is precisely what must be done for a causal explanation to be offered. That is the reason that theories exist more as goals than monuments in political science. How, then, can these goals be achieved?

The first step is to put on some conceptual blinders. It is necessary to direct vision in order to see more clearly. Adopting a conceptual *approach* and a *framework* for analysis helps to do this by suggesting what kind of phenomenon to examine and how to examine it.

Of the two, approaches are more basic. Broadly conceived, they are simply orientations. Organized around a central concept or set of concepts, approaches indicate classifications of phenomena. Political scientists have utilized legal, institutional, political, and psychological approaches to study the presidency. Concepts central to these approaches include authority, precedent, role, organization, power, decision making, character, and style.

A framework is more comprehensive than an approach. It stimulates research by focusing on certain relationships. These relationships provide simplified versions of reality. They are shortcuts. That is their value as well as their danger. They help in framing questions, mobilizing data, and finding satisfactory answers. One potential problem with utilizing a framework is that the data that do not fit and thus are excluded may be important.

Another term, frequently used synonomously with framework, is *model*. A model is a relationship or a set of relationships that offers a potential explanation. It is not yet a theory but can be converted into one if the relationships specified by the model are confirmed by empirical evidence. Some models lend themselves to this confirmation process more easily than others. In general, the more abstract the model, the more difficult it is to confirm, and therefore, the less useful it is as an explanation of empirical reality. It might still have predictive potential, however. A mathematical model would be an example of one that frequently has greater predictive than explanatory value.

For the most part, those models that have greater explanatory payoffs have attracted students of the presidency. Organizational and bureaucratic ones in particular have provided frameworks for examining presidential advisory systems and decision-making situations.

The remainder of this chapter will explore approaches to studying the presidency by describing their basic assumptions, discussing their central concepts, and in the case of models, evaluating their analytic capabilities.

LEGAL PERSPECTIVES

WHAT a president does is a consequence of the powers he has. Some of these powers are inscribed in law; others are the product of prerogative, precedent, and personality. Throughout American history, the scope of the president's authority has been subject to controversy. Much of that controversy has focused on the Constitution itself and on the foundation on which it is built. That foundation has shaped the kinds of questions that have been asked, the information that has been sought, and the answers that have been given. It has also affected terminology that has been used, prescriptions that have been proposed, and assessments that have been made of presidents and their administrations.

The foundation is the familiar one of checks and balances, of separate institutions and shared powers. Predicated on Newtonian mechanics, it is based on a model of government described by Montesquieu in his chapter on the British system in *The Spirit of the Laws* and practiced to some extent in the states of New York and Massachusetts after independence and during the Confederation period.[1]

The model assumes that each institution will naturally promote its own interests and try to accumulate power. If successful, this accumulation could undo the precarious equilibrium among institutions and make one dominant. According to Montesquieu, the equilibrium preserves liberty by preventing this domination. To prevent an accumulation of power from occurring, the system requires the operation of internal checks. They protect legitimate spheres of authority by constraining behavior that encroaches upon the exercise of power within those spheres. Checks thus regulate the natural tension within the system. The Montesquieuian model is not designed to promote efficient government; it is designed to ensure safe government by maintaining a durable balance as long as possible.

Created within the context of this model, the presidency has been judged by it ever since. Concepts central to that judgment include those relating to the sources of its powers, the uses of its powers, and the scope of its powers. The perspective that the model provides is legal and historic. The literature is both descriptive and prescriptive. Those who write about the model tend to do so approvingly. Many see internal tension as both natural and necessary for vigorous, responsible rule.

The sources of authority include the Constitution (general, enumerated, and implied powers), statute, and precedent. They are considered important not only for historic reasons. How the Constitution has been interpreted, which practices become precedent and, in some cases, legally binding, and what laws constrain or require presidential actions affect the legitimization of authority as well as influence its adaptability to changing conditions and demands.

The uses of power have also been subject to considerable scrutiny. Over time the president's functions have increased. Those that derive more or less directly from Article II have remained relatively constant. Those that derive from precedent and/or statute have expanded considerably. Many of these functions have been described in terms of role models: chief executive, chief of state, chief diplomat, commander-in-chief, manager of the economy, legislative leader — to name but a few. The priority given to each of these roles and the vigor with which they have been exercised varies with times and circumstances, the personalities of individual presidents, and, particularly, with their normative theories of power (i.e., how they think they should behave). Whig presidents, such as Taft, Coolidge, and Eisenhower, tended to elevate administrative, judicial, and ceremonial roles, whereas steward presidents, such as Theodore and Franklin Roosevelt and Lyndon Johnson, placed greater emphasis on policymaking and consensus building.[2] In general, the models assume a chieftain position with commensurate authority.

The scope of the president's powers has probably received

more attention from those utilizing a legal perspective than has any other aspect of his authority. Two complementary objectives characterize much of this scholarship: to define the president's powers at a particular point in time and to measure those powers over time. In defining the powers, comparison is frequently made with the designation of powers in Article II. This comparison naturally highlights the growth of the presidency. Traditionally, it also 'stresses the elasticity of the Constitution and the relatively undefined grant of executive authority.

To illustrate the limits of this authority as well as its expansiveness, the struggle between the legislative and executive branches is frequently emphasized. This struggle directs attention to shifting powers. The metaphor often used to describe those shifts is a swinging pendulum. Its movement reflects the changing institutional balance, the range of competitive powers, and the joint, even cooperative, exercise of some of them. The advantage of using a pendulum as a metaphor is that it permits a historical overview consistent with the original design. Explanations can thus be couched in familiar terminology and evaluations predicated on a concept that has achieved general acceptance — that of institutional balance.

In conception and in content, Edward S. Corwin's *The President: Office and Powers* exemplifies the legal perspective.[3] Regarded as a classic since it was first published in 1940, the work provides a public law approach within a historical and an analytic context. Corwin is concerned with the creation and evolution of the president's powers, with the functions that derive more or less directly from them, and, to a much lesser extent, with their structural derivatives. Personal and political considerations are mentioned but not emphasized.

Others adopting a similar approach include Joseph E. Kallenbach, Louis Fisher, and Richard Pious.[4] Each focuses on the range of presidential powers. Each provides a historical perspective from which to assess the enlargment of those powers as well as the tension which that enlargement has generated, particularly with Congress. In addition, each raises important normative questions, questions about accountability and responsiveness, roles and responsibilities, and prescriptions and prohibitions.

It is hard to imagine a period of time in which a discussion of these questions has not occurred in the halls of Congress, courts of law, or the public arena. "An invitation to struggle" is how Corwin described the constitutional system. That struggle inevitably generates concerns about the expansiveness and limits of authority. This is the beauty of a legal perspective. It raises issues that have practical as well as theoretical consequences. Moreover, it addresses them in language that is comprehensible and potentially useful to those who must try to resolve these problems by legislation or through adjudication.

What the perspective neglects, however, is equally important, particularly to political scientists. The president's extraconstitutional roles have not been given nearly as much attention as those derived expressly or implicitly from Article II. The growth of the institution and the development of policy processes have not been scrutinized to the extent that the expansion of the institution's powers has. In general, the distinction between formal and informal powers, between constitutional and statutory authority and the actual ability of a president to meet contemporary demands and expectations and provide effective leadership, has not been emphasized by those adopting a legal perspective.[5]

Not only have there been substantive limits to a legal perspective, there have been methodological ones as well. The approach does not readily lend itself to hypothesis testing or theory building. Interpreting authority and judging its evolution produces argumentation and even analysis but not a body of data from which empirical generalizations can be made. Moreover, reliance on case studies within a historical context tends to emphasize idiosyncratic factors with much the same results.

Limitations in subject and method are, of course, not unique to a public-law perspective. All approaches, by definition, suffer from a similar problem. What is so constricting for political scientists, however, is that this particular perspective fails to emphasize the political or utilize the science. It is no small wonder then that the ranks of "legalists" studying the presidency have been so thinly populated by political scientists since 1950 (despite the rush to law school by so many of their students).

Institutional Perspectives

"I offer, not a commentary, but an outspoken presentation of such cardinal facts as may be sources of practical suggestion," wrote Woodrow Wilson in his introduction to *Congressional Government,* first published in 1885 when he was a graduate student.[6] Wilson's objective, to present a plain factual description of the actual workings of government, departed from the legal orientation in several respects. His context was primarily political; his terminology was straightforward and literary; and his substantive focus was on institutional behavior. Subjects previously neglected by students of government occupied his attention. These included organization, process, and mode of operation. This substantive focus led him to consider questions of power and influence. His conclusions about power within Congress and between the president and Congress became generally accepted dogma until Wilson himself revised them during Theodore Roosevelt's presidency.

Wilson recognized that the president's potential stemmed from politics as well as law. Others, such as Henry Jones Ford, Harold J. Laski, and Wilfred E. Binkley, also saw political factors contributing to personal influence.[7] They, too, presented a broadened perspective on the operation of the constitutional system, one that propounded a new answer to an old question: what should the president be doing and how should he be doing it. The president should be an activist, they contended; he should be a steward of the people.

Wilson, Ford, Laski, and Binkley all rejected the Whig model that the president should do only what the Constitution and laws permitted. In rejecting this model, they also rejected the assumptions on which it was predicated, that constitutional and statutory authority limited the scope of the president's job and defined the range of his powers. Instead of checks, they were concerned with activity; instead of authority, they were concerned with influence; instead of just legal obligations, they were also concerned with extraconstitutional roles.

ROLES AND RESPONSIBILITIES

THE need for a more active president was seen as a consequence of expanded functions and increasing demands. In his reappraisal of the presidency, Woodrow Wilson suggested two additional roles for the chief executive: spokesman for public opinion and leader in foreign affairs.[8] Clinton Rossiter, in an essay entitled *The American Presidency,* added three more: chief of party, protector of peace, and manager of prosperity. In all, Rossiter counted ten essential presidential roles.[9]

This proliferation of responsibilities and expectations created conflicting demands on the president. Describing his burdens as monstrous, Rossiter likened the president's task to that of a chamber orchestra conductor forced to play all the instruments himself: "he must learn for himself by hard practice how to blend them together, remembering always that perfect harmony is unattainable."[10]

By emphasizing roles, Rossiter added a new dimension to the institutional literature and provided an initial step in the direction of a more behavioral approach to the office. The concept of role, derived from sociology, suggests that what a person does is in part a product of his social environment. It is affected by what he is expected to do and how he perceives those expectations. Roles orient. They direct activity but do not indicate behavior. Personal beliefs and psychological needs also play a part.

The importance of adopting a role orientation is that it turns attention from the vicissitudes of individual activity to the regularities of institutional behavior. In other words, it provides a framework for understanding behavior within a social setting. Patterns associated with roles can be identified. If the roles themselves can be isolated and their impact, individually and collectively, measured, then they can be used to help explain, and it is hoped, to predict behavior. Rossiter does not get as far as prediction nor do other presidential scholars. Students of the legislature, however, have developed more sophisticated role models from which they hope to be able to generate more precise statements about personal behavior within an institution.[11]

Rossiter's contribution lies in his emphasis, not in his analysis. By describing the presidency in terms of roles, he projected a dynamic office, one that was active on all fronts. By noting the persistence of some of this activity over time, he also was able to convey continuities in institutional behavior. This activism and those continuities are characteristic of the modern presidency.

Rossiter, however, did not get close to the institution he described. He observed it from afar. Only fleeting references were made to how the presidency was organized and how that organization worked. Toward the end of the 1950s, scholars began to look more carefully at the structural and operational aspects of the institution. The president's cabinet and his executive office began to receive attention. Eventually, informal advisory arrangements and internal policy processes also became subjects of inquiry. These studies initiated a second phase of institutionally oriented literature on the presidency.

STRUCTURE AND PROCESS

IT was no accident that the focus shifted from general roles to more specific structures and processes. The Franklin Roosevelt administration had witnessed the creation of a presidential office and the development of policy processes between it and other executive branch agencies. This office and those processes continued and even expanded during subsequent administrations.

Equally important, an increasing number of participant observers who had served in the presidency could talk authoritatively about their experience. Their insight added an additional dimension to the study of the office. Notable among these scholar-practitioners was Richard E. Neustadt. His articles on central clearance and legislative programming presented an *inside* perspective on how the institution actually worked.[12]

Neustadt was concerned with two aspects of these developments. He was interested in the mechanism itself: how it evolved, what functions it served, who participated, how the participants interacted, and what this interaction augured for future presidential responsibilities and activities. He was also interested in the effect of the process and the mechanism on the president and the presidency, on *his* and *its* influence. In the first instance, Neustadt focused on institutionalization; in the second, on power. Each of these subjects was to occupy, almost preoccupy, presidency students for many years to come.

The concept of institutionalization also has been borrowed from sociology. At one time or another it has been used to explain or exemplify the development of roles, structure, and processes. There have been a few attempts to clarify its meaning. Robert S. Gilmour defined institutionalization as "an index of: boundaries, organizational complexity, routinization and role development, and symbolic attachment."[13] Lester Seligman and Carey Covington have described it as an evolutionary process occurring in stages.[14] The value of the concept is that it facilitates the collection of empirical data on a variety of activities. Moreover, its process orientation permits these data to be examined from a longitudinal perspective, which, in turn, allows qualitative analyses that can yield generalizable statements and prescriptive judgments.

There are many contemporary examples in the literature. To cite but three: Larry Berman, *The Office of Management and Budget and the Presidency, 1921–1979;* Michael Baruch Grossman and Martha Joynt Kumar, *Portraying the President*; and Stephen J. Wayne, *The Legislative Presidency.*[15] Berman focuses primarily on an *organization,* tracing its evolution as a presidential agency. Grossman and Kumar examine a *relationship,* the one between the White House and the news media. They characterize it as both conflictual and cooperative. Wayne describes a *process* — the formulation, coordination, promotion, and implementation of legislation by and within the presidency.

Each of these works discusses structure, function, and operation. Each looks at stages of development and attempts to generalize and offer lessons for the future on the basis of the continuities of the past. The assumptions underlying these studies are that most of these continuities will persist; they will influence the behavior of the president and the operation of the presidency; and they will ultimately condition his success in office.

The merits of an institutional approach lie in its longitudinal perspective. By focusing on key institutional relationships across administrations, the approach can yield general statements that have explanatory and predictive potential. Substantively, the focus has been particularly useful for understanding the persistence and adaptation of organizations and processes over time and their effect on individual and group behavior.

The strengths of the approach, however, are also its weaknesses. By conceptualizing behavior as a consequence of institutional forces primarily, the perspective tends to downplay political factors and submerge human qualities and needs. Personal skills, ideology, and perceptions are deemed to be less important for explaining behavior than are organizational mechanisms. Moreover, the methodology on which most institutional studies have been predicated has tended to produce general descriptions and qualitative analyses, not quantitative measures. The precision and accuracy of the assessments and projections that have resulted from this methodology have suffered as a result.

Political Perspectives

POWER ORIENTATION

Institutional factors, of course, are not alone in contributing to political success. Power orientations are also important. They affect behavior and influence personal relationships. In 1960 a book was published that directed attention to the personal qualities of the president operating within a political environment. Its author, Richard E. Neustadt, was an academic who had served in the Bureau of the Budget and the White House during the Truman administration. Perceiving a gap between theory and practice, between the enumeration of authority and functions, the description of structures and procedures, and the actual operation of government, Neustadt addressed what he described as the classic problem in any political system: "how to be on top in fact as well as name."[16]

His response departed from the scope and methodology of the literature in several respects. His focus was different. Instead of describing roles and powers, Neustadt wrote about expectations and constituencies; instead of discussing organization and process, he talked about internal politics and decision-making situations. Instead of being on the outside looking in, up, and to the president, Neustadt assumed a vantage point that peered over and down the president's shoulder.

In rejecting the external focus of the presidency literature, Neustadt also rejected the assumption on which much of it was based—that the president had the capacity to do his job. Corwin and Rossiter indicated that presidential authority was sufficient to meet the president's constitutional duties and extraconstitutional roles. Neustadt suggested that the president could not govern by his constitutional and statutory authority alone. He went on to dramatize the differences between his perspective and that of the existing literature.

The president had been described as a chief and his powers defined in terms of his roles. Neustadt suggested that he could be a clerk and that his problems and potential weaknesses transcended functional bounds. The notion of a weak chief, almost a contradiction in terms, was a major conceptual breakthrough. It led Neustadt to disregard most of the previous studies on the presidency as irrelevant—at least for his purposes. In their stead, he proposed a new schema for understanding and evaluating the president's performance. The key to that schema was the concept of power.

Neustadt treated power as influence, the ability to make someone do what he or she might otherwise not do.[17] By defining power in such a manner, he rejected the notion, prevalent at that time, that power was a function of authority and/or position and that it could be exercised by a vigorous utilization of the chain of command. While conceding that authority and position can contribute to power, Neustadt also noted that the contribution was not automatic. In fact, by increasing obligations, roles, and demands, authority and position can actually increase the gap between expectations and performance. This Neustadt saw as the president's chief problem in 1960 and sees it as a continuing problem today.

Moreover, Neustadt argued that power was a relational concept. It could not be examined in isolation. Since any power situation involves the behavior of two or more individuals, the personal interaction of the president with others became the critical concern. This shifted the primary focus from the institution to the individuals within that institution. Whether the president had sufficient power to do his job and accomplish his goals became the central question for students of the presidency. A secondary concern was the goals themselves.

Reaction to Neustadt's thesis, and particularly, to his concern for a more powerful president varied with the times. In the aftermath of the Eisenhower presidency, many found Neustadt's argument compelling, including John Kennedy, who read the book and consulted with its author during his transition to office. Lyndon Johnson also adopted behavior that conformed to the Neustadtian model. The impact of Vietnam and Watergate on the presidency, however, rendered the thesis much less appealing. Both Johnson and Nixon were accused of personalizing the institution's power, of using the office to further their own political ends. Their actions illustrated the danger of exercising unchecked powers, of maintaining undivided loyalties, and of pursuing unpopular and often unattainable goals. Any approach that neglected legal limits, institutional checks, and personal accountability was deemed to be deficient in the light of this new and sobering experience.

Only a short period of time elapsed, however, before the principal concern once again became the dilemma cited by Neustadt: how to overcome the constraints of the system. Ford and Carter's ineffectiveness in articulating and achieving their policy goals highlighted the problem and turned attention to Neustadt's solution.

Notwithstanding the popularity of the thesis and its applicability for future presidents, the approach has had a profound effect on the scope and methodology of the presidency literature.

In one way or another almost all of the major works on the institution have reflected its perspective. *The Imperial Presidency, Presidential Greatness, Presidential Government, The Power of the Modern Presidency, The State of the Presidency, Presidential Influence in Congress,* and *The Illusion of Presidential Government* are preoccupied with the problem of leadership, with the adequacy or inadequacy of the president's influence, with his capacity to succeed, ability to survive, or tendency to succumb.[18]

The conceptual contributions of the power approach have been manifold. It has refocused attention from external organizations to internal dynamics. Bureaucratic politics has become a principal concern. It has reassessed the hierarchy of presidential decision making, describing it as horizontal not vertical in character. The president is seen as one actor among many and not necessarily the dominant one. It has redefined power, casting it in personal rather than legal or institutional terms. Exploiting political influence, not expanding legal authority or adjusting the institutional mechanism, is seen as the key to the president's success. Finally, it has presented a new conception of leadership based on a stewardship model of duties and a Rooseveltian model of behavior. The president should be a calculating activist who gets his way through persuasion — gentle or otherwise.

Criticism of the orientation in general and its prescriptions in particular focus on its preoccupation with power and its neglect of other possible influences. Does the president really have to bargain all the time in order to succeed? Does his position not afford him other ways to accomplish his goals? Should executive leadership be primarily manipulative?

To a large extent, the answers to these questions are dictated by the assumptions. Those utilizing a power orientation have tended to assume (1) that the president should be the principal decision maker; (2) that the environment for his decision is essentially confrontational; and (3) that conflicting interests create centrifugal forces that the president must try to overcome. The fact of the matter is that these assumptions may not be valid for all or even most presidential decisions. Routine actions, incremental policy, even crisis diplomacy are not likely to engender the amount of opposition that the power approach anticipates. In other words, the environment may be far less hostile and far more cooperative. Hence, a shrewd and manipulative leader may not be necessary or even desirable much of the time.

Moreover, factors other than political self-interest may affect the judgment of those involved in decision making. By focusing primarily on politics, the approach underemphasizes philosophy, ideology, and culture. It also dilutes the effect of personality. These factors singly or together could facilitate or impede the president's ability to get his way.

The definition of power also presents methodological problems to the empiricist. It is a difficult concept to operationalize. While presidential success or effectiveness can be estimated by studying congressional voting behavior, presidential influence is much harder to measure. Moreover, identifying, much less calculating, the effect of variables individually and collectively on complex presidential decisions is also extremely difficult. Neustadt and others have contributed to this problem by generalizing at a fairly high level of abstraction, thereby making their propositions harder to disconfirm.

One of Neustadt's propositions, however, has received some empirical scrutiny. The hypothesis that prestige (popularity) contributes to power has been tested and generally confirmed. George C. Edwards III has found that increases in presidential popularity (as indicated by Gallup polls) tend to increase presidential support in Congress.[19]

DECISION MAKING

As an orientation, power offers an individualistic perspective, but one that is also sensitive to the setting in which the president must operate. By emphasizing multiple constituencies and pressures, by conveying the increasing pluralism of the system, the power orientation helped shift attention from structure, role, and process to internal politics and from the sources of power to the exercise of power. With that shift came a focus on decision making itself.

By the early 1950s, political scientists had·begun to identify the important influences on decisions. Who were the participants? What were their activities? How did they communicate with one another? What were the pertinent environmental factors that affected their judgment? Neustadt was concerned with these questions as well. *Presidential Power* had described decision-making situations that provided the basis on which the book's analytic framework was predicated. Often referred to as the bureaucratic politics model, this framework featured individuals inside and outside the government in a constant struggle for power. Graham T. Allison has likened that struggle to a game with players, rules, activity, and results.[20]

In Allison's description, the players constitute the officials, interest-group leaders, and at the extreme, members of the attentive and mass public who are concerned about a particular decision and try to influence it. Some play key roles, others marginal ones, and still others seem to have little effect on the decision. The inner circle is the group Neustadt referred to as the Washington community—senior political, military, and business leaders, the press corps, civil servants; even a few academicians. The president is positioned at the center, near the point of final decision. His advisers form a flange about him. All are keyed for battle.

The rules for play are established by the legal and institutional setting, by custom, and to some extent, by the expectations of the players themselves. The rules help determine the position of the players and their access to the chief decision maker. The timing of the decision is frequently a consequence of action-forcing processes. All players, including the president, are expected to operate according to the rules or face the possibility of sanctions. These include bad publicity, loss of present or future support, denial of reelection or reappointment, and, in cases of serious violation, the threat of removal from office. Johnson's and Nixon's "premature" departures were, in large part, a consequence of sanctions imposed for rule violations.

The principal form of activity is bargaining. It is neither haphazard nor random. Players attempt to influence a particular decision in accordance with discernible interests, defined by their position and affected by their constituency. Perceptions, attitudes, and personalities also affect the behavior of the participants, particularly their motivation, intensity, and direction. Knowledge and skill contribute primarily to tactics.

Since the basic assumption is that self-interest underlies behavior, benefits are likely to be judged by the immediacy of their impact. The time-frame, like the tenure of many of the participants, tends to be short. The future is usually the present or near-present. Under the circumstances, long-range planning frequently falls victim to short-range problems. That is why deadlines and action-forcing processes are needed to drive decision makers to decisions.

The results of decisions made in this fashion tend to be compromises rather than extreme solutions. The struggle, with its give and take, produces outputs that are practicable, not necessarily optimal or best. Only during emergencies, when political opposition is momentarily silenced, or during extended honeymoon periods, when it is absent or in disarray, is the neat and rational likely to emerge and a strong authoritative figure able to impose his choices and judgments on others. In the bureaucratic model, "politics as usual" means opposition and struggle. It also means that those decisions that have the greatest political fallout are apt to be the toughest.

The model is both dynamic and multivariate. Those individuals who seek to exert influence either separately or in concert with one another may be viewed as independent variables within the model. The dependent variable is the decision itself. Presidential activity can be seen as an independent, intervening, or dependent variable, depending upon the president's position within the decisional process. Since decisions, once made, are likely to affect future decisions, the model is recursive.

Many major works on the presidency incorporate the basic assumptions and tenets of the bureaucratic politics model or variations of it. Aaron Wildavsky's *The Politics of the Budgetary Process* is a good example.[21] In analyzing how executive budget requests are made, Wildavsky focuses on strategy and tactics. He is concerned with the perceptions and calculations of the departments in obtaining their budget allocations. The perceptions are shaped by the agency, by pressures on it from its clientele, and by the president's policy. The calculations are influenced by expectations of what is necessary, what is possible, and what is likely. The consequence of these strategic considerations is apt to be increments modified by strong presidential support or opposition to certain programs.

Hugh Heclo's "Issue Networks and the Executive Establishment" also assumes many of the tenets of this model.[22] His thesis that issue networks, primarily but not exclusively within Washington, operate to monopolize policy debate and shape the contours for decision making suggests a highly political arena in which multiple forces compete for power, thereby reducing the influence of any one organization or individual.

Like the power orientation, the decision-making approach emphasizes the environment in which presidential decisions occur. Its prime focus is on the decision and the decision maker. It emphasizes the president's weaknesses rather than his strengths. Although the approach has been useful in sensitizing students to the multitude of forces that can affect such decisions, it has not been nearly as successful in measuring the impact of the forces individually or collectively.

The kinds of decisions that have interested political science students of the presidency have contributed to the problem. Highly complex, precedent-setting, crisis-oriented decisions are the ones that have attracted the most attention and scrutiny. These tend to be the most idiosyncratic and least subject to systematic (and certainly, quantitative) analysis. Routine decisions, on the other hand, would be more amenable to such analysis, but they have not generated the same amount of interest. As a consequence, explanatory and predictive propositions about presidential decision making are rare.[23]

A limitation of the decision-making approach, at least as it has been employed by political scientists, has been the relative inattention given to personality factors. Decisions are usually described as conscious and intentional. Neustadt, in particular, was concerned with manipulation and the exercise of political skills. Lack of training in psychology and the reluctance to speculate on nonobservable forces has undoubtedly contributed to the tendency to see concrete policy goals and political objec-

STEPHEN J. WAYNE

tives as primary motivations for (and explanations of) presidential decisions. Whereas the style and ideology of individual presidents has often been described, sometimes in excruciating detail, personality factors have rarely been analyzed systematically by political scientists.

PSYCHOLOGICAL PERSPECTIVES

PSYCHOLOGICAL studies of behavior are predicated on a basic assumption. When personal needs are displaced onto political objects, they can become unconscious motivations for verbal and physical responses. This suggests the merits as well as the dangers of taking such a perspective. On the one hand, it opens vistas to a range of proximate causes that might not be perceived because they are not easily observable except perhaps to those trained in psychological interpretations. On the other hand, it creates confirmation problems. The difficulty of discerning unconscious motivations and of differentiating them from external factors has discouraged political scientists from moving beyond (and behind) data that are either directly or indirectly observable. There have been some attempts, however.

Of the presidency studies that would be considered psychological, two kinds stand out: psychobiographies and psychotypologies. Psychobiographies are analyses of individual presidents set within the context of a particular administration. Predicated on the notion that personality remains fairly constant throughout life, these biographies seek to explain behavior by relating it to the personal needs of individual presidents. Thus, Woodrow Wilson's refusal to compromise on the League of Nations might be traced to insecurities stemming from his relationship to an overbearing and perfectionist father; Richard Nixon's coverup of the Watergate affair might be explained by his tendency to become rigid, inflexible, and very defensive when threatened, particularly during crisis situations.

Examples of psychobiographies of recent presidents include

3 8

Alexander and Juliette George's study of Woodrow Wilson, Doris M. Kearns's analysis of Lyndon Johnson, Fawn Brodie's biography of Richard Nixon, and Betty Glad's book on Jimmy Carter. All of these works present a great deal of information about an individual president and provide insight into a specific administration, including seemingly irrational actions of the president. In this sense, they reveal unconscious needs and thereby contribute to a fuller explanation of presidential behavior.[24]

By focusing on a single actor within a single set of circumstances, psychobiographies are idiosyncratic. Their explanations turn into themselves. Usually, they convey little about the institution of the presidency or even about the relationship between psychological and institutional variables. In order to generalize, it is necessary to overcome idiosyncrasy. This involves typecasting, that is, creating typologies into which data can be categorized and then counted. In psychological studies, categories may be defined in terms of personality dimensions. By identifying and measuring these dimensions, generalizations can be made and the relationship of personalities to behavior assessed. The study by Adorno and colleagues of the authoritarian personality is one of the best known of these typological studies.[25] James David Barber's *The Presidential Character* is another.[26]

Barber's objective was to develop a framework that could be used to study psychological aspects of presidential behavior. He did not regard personal psychology as the sole cause of behavior but as a primary motivation for it. In addition to the development of a psychological theory to explain and predict political behavior, Barber had a prescriptive goal. Believing that certain types of personalities are better suited to the office of the presidency than others, he attempted to demonstrate which were the most desirable and most dangerous types. His message was directed beyond political scientists to others in the electorate.

Key to Barber's formulation was the concept of character. Barber regarded it as the core of personality. Developed early in life, it affects the general stance a person has toward himself and toward the environment. Directly or indirectly, it influences behavior.[27] Other important concepts in Barber's formulation are style and world view. Barber has described style as the garb a person wears, a way of acting. Viewed from the outside, it is the observed quality and character of performance. Viewed from inside, it is a strategy for adapting, protecting, and enhancing self-esteem.[28] World view consists of beliefs about reality. It has both an ideological and philosophic dimension. Although Barber was not explicit about how character, style, and world view interrelate, he regarded that interrelationship as crucial for understanding personality and for assessing behavior in office.

Barber's efforts have engendered considerable criticism. His prescriptions, his methodology, and his analysis have all been the subjects of controversy. The brunt of the criticism has been directed at Barber's methodology: the utility of the psychological categories he has employed, the way in which he has operationalized these categories, and his interpretation and coding of the data.[29] Although directed at Barber, much of the criticism at its core questions whether any psychological model can ever generate an empirically based theory that has explanatory and predictive value. At issue are the validity of typologies for assessing personality, the reliability of coding qualitative data, the collection of these data primarily from secondary sources, and the presentation of alternative explanations (psychological as well as nonpsychological).

Admittedly, personality is very complex. A lot has to be lost when individuals are categorized on the basis of some broad ideal type. They are divested of their uniqueness. Generalizing from a typology cannot reflect this personal dimension. In fact, it reflects little more than the classification itself. This is why it is difficult, if not impossible, to ever explain or predict individual behavior from a typology. Moreover, there can be many explanations of behavior. Ideology, culture, attitudes, and information are all potential influences in addition to or in lieu of psychological factors. Unfortunately, the typology tends to produce a single rather than multicaused explanation. In this sense, it can be chided for its narrowness.

Psychobiography is equally unsatisfactory as an alternative. It, too, can be narrowly focused and highly interpretive. It, too, raises questions of validity and reliability, and those questions underlie the difficulty with all psychological approaches. There is always a leap of faith from observable behavior to the unconscious motivations that are proposed as causes of that behavior. The problem is more than simply what does not meet the eye. Even if it were possible to ascertain the presence of psychological needs, it would be impossible to confirm that those needs were the cause of any given action. Alternative psychological explanations are almost always possible and frequently as probable. In short, psychological approaches inevitably yield speculative findings. This is not to suggest that they are valueless, however.

Psychological perspectives add an important dimension to our knowledge of the presidency. How else would it be possible to explain why individuals with similar values, beliefs, and skills, perhaps even in very similar situations, behave differently? How else would it be possible to explain why those with dissimilar values, beliefs, and skills behave in a similar manner? Psychological insight broadens our understanding. The danger is when it constitutes the sole explanation, a danger that can also result from explanations derived from any of the other approaches.

CONCLUSION

CONCEPTUAL awareness is important for the study of the presidency. It is important for pedagogy as well as for scholarship. By uncovering assumptions, both descriptive and prescriptive, it reveals the implicit beliefs and values on which theoretical frameworks, research methodology, and substantive findings rest. Such revelations are critical for evaluating the merits and limitations of scholarship as well as for accepting, rejecting, or modifying explanations of behavior.

Explanations are achieved through theory. Theory makes cumulative knowledge possible. Without such knowledge, it would be difficult to know how much we know, much less to assess the scope and substance of that knowledge. Without theory, we could not effectively use the past as a guide to the future.

Theory clarifies through definition. Definitions, of course, are essential for communication. Without them, meaning is unclear. Moreover, to demonstrate the validity of a study, there must be a consensus on meaning, including the operationalization of key concepts.

Theory targets through organization. It facilitates the testing and replication of empirical propositions. Only by formulating and testing such propositions can claims of truth be made. Theory also directs attention to the examination of logical relationships by which such propositions can be combined and extended through deduction into explanations and even predictions.

The presidency lacks a rich theoretical literature. There is no one generally accepted model for studying presidential behavior. There have, however, been a plethora of approaches to the office — its powers, roles, operations, and occupants — that provide perspectives from which the institution can be viewed. Together, these approaches constitute a discontinuous, semicumulative body of knowledge that has enlarged our comprehension of the office far more than it has improved our capacity for studying it.

These approaches include certain theoretical frameworks. The frameworks are similar in form even though they are dissimilar in content. They all utilize key concepts and are predicated, implicitly or explicitly, on assumptions about the causes and goals of behavior. They all postulate a means-end relationship and a desired course of behavior.

Legalists focus on constitutional and statutory authority; institutionalists on roles, structure, and process; politicists on leadership and decision making; and psychologists on character and style primarily and on belief systems secondarily. Each of these foci can be and has been operationalized, although the validity of the concepts that are least observable have been subject to the most controversy.

In general, the centralizing concepts of each approach have been considered independent variables that affect what presidents can and should be doing (the dependent variable). The concepts are, however, also amenable to treatment as dependent variables, since they are potentially affected by presidential behavior as well as by the institutional and situational setting in which that behavior occurs. Neustadt, for example, saw power as both cause and effect. His orientation, however, was to use it to explain and prescribe presidential activity rather than the other way around.

The assumptions underlying each of these approaches have varied. The legalists assume the existence of natural institutional tension and have promoted the separation of powers accordingly. In urging a strong, independent, but restrained president, they have not as a general rule questioned his capacity to do the job. The institutionalists perceive role, structure, and process as interrelated, even complementary. They suggest that the enlarged scope of presidential activities requires a greater organizational capacity and a more highly developed procedural mechanism. Politicists, on the other hand, see self-interest as generating expectations, motivating behavior, and creating diverse pressures on the president. Assuming the persistence of these interests over time and in most situations, they see the need for the president to convince, not simply command, if he is to get his way. Unlike the institutionalists, the politicists do not view the enlargement of the presidency as necessarily reducing the president's tasks. Political scientists adopting a psychological perspective point to the intrusion of unconscious and seemingly irrational factors that can impinge on presidential decisions and activities. The president must take these factors into account. Some personalities can do this more easily and effectively than others.

The analytic structures follow from these assumptions. For legalists, the balance among the branches provides the framework in which the presidency functions. Adjustments are necessary to maintain the balance. Recasting authority in the light of precedent and contemporary practices would be the principal way in which this could be accomplished.

Institutionalists tend to describe a process in which demands create roles that beget structures that help to fulfill as well as refuel demands. The implicit model is that of a system with inputs, outputs, and a processing mechanism. For the mechanism to work efficiently, an equilibrium between needs and capacity must be attained and maintained. This is accomplished by structural adjustments to changes in the environment that affect the presidency, changes in what is expected of and demanded from the president.

Perceiving a multitude of situational forces impinging on the president as well as on other actors within his decision-making environment, politicists have tended to describe presidential actions as a consequence of those forces but not totally determined by them. Within this model the president can affect others as well as influence his environment by his intentions, his skills, and his decisions. He is both reactive and proactive. His actions are and should be motivated by his own interests.

The psychologists go a step further. The president and implicitly others as well are also motivated by unconscious needs and seemingly irrational desires. Ego cloaked in style and beliefs sets the parameters for individual behavior and group interaction. In the end it is the power of personality reinforced or reduced by the political and situational milieu that determines the level and kind of activity.

These frameworks, in turn, have affected the kinds of explanations that can be made. The legalists, for the most part, have adopted a historical perspective and pointed to the accumulation of statute, precedent, and judicial opinion as support for their interpretations of the scope, sources, and uses of presidential powers.

The institutionalists also have utilized a longitudinal perspective but have couched their explanation in structural-functional terms. The presidency is described as an organism that develops routines and adjusts to environmental change. The explanation tends to focus on the mechanism and its adjustments.

For the politicists, historical perspective gives way to case studies that serve to illustrate the president's plight. When quantified, the cases also provide empirical substantiation for the general propositions that are derived. The explanation is dictated by the particular setting in which the president finds himself. There are two scenarios: "politics as usual" and "politics suspended." In the first scenario, differing perceptions and goals resulting from the legal, institutional, political, and social diversity within the system, create a hostile, even combative environment that a president must try to overcome. In the second scenario, self-interest is suspended in light of a threat to the system. The suspension generates support that a president must try to direct. In the first case, the president must prevail; to succeed, he must be political. In the second case, he must preside; to lead, he should be apolitical.

The explanations of those utilizing a psychological approach might be described as empirically interpretive, meaning that interpretations, predicated on a psychological theory, are used to explain the whys of behavior. The focus is on the unconscious causes of that behavior. Dimensions of personality are proposed as explanatory and predictive variables.

The more direct the observations, the more solid the base from which interpretations can be made, and if possible, generalizations proposed. In general, the more amenable the model to hypothesis testing, the more valuable it is from a scientific perspective because it facilitates the replication and validation of propositions. Measures of presidential popularity and influence have been used to confirm Neustadt's hypothesis about the relationship between prestige and persuasion. Propositions derived from psychological analyses such as Barber's are more difficult to validate.

The model conditions the methodology. The methodology shapes the research process. It affects the data that are collected, the analysis that is performed, and the style by which it is presented.

Social science methodology has been useful for testing propositions, but it has not been useful for constructing theories. None of the major theoretical formulations on the presidency has been inductively derived, that is, built from the ground up. In one way or another, they have all been the product of scholarship, insight, and observation. Various factors have impeded the development of an empirically based and inductively built theory: the predominance of qualitative data on the presidency, the relatively complex units that are studied, the preference given to macroanalysis, and the desire to proffer advice with most explanations.

In the short run, at least, it seems likely that political scientists will have to continue to depend on a variety of perspectives and many semisynthesized models to focus their inquiry. They will have to continue to utilize social science methods to refine these models and to lend credence to the explanations and predictions generated from them. In the absence of a comprehensive theoretical formulation, a synthesis of existing approaches and models seems to offer the best hope for generating and accumulating knowledge about the presidency.

NOTES

1. Baron de Montesquieu, *The Spirit of the Laws,* vol. 1 (New York: Hafner, 1949), 149–162.

2. The whig philosophy is predicated on a literal reading of the Constitution and a conservative exercise of its designated powers. In the words of William Howard Taft, "the President can exercise no power which cannot be fairly and reasonably traced to some specific grant of power or justly implied and included with such express grant or proper and necessary to its exercise. Such specific grant must be either in the Federal Constitution or in an act of Congress passed in pursuance thereof" (William Howard Taft, *Our Chief Magistrate and His Powers,* [New York: Columbia Univ. Press, 1916], 138. The stewardship theory is much more expansive. Theodore Roosevelt articulated it in a much-quoted statement from his autobiography. "My view was that every executive officer, and above all every executive officer in high position, was a steward of the people bound actively and affirmatively to do all he could for the people, and not to content himself with the negative merit of keeping his talents undamaged in a napkin" (Theodore Roosevelt, *Autobiography* [New York: Scribner's, 1958], 197).

3. Edward S. Corwin, *The President: Office and Powers 1787–1957* (New York: New York Univ. Press, 1957).

4. Kallenbach's book updated Corwin and supplemented it with data on state executives. A dispassionate, descriptive treatise, it adopted a legal perspective, discussed the president's traditional functions and powers, and also presented considerable information on the politics of presidential selection. (Joseph E. Kallenbach, *The American Chief Executive* [New York: Harper & Row, 1966].) Fisher's numerous monographs and articles provide a detailed accounting of expanded presidential powers in the 1970s. His books include *President and Congress* (New York:

Free Press, 1972); *Presidential Spending Powers* (Princeton, N.J.: Princeton Univ. Press, 1975); *The Constitution Between Friends* (New York: St. Martin's, 1978); and *The Politics of Shared Power* (Washington, D.C.: Congressional Quarterly, 1981). Richard Pious's *The American Presidency* (New York: Basic Books, 1979) provides a comprehensive overview of the institution. In taking a legal perspective, Pious offers the thesis that constitutional authority and not political power is most significant in determining what a president can do. Arguing that an excess of checks encumbers the president, he urges more collaborative government to overcome these checks.

5. Pious is an exception. See Pious, *American Presidency*.

6. Woodrow Wilson, *Congressional Government* (New York: Meridan Books, 1956).

7. Henry Jones Ford, *The Rise and Growth of American Politics* (London: Macmillan, 1880); Harold J. Laski, *The American Presidency* (New York: Harper, 1940); Wilfred E. Binkley, *President and Congress* (New York: Vintage Books, 1962).

8. Woodrow Wilson, *Constitutional Government in the United States* (New York: Columbia Univ. Press, 1961).

9. Clinton Rossiter, *The American Presidency* (New York: Harcourt, Brace & World, 1960), 30–43.

10. Ibid., p. 42.

11. See, for example, John C. Wahlke, Heinz Eulau, William Buchanan, and LeRoy C. Ferguson, *The Legislative System* (New York: Wiley, 1962); James David Barber, *The Lawmakers* (New Haven, Conn.: Yale Univ. Press, 1965).

12. Richard E. Neustadt. "Presidency and Legislation: The Growth of Central Clearance," *American Political Science Review* 48 (Sept. 1954): 641–71; "Presidency and Legislation: Planning the President's Program," *American Political Science Review* 49 (Dec. 1955): 980–1021.

13. Robert S. Gilmour, "The Institutionalized Presidency: A Conceptual Clarification," in Norman C. Thomas, ed., *The Presidency in Contemporary Context* (New York: Dodd, Mead, 1975), 152.

14. Lester Seligman and Carey Covington, "The Process of Presidential Institutionalization" (paper presented at the Annual Meeting of the Midwest Political Science Association, Chicago, April 1979).

15. Larry Berman, *The Office of Management and Budget and the Presidency, 1921–1979* (Princeton, N.J.: Princeton Univ. Press, 1979); Michael Baruch Grossman and Martha Joynt Kumar, *Portraying the President* (Baltimore: Johns Hopkins Univ. Press, 1981); Stephen J. Wayne, *The Legislative Presidency* (New York: Harper & Row, 1978).

16. Richard E. Neustadt, *Presidential Power: The Politics of Leadership from FDR to Carter* (New York: Wiley 1980), v.

17. Ibid., 4.

Neustadt's use of the term *power* is similar to Robert Dahl's in his well-known essay "The Concept of Power," *Behavioral Science* 2 (July 1957): 202–03.

18. Arthur M. Schlesinger, Jr., *The Imperial Presidency* (New York: Popular Library, 1973); Thomas A. Bailey, *Presidential Greatness* (New York: Appleton-Century-Crofts, 1966); James MacGregor Burns, *Presidential Government* (Boston: Houghton Mifflin, 1965); Erwin C. Hargrove, *The Power of the Modern Presidency* (New York: Knopf, 1974); Thomas E. Cronin *The State of the Presidency* (Boston: Little, Brown, 1980); George C. Edwards III, *Presidential Influence in Congress* (San Francisco: Freeman, 1980); Hugh Heclo and Lester M. Salamon, *The Illusion of Presidential Government* (Boulder, Colo.: Westview Press, 1981).

19. Edwards, *Presidential Influence,* 86–100.

20. Graham T. Allison. *Essence of Decision* (Boston: Little, Brown, 1971), 144–84.

21. Aaron Wildavsky, *The Politics of the Budgetary Process* (Boston: Little, Brown, 1974).

22. Hugh Heclo, "Issue Networks and the Executive Establishment," in Anthony King, ed., *The New American Political System* (Washington, D.C.: American Enterprise Institute, 1978).

23. For a study of both routine and nonroutine presidential decision making that has generated predictive propositions see Richard L. Cole and Stephen J. Wayne, "Predicting Presidential Decisions on Enrolled Bills: A Computer Simulation," *Simulation and Games* 11 (Sept. 1980): 313–25.

24. Alexander George and Juliette George, *Woodrow Wilson and Colonel House* (New York: Dover, 1964); Doris Kearns, *Lyndon Johnson and the American Dream,* (New York: Harper & Row, 1976); Fawn M. Brodie, *Richard M. Nixon: The Shaping of His Character* (New York: Norton, 1981); Betty Glad, *Jimmy Carter* (New York: Norton, 1980).

25. Theodor W. Adorno, Else Frenkel-Brunswik, Daniel J. Levinson, and Sanford R. Nevitt, *The Authoritarian Personality* (New York: Harper & Row, 1950).

26. James David Barber, *The Presidential Character* (Englewood Cliffs, N.J.: Prentice-Hall, 1977).

27. Ibid., 8–11.

28. James David Barber, "Classifying and Predicting Presidential Styles: Two 'Weak' Presidents," *Journal of Social Issues* 24 (1968): 1.

29. Erwin C. Hargrove, "Presidential Personality and Revisionist Views of the Presidency," in Harry A. Bailey, Jr., ed., *Classics of the American Presidency* (Oak Park, Ill.: Moore Publishing, 1980). Alexander George, "Assessing Presidential Character," in Aaron Wildavsky, ed., *Perspectives on the Presidency* (Boston: Little, Brown, 1975).

2

Case Studies

NORMAN C. THOMAS

CASE STUDIES have been the stock in trade for many students of the presidency. The literature abounds with studies of individual presidents, important presidential decisions, presidential involvement in the enactment of bills and legislative programs, and presidential handling of specific policy areas. Indeed, it is more difficult to think of presidential scholarship that does not rely on case analysis than to cite that which does. At the same time, however, case studies have a bad reputation, methodologically at least, among political scientists.[1] Case studies draw criticism for their idiosyncratic nature, their lack of utility for theory-building purposes, and their descriptive rather than analytical orientation. They are contrasted unfavorably with comparative study, which is held to be more productive of systematic knowledge about the regularities of the political process.

The standing of case studies in the conventional wisdom of political science has perhaps best been typified by Wirt and Kirst, who commented that an "anecdote about how a bond issue was successfully adopted in Round Bottom, Ohio is not scholarship but vanity; it performs a function for one's vita that a filler about a six-legged dog does at the bottom of a newspaper column."[2] Primarily, case studies receive favorable recognition as teaching devices. The Inter-university Case Program studies, which are concentrated in public administration, are most notable in this regard.

Interestingly, students of the presidency have not seriously examined the implications of their reliance on case studies. Either they accept as axiomatic the conventional wisdom's negative assessment[3] or they appear to assume that the merits of case studies as empirical bases for analysis are so manifest that discussion of their methodological strengths and limitations is unnecessary.[4] In this chapter I will review the political science critique and Harry Eckstein's defense of case studies, examine representative examples of the use of case studies in the study of the presidency, and evaluate case analysis of the presidency. My objective is to develop suggestions for scholars preparing case studies related to the presidency.

THE POLITICAL SCIENCE CASE AGAINST CASE STUDIES

THE notion of a "case study" is not clearly defined within political science. In his discussion of case studies in *The Handbook of Political Science,* Eckstein defines a case "technically as a phenomenon for which we report and interpret only a single measure on any pertinent variable."[5] This is, however, a narrow definition derived from the distinction made in medicine and psychology between experimental and clinical studies. The former are concerned with general knowledge and involve many cases arrayed in statistically representative samples of an entire population. The latter are concerned with what is unique and distinctive about the subject of the study. Experimental studies are seen as contributing to the development and testing of theory, whereas clinical studies produce descriptive reports.

The problem with Eckstein's "technical definition" of case studies is that in political science the study of collective individuals or groups (e.g., parties, interest groups, legislatures, bureaucracies) involves complex relationships among many variables; attempts to disaggregate them into "single measures" of "pertinent" variables risk losing sight of the interrelationships between variables in the phenomena under study. Although seldom defined with Eckstein's precision, case studies generally are regarded as narrative descriptions of a wide range of individual and collective behavior, such as decisions, processes, and policies, that tend to be resistant to systematic analysis. There is substantial argument about the value of case studies, since it is difficult to generalize from them about the political process. It is my contention that case studies are worth "doing" if one is aware of their limitations and their potential for increasing general knowledge of politics.

In addition to the belief that case studies are more suitable for description than for analysis, the case against them holds that they do not lead to the accumulation of knowledge that can be analyzed through the use of accepted theoretical frameworks. Also, efforts to aggregate case-study findings have not been highly successful.[6]

The inability of scholars to use case studies for the accumulation of knowledge stems from the idiosyncratic nature of the studies and the failure of many of them to employ common research paradigms and analytical frameworks in conducting the studies. The unique features of every case—personalities, external events and conditions, and organizational arrangements—virtually ensure that studies conducted without the use of an explicit analytical framework will not produce findings that can easily be related to existing knowledge or provide a basis for future studies. Although there are notable exceptions to this observation, as I will indicate in the discussion to follow, most writers of case studies have been content to let their readers impose their own analytical frameworks and relate the findings to other knowledge as best they can.[7] The result has been that case studies usually are noncumulative, often interesting, and perhaps marginally useful for enhancing our understanding of the political process and for suggesting further areas of inquiry.

The argument against case studies culminates with the charge that they have little utility for theory-building purposes. Theodore J. Lowi, in a seminal review of Bauer, Pool, and Dexter's

American Business and Public Policy, one of the most complex and highly regarded case studies in the field of American politics, charged that case studies generally and studies of policy in particular were almost wholly atheoretical.[8] Lowi maintained that lack of attention to theory had led scholars to ignore the possibility, which he regarded as manifest, that policy was an independent variable that helped to shape the pattern of politics rather than a dependent variable to be explained by political factors. Lowi's suggestion that policy be classified as regulatory, distributive, and redistributive for purposes of analyzing politics has profoundly affected the study of public policy. It has had much less impact, however, on the conduct of case studies. Most case analysts have continued to show limited interest in using them for developing theory or even in using rudimentary classification schemes, such as Lowi's policy typology, or other devices to order their inquiries in a more systematic manner.

The neglect of theoretical considerations by most case-study writers may be a function of the nature and development of political science as a discipline. Political science is a hybrid, built by borrowing from other disciplines. As such it has never had a dominant intellectual paradigm or set of first principles that serve to guide inquiry and are conducive to the accumulation of knowledge and the development of theory. Indeed, interest in explanatory theory, as distinguished from normative questions and metaphysical issues, is a fairly recent development. Although most contemporary political scientists believe that the development of theory should be a basic goal of scholarship, their conception of theory is "soft" rather than "hard" or formal. According to Eckstein, hard theory uses precisely defined concepts and reasons deductively in the manner of theoretical physics, whereas soft theory is "any mental construct that orders phenomena or inquiry into them."[9] Most of the theory employed in or suitable for case studies is of the latter type.

In a polyglot discipline that includes no central theoretical paradigm and that has only recently come to an awareness of the importance of explanatory theory, albeit "soft," it is hardly surprising that large areas of inquiry remain unaffected by theoretical concerns. Given the problems of applying formal theoretical analysis to case studies, in which $n = 1$, it is quite likely that scholars with little interest in theory have been attracted to them.

Eckstein's Defense of Case Studies

The goals of theory in political science are by no means universally agreed upon. In defining theory, however, it is essential that the goals be made explicit. Briefly, according to Eckstein, theory strives for "regularity, reliability, validity, foreknowledge, and parsimony."[10] A mental construct qualifies as theory if it states "a presumed regularity in observations that is susceptible to reliability and validity tests, permits the deduction of some unknowns, and is parsimonious enough to prevent the deduction of so many that virtually any occurrence can be held to bear it out."[11]

In evaluating the utility of case studies for theory building in comparative politics, Eckstein identifies six positions, ranging from the view that there is almost no value in case studies to the belief that they are of far greater value than comparative studies. He links those positions to specific classes of case studies that are characterized by a progression in which intuition is of decreasing importance relative to systematic analysis.[12] The positions, or "options" as Eckstein calls them, and associated types of case studies are summarized in Table 2.1. He observes, quite correctly, I believe, that the "modal preference" of contemporary political science is for options 2 and 3, that a few scholars choose the fourth option, and that hardly anyone, except himself, sees merit in the final two options. The first option represents the once dominant and still common viewpoint that has been discredited by scholars such as Verba and Eckstein himself.[13]

Eckstein's defense of crucial case studies, as opposed to comparative studies, as the preferred mode of macropolitical analysis is too complex and controversial to be reviewed fully here.

TABLE 2.1

ECKSTEIN'S OPTIONS ON THE UTILITY OF CASE STUDIES
FOR THEORY BUILDING AND TYPES OF CASE STUDY

OPTION	TYPE OF CASE
1. Case studies limited to description and intuitive interpretation; only comparative studies useful for theory building.	*Configurative-Ideographic.* The configurative element is their aim to depict the overall *gestalt* of the subject, i.e., individuals, parties, bureaucracies, etc.; the ideographic element is that they let the facts speak for themselves or interpret them through intuition.
2. Case studies of limited utility for theory building but only because in interpreting cases it is necessary to apply theoretical generalizations.	*Disciplined-Configurative.* Case interpretations based on established or provisional theories or, in the absence of such theory, on "frameworks of inquiry" that will help lead to the development of general laws.
3. Case studies may be useful in the early stages of theory building for the purpose of discovering theoretical questions and possible theories.	*Heuristic.* Case studies designed to find important general problems and possible theoretical solutions; such studies can be conducted sequentially with a view to amending and refining theoretical interpretations; such studies often employ preconceived analytical frameworks.
4. Case studies can shed light on the plausibility of theory even though ultimately only comparative studies can be used to test theories. Careful case studies can be used to determine if it is worthwhile to proceed to the final stage of theory building.	*Plausibility Probes.* Attempts to discover whether the potential validity of a theory is high enough to justify the cost of testing; minimally they may simply entail an effort to determine whether a theoretical construct is worth considering; empirical probes can be suggestive or rigorous.

TABLE 2.1

Eckstein's Options on the Utility of Case Studies for Theory Building and Types of Case Study

OPTION	TYPE OF CASE
5. Case studies and comparative studies have equal utility for validating theory; they are alternative means to the same end.	*Crucial.* Cases that function as a test of theory by virtue of the fact that either they must "closely fit" a theory if we are to have any confidence in its validity, or alternatively "must not fit equally well."* (The other types of case studies may also be used with option 5. Crucial case studies are limited to options 5 and 6.)
6. Case studies are better suited to theory building than comparative studies, which are most useful as preliminaries to conclusive case studies.	All types of case studies may be used with option 6.

Source: Adapted from Harry Eckstein, "Case Study and Theory in Political Science," in Fred I. Greenstein and Nelson W. Polsby, eds., *The Handbook of Political Science,* vol. 7, *Strategies of Inquiry* (Reading, Mass.: Addison-Wesley, 1975), 92–123.

*Eckstein, "Case Study and Theory," 118.

Still, it contains at least two important arguments relevant to my assessment of case studies involving the presidency. First, case studies offer practical advantages. They cost less money and require less manpower, time, and effort than data-based comparative studies, and they are not susceptible to the problems of sampling macropolitical units.

More important, Eckstein argues that crucial case studies have advantages for theory-building purposes. They avoid the "inductive fallacy," which assumes that theories lie in phenomena and can be derived through data processing.[14] Scholars conducting a crucial case study are constrained to state theories carefully "in a manner that permits their deductive and predictive application to cases."[15] Moreover, case studies are useful for disconfirming theories, and comparative case studies can provide substantial if not conclusive confirmation. To the objection that crucial case studies cannot confirm multivariate theories or deal with complex interaction effects, Eckstein responds that theory should be regarded as a "tool of explanation" of behavior "rather than as total explanation."[16]

Whether or not one accepts all of Eckstein's defense of crucial case studies is not at issue here. His conclusion, however, that case studies have been underutilized for the purposes of finding clues to general theories in the study of macropolitics and for confirming or disconfirming them seems quite sound. That point of view will serve as the basis for the following examination and evaluation of case studies of the presidency.

CASE STUDIES AND THE PRESIDENCY

IN this discussion, I will attempt neither to make a comprehensive listing of the voluminous case-study literature involving the presidency nor to explore specific studies in depth. Rather, I shall identify two principal types of case studies and use examples of each type to examine the strengths and limitations of the type for theory-building purposes.

Undoubtedly there are many possible ways of classifying presidency case studies. For the purpose of analyzing presidential behavior, it seems logical and appropriate to distinguish between studies of areas of presidential activity such as foreign policy and studies of specific presidential decisions. This is an obvious classification scheme that can easily be applied to most of the case-study literature. Policy-area case studies treat substantive policy as the dependent variable and seek to identify and assess the impact of independent variables. Decision-making studies, most of which involve crisis situations, focus on the actions of the president.

POLICY-AREA STUDIES

AMONG policy-area case studies, those of foreign policy and national security are more numerous and display greater attention to theory than 'studies of various domestic policy areas or of economic policy. Among the analyses of foreign policy that are case studies themselves and that often rely on other case studies as important sources of data are works by scholars such as Huntington, Hilsman, Halperin, Destler, and George.[17] Also notable is the employment of case studies by the U.S. Commission on the Organization of the Government for the Conduct of Foreign Policy (Murphy Commission) as the primary basis of its 1975 report.[18]

Huntington and Hilsman use an implicit model of policymaking that regards the president as the major participant in a Washington-based process of bargaining, negotiating, and persuading and that explains policymaking as governmental response to conflicting pressures from foreign and domestic environments. Halperin, seeking greater analytical precision, employs a bureaucratic politics model that explains foreign policy as the result of unintended bargaining games within the government. The model concentrates on the organizational factors that cause slippage between presidential intentions and the implementation of policy.

Destler employs an analytical framework that combines policy concerns (issues) and organizational factors to case studies of food and trade policy in his study of foreign economic policymaking. The central question that guides Destler's analysis is "what policy concerns, represented by whom, were competing for influence?"[19] George's objective is to improve the quality of presidential foreign-policy decisions. He focuses on impediments imposed by trade-offs between high-quality decisions, the need for public acceptability and support, and the management of presidential time and resources.[20] George concludes that the key to effective foreign-policy decision making is "policy-relevant theory" based on "competent generalizations" about how such phenomena as crisis management, deterrence, and detente vary under different conditions.[21]

Each of these analyses of the making of foreign policy, a process in which the president is the central participant, relies heavily on case studies as empirical evidence. The case-study data are used to suggest theories (George and Destler) and to serve as reference points for developing theory (Halperin and Destler). Each analyst, however, employs his own theoretical constructs, and the studies do not lead to common theoretical frameworks, let alone general theories, that help to make their findings comparable and cumulative.

Case studies of domestic-policy areas manifest less concern for theory than do foreign-policy analyses. Studies of housing,[22] education,[23] and civil rights[24] tend to focus primarily on the Johnson administration (except for those of Finn and Morgan). Wolman and Thomas view presidential policymaking for housing and education as taking place in subsystems within which the president is the principal participant in a pluralistic bargaining process. Both use analyses of specific actions to illustrate their models, but they do not suggest that the relationships they found operating during the Johnson presidency will necessarily characterize subsequent administrations.[25] In fact, Thomas later notes that significant differences existed between the handling of education policy by the Johnson and Nixon administrations, as Finn clearly demonstrates in his participant-observer's report on Nixon's approach to education in the period 1969–70.[26] Also, Wolman and Merget's brief case study of the Carter administration's treatment of housing policy shows that it was quite different procedurally from that in the Johnson years.[27]

Morgan's study of civil rights policymaking compares the use of a single tool, the executive order, by five presidents from FDR through LBJ to achieve such goals as equality in the armed forces, fair employment practices, and fair housing. Her conclusions specify the factors that lead presidents to use executive orders in preference to the alternative of proposing legislation to Congress. She also identifies the conditions that affect the effectiveness and constitutionality of executive orders. Although her case study of the executive order is informative, it is issue specific and lacks theoretical relevance.

Bruce Miroff's analysis of the relationship between the

59

Johnson White House and the civil rights movement provides an excellent example of the value of a case study for exploring the validity of existing theories and for developing new ones. Miroff argues that the literature of presidential policymaking concentrates almost exclusively on elite negotiations within the Washington community. Such negotiations lead to consensus and produce incremental change. In contrast, social movements rely on mass mobilization and confrontation and seek major social change immediately. Consequently there is, Miroff asserts, a need to expand the conceptualization of the president's domestic political role derived from the literature. He accomplishes this objective through an examination of the Johnson administration's three-pronged strategy for gaining leverage over the civil rights movement. That strategy involved moderating the actions of the movement, managing the appearances of its relationship with the movement so as to find a "symbolic balance point" between commitment to the movement's goals and social stability,[28] and shifting the channels of action for adherents of civil rights from the movement toward party politics.

Miroff's findings, which he describes as suggestive, should be useful to practitioners and students of presidential politics concerned with the problem of White House relationships with social movements. Influence over the movement depends on maintaining congruence between the objectives of the movement and the administration. If the movement demands radical changes in societal institutions and values, no administration can afford to maintain a close relationship with it. Such a relationship will also be jeopardized if the White House increases its distance from the leaders and activities of the movement. Inability to influence a social movement results in loss of control over the issue(s) it espouses, yet the cost of maintaining that leverage may be more than an administration is willing to pay. Although he appreciates the White House perspective on social movements, Miroff cautions against presidential efforts to control them lest their value as stimuli for political change and vehicles for mass political participation be damaged. Those persons interested in the Reagan administration's relationships with the "New Right"/

Moral Majority could profit greatly from a reading of Miroff's case study.

Studies of economic policymaking are fewer in number than studies of foreign and domestic policy, but they also vary substantially in their concern for theory. James E. Anderson offers a straightforward description of how the "Johnson Administration was organized and how it operated to assist the president in his role as economic manager."[29] Anderson focused his analysis on the "economic subpresidency," or that system of advice, information, and staff assistance that aid the president in developing and implementing economic policy. He found a "loose and unstructured system," quite well suited to Johnson's style of leadership.[30] He did not, however, suggest generalizations or hypotheses about presidential management of the economy that can be related to other analyses or tested in other administrations.

Lawrence C. Pierce also studied economic policymaking in the Johnson administration. Using a more explicit analytical framework than Anderson, Pierce concentrated on the impact of organizational factors on fiscal policy decisions. Organizations, he argued, influence policymaking by defining specific goals, creating structures and procedures to facilitate consideration of policy objectives, and establishing rules for choosing among the alternatives.[31] A central feature of Pierce's study is the grounding of the empirical description of fiscal policymaking in a case study of the development and enactment of the 1967 income tax surcharge. Pierce found "two sequential processes operating simultaneously," one providing technical economic analysis and advice relevant to the president's economic goals, the other a complex organizational process that relates fiscal policy to bureaucratic goals, interest group demands, and the need for public support.[32] The fiscal policy process is highlighted by conflict within the executive branch and between the executive branch and Congress. Fiscal theory and analysis require consideration of long-range consequences of policy choices, and they tend to force action to achieve desired results, whereas political considerations based on the next election tend to delay or limit action. Increasingly, Pierce suggests, the president and his economic advisers find themselves taking the perspective of economic analysis while Congress, with its bargaining bias, sees things differently.[33] Pierce concluded with the prediction that the somewhat informal fiscal policymaking process that he studied would be less successful in controlling inflation in the 1970s than it had been in achieving prosperity in the early 1960s.[34]

Much in Pierce's organizational analysis of the Johnson administration facilitates our understanding of economic management by subsequent administrations. For example, the extensive commitment of the Reagan administration to a particular economic theory (monetarism/supply-side economics) and its insensitivity to the political constraints imposed by the organizational process contributed to an impasse between the White House and Congress and worsening economic conditions by late 1981. Pierce's work also illustrates how a case study conducted with an analytical framework can have predictive and explanatory value when applied to similar phenomena.

A third study of economic policymaking also applies a variant of organizational theory with positive results. Roger B. Porter's case study of the Ford administration's Economic Policy Board (EPB) uses as its analytical framework three basic strategies that presidents have employed to organize the advice, information, and assistance they receive from their staff and from the federal bureaucracy.[35] The first strategy, adhocracy, is relatively open-ended and unstructured, except for the regularizing influence of permanent staff units such as the Office of Management and Budget. It eschews systematic collection and processing of advice and relies instead on the president to distribute assignments, which may often be competitive, and to decide whom he will consult. Adhocracy is generally associated with FDR and his free-wheeling approach to running the presidency. The second approach is the antithesis of adhocracy, centralized management. It relies heavily on staff units in the White House and the Executive Office of the President to analyze ideas and information and to present its analysis to the president in a systematic format that synthesizes his options. It also uses presidential staff members and units to coordinate the activities of departments and agencies and to ensure that policies reflect presidential priorities rather than parochial departmental interests. It is an approach that was most characteristic of the Eisenhower and early Nixon administrations.

The third organizational strategy is multiple advocacy, which Porter characterizes an "an open system designed to expose the President systematically to competing arguments and viewpoints made by the advocates themselves."[36] These include representation of all points of view through examination of alternative courses of action, a means of linking policy formulation with policy implementation, a strengthening of presidential influence in the executive branch, systematic mobilization of executive-branch resources, and enhanced sensitivity to the political forces that will be affected by the policy. He warns, however, that multiple advocacy requires a stable group of high-level advisers who are able to work together effectively.

In his study, Porter first examines the establishment, structure, and operating procedures of the EPB and then presents case studies of its handling of three issues: the 1975 State of the Union tax proposals, the U.S.-U.S.S.R. grain agreement, and the 1976 footwear import decision. He finds that the EPB met many of the requirements for a multiple advocacy system as stipulated by Alexander L. George, who originated the concept:[37] it had an "honest broker" to manage the process (William Seidman, Assistant to the President for Economic Affairs); the president acted as a "magistrate" and evaluated the arguments, weighed the evidence, and then decided on a course of action; a stable core of senior advisers shared responsibility for advising the president, and the members of that group had effective access to the president; and the EPB served only the president, it was his "exclusive instrument." Porter concludes that the EPB successfully performed such functions as identifying issues and problems meriting presidential consideration, limiting presidential attention to major issues, presenting information and analysis, ensuring adequate consideration of the interests affected by an issue, developing a full range of options and identifying their costs and benefits, aiding in the implementation of presidential decisions, and evaluating policy results. The major limitations of the EPB as a mul-

tiple advocacy system were political insensitivity, the domination of a single (conservative) ideology, and insufficient attention
to strategic planning.

Porter offers a set of organizational principles, based on the
EPB experience, as guidelines for multiple advocacy systems.[38]
He suggests that presidents can best achieve policy integration
and coordination through the establishment of three cabinet-level
councils, for national security, economic policy, and social policy,
each managed by senior presidential assistants functioning as
brokers and each organized as multiple advocacy systems.[39]
Whether the multiple advocacy approach will work for other presidents in other policy areas as well as it did for Ford in economics
cannot be determined on the basis of Porter's study, but by organizing his analysis around the requirements of a strategy for
systematically processing presidential advice and information,
Porter has given his book a degree of relevancy that extends beyond a "mere case study." He may have provided a blueprint for
future presidents contemplating the organization of the White
House. At the very least, his effort should invite replication by
other scholars interested in economic policymaking and presidential advisory systems.

DECISION-MAKING STUDIES

CASE studies of presidential decision making fall into two general categories: intensive studies of specific decisions and studies
of more than one decision in which the cases are used to develop
or illustrate a theory. Studies of specific decisions can be further
classified according to the kind of policy involved, the most obvious distinctions being between foreign and domestic policy and
between crisis and noncrisis situations.

Studies of Specific Decisions. Foreign-policy decisions, especially
those involving crisis situations, have been examined extensively.
Two of the most important case studies of crisis decisions from
the standpoint of their contribution to theory building are Paige's
analysis of the 1950 decision to intervene in Korea, and Allison's

analysis of the Cuban missile crisis of 1962.[40] A crisis is an unanticipated situation that threatens the highest priorities of the president and other major decision makers and that must be dealt with in a limited period of time.[41] Both Paige and Allison employ analytical frameworks to shape their analyses, to serve as the basis for inducing prospective hypotheses from the facts of the case, and as a source of theories to explain the decisions in the case. Their frameworks are quite different, however, and do not permit comparative analysis of their results.

In his study of the Korean intervention, Paige uses a decision-making approach that explains organizational decision as the result of the interaction of three general variables or "sets of variables": the internal and external setting of the decision, information (both content and processing), and the motivations (values) of the decision makers.[42] After providing a background that describes conditions at the time of the decision in terms of the internal and external settings, he presents a narrative reconstruction of the decision-making events during the period June 24–30, 1950. He organizes the presentation so as to emphasize the categories of the conceptual framework. The distinctive features of Paige's work constitute its concluding section and principal contribution: the induction from the narrative of a set of empirical propositions regarding the effect of crisis on the independent variables of the decision-making framework and the impact of crisis on relationships between the decision makers and their settings; and the development of suggested operational guidelines for managing crisis situations involving national security.[43] Unfortunately, most of Paige's propositions and implications have not been tested through applications of his approach to other crisis decisions. A probable reason for the reluctance of other scholars to adopt his approach is its complexity; it requires extensive amounts of information and time. Still, it stands as an excellent example of how a single case study can have theoretical significance. Paige goes far beyond describing *what* happened to an analysis of *why* it happened and a consideration of *so what?*

In contrast to Paige's decision-making approach, the three conceptual models that Allison employs in his study of the Cuban missile crisis are less elaborately structured. He argues that ex-

planation and prediction in the study of national security policymaking can be enhanced by going beyond the model employed
by most analysts, which conceives of the nation-state as a rational
actor pursuing specific goals. He offers two alternative models:
the organizational process model views decisions as the outputs
of organizations within government functioning according to routines and standard operating procedures; the governmental, or
bureaucratic, politics model sees governmental actions as the
resultants of intragovernmental bargaining games among individuals acting "according to various conceptions of national, organizational, and personal goals."[44]

The three models contain different sets of assumptions and
categories of analysis that shape the kinds of questions asked and
the type of information sought by the analyst. The models provide three distinct "cuts" at the decision under study, each at a
different level of analysis; the entire government, organizations
within the government, and individual actors. Allison shows that
explanation is clarified and made more precise through successive
use of the three analytical cuts. The models are complementary
and not mutually exclusive. In a rather chilling conclusion, Allison
asserts that organizational rigidities and human limitations substantially reduce the ability of nations to avoid nuclear war on
rational grounds.

Allison does not claim that his models have general validity,
but he suggests that they can be applied, with appropriate mod-
ifications, to policy decisions in other areas.[45] It is also possible
to apply Allison's models selectively to various phenomena, for
example, strategic decisions, organizational actions, or decisions
emerging from intragovernmental debate.[46] The lack of formality
and precision in Allison's models may limit their utility for suggesting testable hypotheses, but it should also make it relatively
easy for other scholars to employ them. Given a sufficient number
of applications to other situations, it should be possible to make
refinements that could lead to formulation of general theories.
Minimally, Allison offers a framework for making comparative
case analyses that should encourage movement toward limited
but validated theoretical generalizations.

American involvement in the Vietnam War is the final national security case study I shall examine. Although Vietnam involvement did not necessitate crisis decision making, it having occurred as the result of a long series of incremental decisions, it was of crucial importance to the nation in terms of its impact on politics, social values and institutions, and foreign and military policy. The literature on Vietnam is vast and offers several explanations of why the United States became so deeply committed to what is almost universally regarded as an unsuccessful venture.[47] In one of the most systematic attempts to answer the question objectively, Leslie H. Gelb explores the decision-making process that led to steadily increasing American involvement in the period from 1947 until 1968, when President Johnson called a halt to the escalation.[48] Gelb organizes his analysis around the paradoxical proposition that although the policy failed, the decision-making system that produced it worked as it should given that the United States is a pluralistic constitutional democracy.[49] Gelb accepts the pluralistic model of policymaking and bases his argument that the system worked on three points: (1) the consensual foreign policy goal of containing communism was pursued consistently; (2) opinion differences in the policymaking elites and the mass public "were accommodated by compromise," and policy toward Vietnam deviated only slightly from the center of those opinions; and (3) the decision makers considered "virtually all" viable alternatives and made their choices with few illusions that a quick and easy victory was possible.[50]

If the system worked so well, why did it produce such a disastrous result? According to Gelb, elevation of the military containment of communism to the status of a foreign-policy doctrine not subject to challenge or debate made intervention in Vietnam an operational necessity. The intervention was gradual and did not seek immediate military victory, because the opinion consensus that supported containment did not include acceptance of the risks of a wider war with the Soviet Union or China. Perceived domestic political costs of losing — a revival of McCarthyism and electoral retribution — and of winning — isolationism and pacifism — resulted in decisions in which each president did only what was minimally necessary to keep Vietnam from falling to communism.[51] Moreover, the presidents and other high-level policymakers knew that a stalemate was the likely result.[52] Their long-range strategy was one of perseverance by which it was hoped that eventually the Communist forces would relent and seek a negotiated peace. It was not until the consensus broke up, following the Tet Offensive in 1968, that the decision to cease the escalation was made, and it was not until 1975, when a new consensus indicated that the American people had had enough, that a congressional majority ended the involvement.[53]

Gelb's principal conclusion is that presidents, in making and implementing foreign policy, should avoid the temptation to cast their policy in the framework of overall doctrines supported by consensus.[54] The problem with such policy doctrines, such as containment, is that they create a "framework of necessity. Anything that becomes necessary to do in the first place becomes virtually impossible to undo thereafter."[55] Ambitious, overarching policy doctrines also stifle dissent and lead to conceptual and operational rigidity. What is needed, Gelb maintains, are limited policy doctrines that are adaptive and conditional. Such a pragmatic, workable foreign policy can be obtained by enhancing checks and balances on the president and allowing competing centers of power, primarily Congress, to share responsibility.[56]

The theoretical contribution of Gelb's study is limited in that he does not use an explicit analytical framework that invites replication or comparison with similar studies of other long-range policy decisions. He does, however, raise important issues regarding the problems a pluralistic democracy encounters in defining and achieving its foreign-policy objectives. In this respect, his study reinforces the findings of more general studies of foreign policy that hold that policies reflecting popular attitudes and made by bargaining among a wide range of participants acquire a life of their own as a consequence of the quest for consensus.[57] Such policies drive out options, create their own imperatives, and lead to rigidity if not irrationality. Gelb's "lessons" and recommendations stand as hypotheses that invite further testing in other situations. Finally, the longitudinal dimension of the study — decisions of four presidents over a twenty-year period — increases the ability of his findings to be generalized.

The Vietnam experience is also the subject of an article-length case study that empirically tests three interrelated hypotheses concerning crisis decision making. In an analysis of President Johnson's interactions with his national security advisers during a nine-month period that included the Tet Offensive of 1968, Sigelman and McNeil test the propositions that stress leads to a contraction of the size of the decision-making unit, concentration of decision-making functions, and activation of decision-making resources. Using data obtained from the president's appointment book, they found "virtually no empirical support" for the propositions tested.[58] Still, they warn that their tests may not be valid and that their findings may be an artifact of Johnson's personality and decision-making style. Their study does demonstrate that certain widely held beliefs about the impact of stress on high-level organizational decision making are less than universally valid and that further testing is in order.

Case studies of domestic policy decisions abound, but for the most part they tend to be descriptive narratives of the configurative-ideographic type. Examples of such treatments of crisis decision making include Maeva Marcus's study of President Truman's seizure of the steel industry in 1952 and Grant McConnell's account of President Kennedy's confrontation with the United States Steel Corporation over a price increase.[59] Thomas E. Cronin's brief recounting of presidential involvement in the establishment and operation of the Teacher Corps provides a good example of the study of noncrisis decision making.[60]

Marcus approaches the steel-seizure decision and its aftermath from the perspective of presidential power and the constitutional separation of powers. She is more concerned with the impact of Truman's decision than the reasons why it was made and the process of decision making. McConnell tells the story of the steel-price crisis, and then reflects on its implications in terms of a power struggle between big business and big government. Cronin concludes his analytical study of the Teacher Corps with several suggested "lessons" of general application concerning factors that influence the achievement of policy objectives.[61] He also relates his findings to those of analysts in other policy areas, such as Moynihan and Pressman and Wildavsky.[62] His analysis of what was ultimately an unsuccessful program shows that case studies need not be dramatic nor elaborate in order to have significance beyond the facts at hand.

Studies Involving More than One Case. The second format for the employment of case studies in the analysis of presidential decision making entails the use of more than one case to provide empirical illustration of previously held theories and/or to develop hypotheses and testable generalizations. Two major works of this type are Richard E. Neustadt's *Presidential Power* and Irving L. Janis's *Victims of Groupthink.* [63] Neustadt builds a theory of presidential power and leadership on five short case studies. Three of the cases involve command decisions: President Truman's dismissal of General Douglas MacArthur in 1951, Truman's seizure of the steel industry in 1952, and President Eisenhower's dispatch of federal troops to Little Rock, Arkansas, in 1957 to enforce a judicial school-integration decree. In the other two cases the issues were less clear-cut and involved discretionary choices: Eisenhower's acceptance and support of the attack on his proposed budget by his secretary of the treasury, George Humphrey, in January 1957 and Truman's extension of the Korean War north of the thirty-eighth parallel in response to strong urging by General MacArthur in October 1950.

Neustadt's basic assumption is that the presidency is a weak office in terms of its formal powers and that presidential power depends largely on the power to persuade. Although the three cases of command resulted in achievement of presidential goals, the fact that the presidents had to resort to command was a manifestation of their weaknesses as persuaders. The damage done to the presidents in the matters of choice resulted from their failure to perceive the nature of their personal power stakes. What the country needs, Neustadt concludes, are power-sensitive presidents who are aware of the fundamental weakness of their office and who consciously seek to increase their influence so that they may persuade more effectively. The basic mode of action for such presidents should be bargaining, not command or muddled choice made primarily in response to the interests of others. In a later book, Neustadt uses case studies of foreign-policy decisions—

the Suez crisis of 1956 and the cancellation of the Skybolt rocket in 1962 — to apply the theory comparatively to the United States and the United Kingdom.[64]

Although Neustadt's theory is never explicitly stated or formally outlined, it has served as the dominant model for the study of presidential behavior since shortly after its publication.[65] Scholars routinely refer to it in framing research designs and assessing their findings. More than anyone else, Neustadt demonstrates how case analysis can produce theoretical generalizations and testable hypotheses and serve as the basis for comparative study. Moreover, Neustadt's achievement shows that creative and theoretically significant case studies need not have a quantitative empirical basis or be cast in the elaborate language of formal theory.

Janis makes a somewhat different use of six case studies in *Victims of Groupthink*. He is concerned with the causes of high-level decision-making failures involving the president and a small group of advisers. His approach is a hypothesis drawn from group-dynamics studies in social psychology: members of small, cohesive decision-making groups tend to be subjected to intense pressures for consensus and group approval that stifle dissent and prevent consideration of alternatives. The result is "groupthink" or the "deterioration of mental efficiency, reality testing and moral judgment."[66] A primary source of policy fiascoes, then, lies in defective judgment that is inherent in small, cohesive groups.

Janis tests the groupthink hypothesis through an examination of four cases involving highly cohesive groups that made defective decisions and two counterpoint cases in which groupthink was avoided. The fiascoes include the April 1961 Bay of Pigs invasion, the decision to expand the Korean War in October 1951, the failure to be prepared for the Japanese attack on Pearl Harbor in December 1941, and the escalation of the Vietnam War between 1964 and 1967. The counterpoint cases, which show that groupthink is not inevitable, are the Cuban missile crisis of 1962 and the formulation and implementation of the Marshall Plan in 1948.

From his case analyses, Janis draws some cautious generalizations and suggests hypotheses regarding the conditions under which groupthink is likely to occur. He also identifies the symptoms of groupthink and suggests "prescriptions" for avoiding it. The major generalizations are that all policymakers are susceptible to groupthink in circumstances that encourage them to seek consensus and the approval of their peers and that "groupthink tendencies sometimes play a major role in producing large-scale fiascoes."[67] Janis proposes three hypotheses: the likelihood of the occurrence of groupthink increases with the degree of group cohesiveness, with the insulation of the group members from outside influences, and with the active pursuit by the group leader of his or her preferred solution.[68]

Janis makes the concept of groupthink operational by describing eight symptoms that characterize it: (1) "an illusion of invulnerability"; (2) collective rationalizations to discount information that might lead to reconsideration; (3) "unquestioned belief " in the morality of the group; (4) stereotypical perceptions of adversaries; (5) strong pressures on members who challenge the group's stereotypes, assumptions, or commitments; (6) "self-censorship of deviations from the apparent group consensus"; (7) "a shared illusion of unanimity" concerning group judgments; and (8) the voluntary adoption of a "mindguard" role by some members who "protect the group from adverse information that might shatter their shared complacency."[69]

Janis's concluding hypothesis is that the symptoms of groupthink are most likely to occur when decision makers face a moral dilemma in which the most expedient course of action forces them to violate personal standards of humane conduct.[70] His prescriptions for avoiding groupthink are set forth as "speculative inferences" based on the case studies and general knowledge of group dynamics. They specify procedures designed to promote conscious consideration of adverse information and alternative courses of action as well as careful and deliberate reconsiderations.

More than most scholars, Janis effectively exploits the theory-building potential of his case studies. Starting with a general hypothesis — groupthink tendencies in small, cohesive groups —

he analyzes six high-level governmental decisions and finds that the failures are to a significant extent the result of groupthink. He concludes with a "rudimentary explanatory theory" that "concurrence-seeking" within decision-making groups tends to suppress rational, empirical assessments of the efficacy and morality of the alternatives under consideration.[71] His prescriptions can serve both as a guide to policymakers and as hypotheses for testing in further studies. Janis's theory has been widely applied in subsequent studies of decision making.[72]

Conclusion: Presidency Case Studies and Theory Building

Most case studies of the presidency fall within Eckstein's first three options in terms of their utility for theory-building purposes and are of the configurative-ideographic, disciplined-configurative, or heuristic types. Even the most highly regarded case studies, such as those in the work of Allison, Neustadt, and Janis, are primarily of heuristic value, although it might be argued that they have certain attributes that qualify them for inclusion under options 5 and 6.

I assume that case studies involving the presidency will continue to be written, because they are a manageable way of presenting complex information and because the obstacles to generating quantifiable data that can serve as the basis for comparative study in the field are so formidable that most scholars will continue to opt for case analysis. (The Sigelman and McNeil undertaking suggests that those who do generate quantitative information may find that it is so tenuously related to the phenomena under study that it cannot carry the weight of the analytical task of testing complex theory. Their article is but one case study, however, and one should not make sweeping conclusions on the basis of such limited evidence.) I also assume that presidency case analysts will increasingly want to go beyond option 1 and the configurative-ideographic mode and exploit the theory-building potential of their research — if only to invalidate, disprove, or call into question widely held generalizations.

These assumptions pose obvious questions. Given the nature of research problems in studying the presidency — the paucity of quantitative information and the small number of cases — how much further can scholars go in using case studies for theory building? How should they proceed? What considerations should they bear in mind as they design and conduct their research? Clearly, additional configurative-ideographic studies are of little value beyond their contribution to the historical record. Most case studies will probably be of the disciplined-configurative and heuristic types. True comparative analysis in this area is out of reach. Crucial case studies that function as tests of theory (option 5), however, are a possibility, as is evidenced by Allison's study of the Cuban missile crisis and Janis's exploration of the groupthink hypothesis.

At the very least, scholars contemplating the use of case analysis, either to study a major presidential decision of historic importance or as a means of testing and exploring hypotheses about presidential behavior, need to be aware of the prospects for and pitfalls of theory building in this form of inquiry. They should consciously use an analytical framework, in the manner of Porter, and they should design their studies so that their findings can be related to the efforts of other scholars. Some degree of comparability across presidential administrations, such as Gelb provides, will make their conclusions better able to be generalized and will facilitate replication and further study in other situations.

I have tried to show in this survey of the use of case studies in presidential scholarship that case analysis need not be purely descriptive and atheoretical. Case studies have considerable potential for theory building if only scholars will recognize and exploit it. Although we may never discover the methodological grail of a general theory of presidential politics and behavior, we can and have through case studies increased the precision of existing paradigms and more systematically produced knowledge that is cumulative and that moves closer to that illusive goal.

NOTES

1. See Sidney Verba, "Some Dilemmas in Comparative Research," *World Politics* 20 (Oct. 1967), 111–27, and Frederick M. Wirt and Michael W. Kirst, *The Political Web of American Schools* (Boston: Little, Brown, 1972), 1–3.

2. Wirt and Kirst, *Political Web,* 2.

3. See, for example, Hugh Heclo, *Studying the Presidency: A Report to the Ford Foundation* (New York: Ford Foundation, 1977), 17, 19.

4. In this respect, see Richard E. Neustadt, *Presidential Power: The Politics of Leadership* (New York: Wiley, 1960), and *Alliance Politics* (New York: Columbia Univ. Press, 1970); Maeva Marcus, *Truman and the Steel Seizure Case: The Limits of Presidential Power* (New York: Columbia Univ. Press, 1977).

5. Harry Eckstein, "Case Study and Theory in Political Science," in Fred I. Greenstein and Nelson W. Polsby, eds., *The Handbook of Political Science,* vol. 7, *Strategies of Inquiry* (Reading, Mass.: Addison-Wesley, 1975), 79–137.

6. Cf. Stephen K. Bailey and Edith K. Mosher, *ESEA: The Office of Education Administers a Law* (Syracuse, N.Y.: Syracuse Univ. Press, 1968).

7. Robert K. Yin and Karen A. Heald, "Using the Case Survey Method to Analyze Policy Studies," *Administrative Science Quarterly* 20 (Sept. 1975), 371–81.

8. Theodore J. Lowi, "American Business, Public Policy, Case-Studies, and Political Theory," *World Politics* 16 (July 1964): 677–715; Raymond A. Bauer, Ithiel De Sola Pool, and Lewis Anthony Dexter, *American Business and Public Policy: The Politics of Foreign Trade* (New York: Atherton Press, 1963).

9. Eckstein, "Case Study and Theory," 86.

10. Ibid., 87.

11. Ibid., 90.

12. Ibid., 92.

13. Verba, "Some Dilemmas,"; Eckstein, "Case Study and Theory."

14. Eckstein, "Case Study and Theory," 113.

15. Ibid., 123.

16. Ibid., 130.

17. Samuel P. Huntington, *The Common Defense: Strategic Programs in National Politics* (New York: Columbia Univ. Press, 1977); Roger Hilsman, *The Politics of Policy-Making in Defense and Foreign Affairs* (New York:

Harper & Row, 1971); Morton H. Halperin, *National Security Policy-Making* (Lexington, Mass.: Lexington Books, 1975); I.M. Destler, *Making Foreign Economic Policy* (Washington, D.C.: Brookings Institution, 1980); and Alexander L. George, *Presidential Decisionmaking in Foreign Policy: The Effective Use of Information and Advice* (Boulder, Colo.: Westview Press, 1980).

18. U.S. Commission on the Organization of the Government for the Conduct of Foreign Policy, *Appendices* (Washington, D.C.: U.S. Government Printing Office, 1975).

19. Destler, *Making Foreign Economic Policy*, 18.

20. George defines high-quality decisions as those "in which the president correctly weighs the national interest in a particular situation and chooses a policy or option that is most likely to achieve national interest at acceptable cost and risk." (*Presidential Decisionmaking*, 2–3.)

21. Ibid., 243.

22. Harold L. Wolman, *Politics of Federal Housing* (New York: Dodd, Mead, 1971); H.L. Wolman and Astrid E. Merget, "The Presidency and Policy Formulation," *Presidential Studies Quarterly* 10 (summer 1980): 402–15.

23. Norman C. Thomas, *Education in National Politics* (New York: David McKay, 1975), and "The President and Education Policy," in Steven A. Shull and Lance T. LeLoup, eds., *The Presidency: Studies in Policy Making* (Brunswick, Ohio: King's Court Communications, 1979), 152–73; Chester E. Finn, Jr., *Education and the Presidency* (Lexington, Mass.: Lexington Books, 1977).

24. Ruth P. Morgan, *The President and Civil Rights: Policy-Making by Executive Order* (New York: St. Martin's, 1970); Bruce Miroff, "Presidential Leverage Over Social Movements: The Johnson White House and Civil Rights," *Journal of Politics* 43 (Feb. 1981): 2–23.

25. Wolman, *Politics of Federal Housing;* and Thomas, *Education in National Politics.*

26. Finn, *Education and the Presidency.*

27. Wolman and Merget, "The Presidency and Policy Formulation."

28. Miroff, "Presidential Leverage Over Social Movements," 14.

29. James E. Anderson, "Managing the Economy: The Johnson Administration Experience" (paper presented at the Annual Meeting of the American Political Science Association, Washington, D.C., Aug. 27–30, 1980).

30. Ibid., 21.

31. Lawrence C. Pierce, *The Politics of Fiscal Policy Formation* (Pacific Palisades: Goodyear Publishing, 1971).

32. Ibid., 6.

33. Ibid., 208.

34. Ibid., 211.

35. Roger B. Porter, *Presidential Decision Making: The Economic Policy Board* (New York: Cambridge Univ. Press, 1980).

36. Ibid., 27.

37. Alexander L. George, "The Case for Multiple Advocacy in Making Foreign Policy," *American Political Science Review* 66 (Sept. 1972): 751–85.

38. Porter, *Presidential Decision Making,* 215–30.

39. Ibid., 226–28.

40. Glenn D. Paige, *The Korean Decision* (New York: Free Press, 1968); Richard C. Snyder and G.D. Paige, "The United States Decision to Resist Aggression in Korea: The Application of an Analytical Scheme," *Administrative Science Quarterly* 3 (Dec. 1958): 341–78; Graham T. Allison, *The Essence of Decision: Explaining the Cuban Missile Crisis* (Boston: Little, Brown, 1971), and "Conceptual Models and the Cuban Missile Crisis," *American Political Science Review* 63 (Sept. 1969): 689–718.

41. Charles F. Hermann, *Crises in Foreign Policy: A Simulation Analysis* (Indianapolis: Bobbs-Merrill, 1969).

42. Paige, *Korean Decision,* 6; Snyder and Paige, "United States Decision," 348.

43. Paige, *Korean Decision,* chs. 11, 13.

44. Allison, *Essence of Decision,* 174.

45. Cf. Theodore Marmor, *The Politics of Medicare* (Chicago: Aldine, 1973).

46. Allison, *Essence of Decision,* 276.

47. See, for example, David Halberstam, *The Best and the Brightest* (New York: Random House, 1972); and Daniel Ellsberg, *Papers on the War* (New York: Simon & Shuster, 1972).

48. Leslie H. Gelb with Richard K. Betts, *The Irony of Vietnam: The System Worked* (Washington, D.C.: Brookings Institution, 1979).

49. Ibid., 2.

50. Ibid., 24–26.

51. Ibid., 25.

52. This is also Ellsberg's principal thesis.

53. Gelb with Betts, *Irony of Vietnam,* 351–53.

54. Ibid., 365.

55. Ibid., 362–63.

56. Ibid., 364.

57. See Robert A. Dahl, *Congress and Foreign Policy* (New York: Norton, 1950); Huntington, *Common Defense*; and Hilsman, *Politics of Policymaking*.

58. Lee Sigelman and Dixie Mercer McNeil, "White House Decision-Making Under Stress: A Case Analysis," *American Journal of Political Science* 24 (Nov. 1980): 652–73.

59. Marcus, *Truman and the Steel Seizure Case*; Grant McConnell, *Steel and the Presidency* (New York: Norton, 1963).

60. Thomas E. Cronin, *The State of the Presidency*, 2d ed. (Boston: Little, Brown, 1980), ch. 9.

61. Ibid., 319–21.

62. Daniel P. Moynihan, *Maximum Feasible Misunderstanding* (New York: Free Press, 1969); Jeffrey Pressman and Aaron Wildavsky, *Implementation* (Berkeley: Univ. of California Press, 1973).

63. Neustadt, *Presidential Power*; Irving L. Janis, *Victims of Groupthink* (Boston: Houghton Mifflin, 1972).

64. Neustadt, *Alliance Politics*.

65. For a formal statement of Neustadt's theory, see Peter W. Sperlich, "Bargaining and Overload: An Essay on *Presidential Power*," in Aaron Wildavsky, ed., *The Presidency* (Boston: Little, Brown, 1969), 168–92.

66. Janis, *Victims of Groupthink*, 9.

67. Ibid., 192.

68. Ibid., 197.

69. Ibid., 197–98.

70. Ibid., 206.

71. Ibid., 202.

72. See George, *Presidential Decisionmaking*, 93–94.

3

Concepts

JOHN H. KESSEL

RESEARCH BEGINS in an atmosphere of uncertainty and constraint. At the outset, one is all too aware of the hazards and limitations. Yet certain of the constraints — specifically those stemming from the concepts brought to the research task — enable the researcher to move from uncertain beginnings to a finished research product.

This chapter explains my use of concepts in some of my research on the presidency. Since it is necessarily personal, it is not intended as an account of how research should be done. Rather, it is a record of how some research actually was done, and it provides some examples that other researchers may want to use, adapt, or ignore according to *their* research needs.

One source of uncertainty to a researcher, especially to one working in an area in which little previous study has been done, is the absence of an articulated body of theory. As Charles O. Jones has noted in an article significantly entitled "Doing Before Knowing," good theory is necessary to identify good concepts. Good theory, however, is often unavailable, and when "the search for 'good theory' is likely to be unrewarding, one may simply feel too insecure in proceeding any further."[1] It is one thing to engage in research in voting behavior, in which one can draw on theories of party identification, candidate choice, and so forth. In research on the presidency, however, these familiar guideposts are not available, and this can give the researcher a very lonely feeling.

Additional sources of uncertainty are unfocused plans and an unfamiliar setting. Richard Fenno has provided an excellent account of his feelings during his fieldwork for *Home Style*. At the outset, he writes, "I had no idea what kinds of answers I would get. I had no idea what questions to ask. I knew only that I wanted to get some number of House members to talk about their constituency perceptions . . ."[2] Once in the field, Fenno wondered, "How do I know whether I'll get anything useful? I am 2000 miles from home and $600 poorer, and how do I know I'll have any decent rapport with these people?"[3] Past research experience helps to cope with these doubts, up to a point. But such stage fright is entirely normal when beginning to gather data.

Along with uncertainty, the researcher is aware of limits on what can be accomplished. Access will be available only to certain kinds of data, persons may refuse to be interviewed, and if interviews are obtained, the conditions may be such (the respondent gets an urgent phone call or has to leave to go to a meeting) that the researcher may be able to learn only a fraction of what he or she hoped to discover. Above all, the researcher's time is limited, either because of costs or because of other responsibilities. Hence, the researcher will have to make do with whatever can be learned within a finite opportunity.

Another limiting factor is one's accumulated intellectual capital. This includes, of course, certain data-gathering techniques, certain modes of analysis, and, most important, certain concepts. Once launched on a research enterprise, the time is no longer ripe for enlarging one's intellectual repertoire. This adds to the already present sense of constraint, but it also sets the eventual course. The very limits on the concepts available provide the discipline that will shape the data gathered and fashion the eventual report. It is this thesis that I will illustrate from my own experience.

RAW MATERIALS

ANYTHING that one constructs must be fashioned from the raw materials available to the builder. This is true of intellectual products as well as buildings and other artifacts. The only difference is that the raw materials available to the intellectual are the concepts he or she already knows, those that can be borrowed, and the ideas that occur because of other things that engage his or her attention at the same time.

In the autumn of 1972, I had just completed writing "The Parameters of Presidential Politics."[4] This was a content analysis of the State of the Union messages delivered by Presidents Truman, Eisenhower, Kennedy, and Johnson. It revealed six policy areas — international involvement, economic management, social benefits, civil liberties, natural resources, and agriculture — that could be defined both by subject matter and by characteristic behavior. Although I was satisfied that these policy areas suggested a general pattern to presidential politics, they did not give me much of a feeling for the institution. I wanted to do some research that would bring me into personal contact with presidential staff members. My hope was that it would provide some sense of the activities that I thought must be subsumed within the general pattern that had been identified.

Two other projects were going forward at the same time. Richard Hofstetter, then at Ohio State, had been given a grant by the American Enterprise Institute to study the media content of the 1972 campaign, and his research design included parallel surveys of campaign activists and of the electorate. I had begun a content analysis of texts from nomination, electoral, and executive politics with the support of the National Science Foundation. This was a successor study to "Parameters" that made comparisons across institutional domains in a single year rather than across time within a single institutional domain. Hofstetter and I had made plans for parallel studies, and data were being collected. The research that I thought would make sense in this context was a case study of the 1973 State of the Union message. Tracing the decisions about what did and did not go into this message would give me some sense of the presidency that was missing from the more abstract factor analysis, and whatever information I got could be interpreted in the light of these two other studies.

In early September, I saw Raymond K. Price, the speechwriter who was the author of most of Nixon's State of the Union messages. He told me that the composition of the messages was too personal to the president to permit an outside scholar to come in and gather data, but he made another suggestion. The Domestic Council was the source of many of the policy proposals in the Nixon White House, and no study of it had yet been done. Preliminary inquiries indicated that I *might* be able to interview members of the Domestic Council staff. With this altered research target in mind, I went back home to make some plans.

This situation is, at least in my experience, fairly typical of the beginning of research. I knew nothing about the Domestic Council, beyond the simple fact of its existence, and since little had been written about it, my innocence was not going to be alleviated prior to the interviews. I had never done any interviewing with White House personnel and knew only that those who had been most successful (such as Richard E. Neustadt and Thomas E. Cronin) had had the advantage of familiarity from their own experience on White House staffs. I needed to complete the research quickly because I was soon going to take on the editorship of the *American Journal of Political Science,* and once manuscripts began arriving in early 1973, further research would be impossible. In other words, I found myself very conscious of uncertainties and constraints.

The proclivities that I brought to this situation can be divided into two classes: general intellectual premises and the background of research with which I was familiar.[5] The first general premise was that there should be a good fit between any theory and the subject matter to which it is applied. This may be nothing more than saying that material validity should be a test of the appropriateness of theory as well as logical validity. Although both of these tests are traditional, many persons working with axiomatic theory seem more concerned with a closed system than with a good fit with real-world data. I am one of those who, as Donald Matthews once put it, likes to "muddle along rather close to the data."[6]

The second general premise was that political behavior is not a separate field but, rather, an approach that is at least potentially applicable to all traditional political topics. Heinz Eulau has explained it thus:

Political behavior is invariably "electoral behavior," "administrative behavior," "judicial behavior," and so on. . . . This implies that behavior in one context or institutional setting differs from behavior in others, and the context or setting is the critical factor in behavior. . . . Our concern is with those characteristics of behavior that we expect to occur because the behavior is relevant to the institutional political order of which it is a part. For this reason, political behavior is not a separate field òf investigation.[7]

Professor Eulau rightly stresses explicit recognition of institutional factors, but this posture also means that as long as human beings are involved, and as long as the observer aspires to systematic explanation, the whole panoply of behavioral concepts is available for use. This obviously is consistent with my first general premise that the theories employed ought to be isomorphic with the data.

The third general premise concerned the utility of levels of analysis. This was introduced in political science in 1952 by Herbert A. Simon, who wrote:

Complexity in any body of phenomena has generally led to the construction of specialized theories, each dealing with the phenomena at a particular "level." Levels are defined by specifying certain units as the objects of study and by stating the propositions of theory in terms of intra-unit and inter-unit behavior. (Cf. the sequence of elementary particle-atom-molecule in physics and the sequence: gene-chromosome-nucleus-cell-tissue-organ-organism in biology.) . . . The phenomena of organization constitute an important level of theory — a level that is encompassed neither by the usual conceptualizations of small group processes nor by those of the more macroscopic analyses of cultures and institutions.[8]

In two preceding works, a book written in the mid-1960s, and a review of the literature written in the summer of 1971, I had used four levels of analysis to interpret political parties, arguing that actors combine into groups, that groups combine into coalitions, and so forth.[9]

During the time I was planning this research, I read three other studies. One was in page proof, and the other two were in manuscript. The first was *Labyrynths of Democracy* by Heinz Eulau and Kenneth Prewitt.[10] I had sought a copy of this study of

San Francisco Bay area city councils because it was the one major study since David Truman's *The Congressional Party* that both addressed important political questions and sought to operationalize group phenomena.[11] It seemed evident to me that the Domestic Council staff was a group, and in order to address the topic in this way I needed measures for group-level phenomena. The second source was Thomas Cronin's *State of the Presidency,* which presented the fruit of his interviews with members of the Kennedy, Johnson, and Nixon staffs.[12] The third source was Aage Clausen's *How Congressmen Decide.*[13] Among other things, this contained Clausen's discussion of the content of his policy dimensions.

Selecting the Concepts

As it developed, I had little more than a month, from early September to mid-October, to review this material and plan the research. My choice of concepts — and the measures used to operationalize them — are not all that surprising given the nature of the research opportunity, my own predilections, and the material I had been reading. From the Eulau-Prewitt study, I took several measures of influence resting on identification, legitimacy, sanctions, and expertise; a question about bargaining that had been crucial to their discussion of governing practices; and a general question they had used as the basis for their conceptualization of governing style. I also included a couple of questions that could be seen as reflecting their concern for contextual properties. The first, which I would ask respondents early in the interview, was "What would you say are the things the Council *must* do in order to serve the needs of the president?" The other question was to be asked at the end: "What presidential actions are most critical to the success or failure of an administration?" These two items could also be seen as coming from Richard Fenno's environmental constraints or from my discovery that two of the policy areas (international involvement and economic management) were treated by presidents as imperative, whereas the others were not.

The part of the Cronin study that was most germane to domestic policy coordination was his discussion of White House-department relations, some of which had been in his earlier "'Everybody Believes in Democracy until He Gets to the White House'."[14] From Aage Clausen's careful analysis of the content of policy dimensions came questions about the staff members' attitudes in each of the policy areas as well as queries about how much time was devoted to each policy area.

Although many of the concepts that shaped my questions came more or less directly from the three works, some concerns arose independently. In order to capitalize on the Hofstetter data set, items were included that asked the respondents where the president was perceived to be, and where the voters were, in each of the policy areas. This meant that Hofstetter and I had identical policy items for the voters, campaign activists, and White House staff members, as well as extensive perceptual data. Since I saw the Domestic Council staff as a group, I also included some items on their norms, intragroup communication, and the salience of other actors with whom they were dealing.[15] I was a good deal more nervous about these questions. The other items had at least borne fruit in other vineyards; I had no idea what would emerge from these seeds.

I also decided on some questions that were not conceptual at all but arose from a strictly substantive need to find out what these people were doing. An open-ended query asked each respondent to pick some project that was fairly typical of the work he or she was doing and to tell me a little bit about it. Another item asked how much time the person was spending on each of five tasks that the Domestic Council had been charged with handling when it was created.

COLLECTING THE DATA

EARLIER I said that researchers should not spend time enlarging their intellectual repertoire when engaged in fieldwork. By this,

I meant that time taken off to study something new reduces time spent on the research. In the course of the research, however, investigators learn something about the measures they have chosen to employ. If they do not add to their intellectual capital in the sense of acquiring some new skill, their understanding is certainly modified as they learn what works and what does not. Unexpected comments made by respondents aside from strict answers to questions will also increase their knowledge.

This process cannot be disentangled from the interviewing itself, particularly in structured interviews. The question sequence has two basic purposes: to elicit data pertaining to the concepts selected for study and to maintain sufficient rapport between the researcher and respondents. Any change made for one purpose affects the other. Consequently, the experience of interviewing affects one's views on the utility of the concepts and the quality of the data.[16] Let me illustrate this with a few examples from my interviews with Domestic Council staff members.

Most of my interviewing was done in November 1972. Although most of the interviews went very well — in some cases lasting half a morning — the general context was set by the post-Watergate atmosphere,[17] by the staff's previous experience with reporters who could put unguarded comments in headlines the next morning, and by the fact that they did not know how far they could trust me. Beyond all this, there were certain topics they simply could not discuss. For example, they could not talk about anything that was then being considered by the president. This was of little concern to me. I was not looking for any secrets: I was much more concerned with ascertaining the basic behavior pattern of the staff. Consequently, in the open-ended question about a typical project the respondent was handling, I emphasized that I was interested in something the respondent was free to talk about. This facilitated the interviews but also meant that I had to handle the resulting data with some care because of the respondents' tendencies to pick projects of which they were relatively proud.

Another question that turned out to be troublesome was that about the relative salience of other actors. As already noted, there was no doubt in my mind that I wanted to ask about this. The question was how. The phrasing I used was:

> Now this is a little more difficult, because it refers to a hypothetical situation. I'm going to name some persons and groups. In each case, I'd like you to assume that you'd found out that they had *very strong* views about some topic you were handling. How much difference would it make in the way *you* handled it — a *very great* difference, a *great* difference, *some* difference, *hardly any* difference, or *no* difference at all?

This was followed by a list of eight types of actors: the president, congressional leaders, colleagues on the Domestic Council staff, and so forth. My assumption was that everyone would say that the president's views would make a very great difference. I wanted to see how the other actors would be ranked in comparison with the president and in comparison with each other. This question proved difficult for the respondents to handle. It generated data, and as far as I could judge after analysis, reliable data, but it took the respondents a long time to answer and made me nervous about the amount of interview time that was being used up. The staff members took time to explain why they were hesitant to give me a flat answer of "a very great difference," "some difference," or whatever, and in the process they told me a good deal about their relationships with congressional leaders, party leaders, interest group leaders, and so on. If I had not employed this "bad" question, I would not have learned nearly as much about White House ties to Congress, parties, or interest groups.

Another part of the interview that proved to be "bad" in a very different way was the pair of questions dealing with White House-department relations. One question asked what strategies were available to the departments if they wanted White House support for their policy positions, and a follow-up question asked what the White House could do to get departments to support their preference. This did not cause the respondents any discomfort; they answered immediately. The problem was that the White House-department relations were so well understood that almost everyone gave much the same answers. I was getting lots of validity checks, but I was wasting precious interview time because I was getting very little new information from successive respondents. The positive, and unpredicted, aspect of these questions, was that in combination with the "bad" series about the salience of various actors, the information began to shape itself into a view of the environment in which the Domestic Council staff was situated.

WRITING

IT is by now a commonplace that the way research results are reported — in books, journal articles, and so on — bears little resemblance to the way the data are gathered or to the thoughts that pass through a researcher's mind as he or she gropes toward the report. Indeed, a principal reason for books such as this is that it is difficult to reconstruct the research process from the report. A key to understanding *why* this is so can be found in Charles O. Jones's "Doing Before Knowing." Jones points out that one way we use concepts is as a *classification of research expectations,* projecting what we suppose we will find, and another way is as a *classification for general understanding,* ordering phenomena in order to be able to communicate with others about it. "'Doing Before Knowing,'" Jones tells us, "is really an exercise in concept development and modification."[18] Seen in this light, a researcher has three chances to array the concepts — or, if you prefer, two chances to repair initial mistakes. The first comes in the selection of the concepts that will guide the data collection. The second comes in the data-gathering stage when the investigator discovers what is working, what is not working, and what is working differently from the way expected. The third comes in the preparation of the research report. The report masks the manner in which the data were collected not only because the sequence in which the data are collected is rarely the most efficient manner in which to communicate the findings but also because the investigator learns more about his concepts when gathering the data and still more in the process of rumination while writing up the results.

In the case of *The Domestic Presidency,* the data gathered during my interviews was presented in chapters 2 through 4.[19] In chapter 2, I wanted to show that it was appropriate to consider the Domestic Council staff as a group. The basic definition of a group, from David Truman's *The Governmental Process,* is that a group must have shared attitudes and a stable pattern of interaction.[20] For the first element, shared attitudes, I used data on the staff members' views in the policy areas. In order to show agreement among staff members, I used a measure of consensus developed from the marginal distributions and a measure of proximity that tapped the extent of agreement between each pair of staff members. (Strictly speaking this did not show sharing, but it was close enough to allow the inference.) In order to show structure I used the data on communication and those on influence. To present these I used a matrix form suggested in *Introduction to Finite Mathematics* by John G. Kemeny, J. Laurie Snell, and Gerald L. Thompson.[21] Although infrequently used in political science, it is a very powerful way to analyze patterns. The analysis showed that the communication and influence patterns were consistent with one another, that some of the communication links were not apparent to the staff members themselves, and that expertise provided a basis of influence that was distinct from identification, sanctions, and legitimacy, three bases of influence that tended to reinforce one another.[22]

In the third chapter, I gathered together material that suggested the staff members' perception of their environment. In one bit of luck, it turned out that voters were the actors who were regarded as most important after the president himself. Since perceptual data had been gathered pertaining to the president and the voters, this provided a beginning for this chapter. Much of the rest of this chapter dealt with the other actors — cabinet members (and their departments), staff colleagues, Congress, interest groups, bureau chiefs, and Republican party leaders — in descending order of importance.

The fourth chapter was more substantive. Here the activities of the staff members were discussed: preparing decisions for the president to make, making some less consequential decisions themselves, backstopping the president by taking care of fire-engine chores, collecting information as a basis for long-range planning, and monitoring agency activity in order to make sure they were fully aware of what was going on. The analysis of time devoted to these activities showed that the staff members were devoting the most time to preparing decisions for the president, the least to monitoring agency activity; the others were ranked in between in the same order that they are listed here.

Afterthoughts

One thesis to this point has been that the research design, data gathering, and writing are focused by the limited number of concepts at the command of the researcher. Another, implicit so far, is that your work is driven by doubt. You pay closer attention to the things that you are less satisfied with, and this attentiveness makes it more likely that you will find some way to modify the concepts, measures, or exposition so as to make them more useful. For instance, because of my concern about the staff members' answers to questions dealing with the salience of other actors, I observed these more closely and ideas began to emerge about the environment in which the staff was situated.

The dual feelings of contentment and skepticism continue after the work is done. The researcher knows better than any readers what has worked reasonably well and what is unsatisfactory. In my case, I was restive with the levels-of-analysis approach. I was quite satisfied that the staff could be properly treated as a group, and there were no difficulties with the aggregative properties of the group. One could begin on the individual (or infra-individual) level, pick up attitudinal data, and aggregate this perfectly well to the group level, reporting measures of central tendency, such as a mean. The difficulties came with the contextual properties, those which come from the more inclusive levels in which the entity being considered is situated. In my previous work, I had used activist, group, coalition, and institution as four levels of analysis. But where do these more inclusive levels stop? An institution is part of a government, and a government — depending on the goal of the analysis — is either part of a culture or an international system. In other words, the concept of contextual properties (or, equivalently, environmental constraints) excludes *nothing* as a possible cause of the unit's behavior.

I had been thinking about how institutional environment could be defined when I happened to read a chapter entitled "The Majestic Clockwork" in Jacob Bronowski's *The Ascent of Man*.[23] The chapter dealt with time as an absolute in Newtonian physics and as a function of space in relativistic physics. What, I found myself wondering, would happen to the concept of environmental constraint if I split out time as a separate concept?[24]

There were certainly temporal patterns that were defining characteristics of institutions. Many cycles arose from the two-year and four-year electoral calendar, and the behavior in the policy areas followed temporal patterns. There were other temporal effects besides. Enough temporal effects were evident to make it worthwhile to group them together, but what would that leave? One possible answer was that executive politics takes place in a structured environment. Certain actors — Congress, the bureaucracy, the media, and so on — command the attention of any incoming president, and there are certain policy areas in which he must act. If the notion of structure was potentially useful when looking outward from the White House, it was certainly useful within. There had not been any problem with aggregative properties in the levels of analysis; it would be quite simple to treat the less inclusive levels of analysis as internal structure. Therefore, temporal patterns could be identified, internal structure could be identified, and there was at least the beginning of a definition of external structure in the idea of other actors with whom the president had necessary relationships. These were the musings that led me to move from a straight levels-of-analysis approach to one that uses internal structure, external structure, and time.

I returned to White House interviewing in the autumn of 1980. My planning was somewhat more straightforward than it had been in 1972 because of my earlier experience. I wanted to do a partial replication of the 1972 study but focusing on the major elements of the White House staff rather than on a single unit. My guiding rule was to keep those concepts and measures that had worked before and to discard the rest, substituting material germane to my newer interests, time and structure. I wanted to ask directly about temporal patterns. I was puzzled about how the various units of the White House staff (i.e., press office, congressional relations office, National Security Council (NSC) staff, and so on) fit together into a decision-making complex of whatever character. I wanted to begin looking at the components of external structure.

As this is written (June 1981), I have completed interviews with thirty members of the Carter White House staff, and have had much shorter initial interviews with thirty members of the Reagan White House staff. I have done a little analysis and am presently pondering some initial results. What are my doubts right now? To begin with, how representative are my respondents of the White House staff? I was able to obtain interviews with more than 90 percent of the persons I contacted in the Carter White House, and with three-quarters of the number I contacted in the Reagan White House.[25] At least three "screens," however, made it more likely that I would see some White House staff members rather than others. First, because I could not include all of the many members of the staff, I chose to focus on the more permanent, more policy-oriented units of the Executive Office of the President (for example, Office of Management and Budget, NSC, and so on) rather than the "political outreach" components. Second, I often sought interviews with individuals who had been mentioned as being particularly intelligent, simply because I could learn more from such respondents. Third, some persons refused to be interviewed. Other things being equal, persons who felt uncomfortable with an academic were the ones more likely to do so. As a result, I ended up with a set of informative interviews from intelligent persons. Still, I do not know how representative of the total White House staff my respondents are.[26]

Another puzzle is how much of the change I am finding is true change, and how much of it is a result of a change in my measures. I replaced the "bad" sequence of questions, about the salience of the other actors, with a question that asked about a hypothetical recommendation the respondent had received, that included a much longer list of actors, and that used responses whose intensity was known through the work of Lodge, Tursky, and Tanenhaus at Stony Brook.[27] For those actors appearing on both the 1972 and 1980 lists, the responses of Nixon staffers and Carter staffers were generally comparable — with one important exception: voters were seen as much less important in the Carter White House than in the Nixon White House. I do question, however, how much of this apparent change should be attributed to the fact that voters rarely "make a recommendation," the 1980 form of the question, even though their "very strongly held views," the 1972 form of the question, may be regarded as quite important.

Finally, should differences between the Carter and Reagan White House staffs be regarded as intrinsic, or are they due to the much greater experience of the Carter respondents at the time of the interview? (Interviewing both staffs close to the same time point is useful for some purposes, such as their perception of the 1980 electorate, but not for others, since the Carter personnel had had four years of experience, whereas the Reagan administration was new to office.) For example, analysis of their attitudes on public policy shows there is much greater consensus among the Reagan staff members than was the case with their predecessors. Is this an intrinsic difference between the two staffs? Or is the greater agreement among Reagan staff members because they have not yet had to consider the range of policy alternatives that they will face during four years? Either is a plausible explanation. Comparison with the attitudes of the Nixon staff (a Republican staff interviewed after four years in office) was inconclusive. Eight items were repeated. On four, the Nixon standard deviations (a measure of consensus) were closer to the Carter pattern; on two, the Nixon pattern was closer to the Reagan pattern; and on two others there was no real difference. One might construe this as a hint, but it certainly does not resolve the question. If my second thesis that research is driven by doubt is true, there are enough puzzles here to sustain analysis for some time.

93

Conclusions

Can any generalizations be drawn from my experience? It is personal, but I suspect that one generalization is that research *is* personal. I have stressed how my approach was shaped by the concepts I have used and my own cognitive style. To the extent that concepts are uniformly understood and used throughout a discipline, and to the extent that persons with similar cognitive styles are recruited into a discipline, there should be comparable research throughout that discipline. These conditions do not prevail in an eclectic discipline such as political science. However one might wish for the ease of communication that exists when most research is being done within the same paradigm, many different concepts are used by researchers with many different cognitive styles. Therefore I suspect this account might be most helpful to those who feel comfortable with these concepts and who think in similar ways.

My approach certainly does not guarantee "success." The reviews of *The Domestic Presidency* provide some insight into peer reaction to research. The most favorable review appeared in the *American Political Science Review*. Peter Sperlich wrote:

> What we have . . . is a case study. . . . The great danger in this approach is that the monograph easily degenerates into story-telling. . . . Anecdote is piled on anecdote, completely smothering whatever systematic theoretical formulations the work once contained. Fortunately, in Kessel, theoretical considerations and interests predominate over the anecdotal components. [He] approaches the subject matter not as a historian-journalist, but as a social scientist, with a theoretical orientation, explicit definitions, and specified hypotheses. He has an explicit methodology, and an awareness of the basic rules of evidence and inference. On these grounds alone, the book is a most welcome change from the more customary literature. . . . *The Domestic Presidency* is a small and unpretentious yet insightful book of considerable importance.

The least favorable review appeared in *Choice*. This (anonymous) reviewer said:

Decision-making in the White House — whether on the domestic front or in the area of international relations — has been a neglected area of academic examination. This book does little to alter that. . . . There have been other better books on the presidency in recent years: George E. Reedy's *The Twilight of the Presidency* and Emmet John Hughes' *The Living Presidency.*

The point here is not that you win some and you lose some (although that is usually the case). Rather, it is that peer reaction depends on what the reader considers important. Peter Sperlich received his Ph.D. from the University of Michigan, and he feels entirely comfortable with a behavioral approach such as mine. The reviewer in *Choice,* judging from his comment about better books on the presidency, thinks well of critiques written by insiders. My book was not a critique, and I am not an insider. The generalization here is that the best any scholar can hope for is to reach the audience that is on his wavelength. Whatever your approach, you cannot expect approbation from those who have tuned you out before you begin.

Another way my research is typical is that it illustrates the continual give-and-take between research and theory. A stick-figure version of research holds that one looks up a theory in the literature, decides on a hypothesis, collects data, announces that the hypothesis has been confirmed or disconfirmed, and that is all there is to it. It does help to have clearly defined concepts. As Robert K. Merton has put it, "If [the investigator] is not to be blocked at the outset, he must devise indices that are observable, fairly precise, and meticulously clear. The entire movement of thought that was christened 'operationalism' is only one conspicuous case of the researcher demanding that the concepts be defined clearly enough for him to go to work."[28] But as Charles O. Jones has pointed out, clear concepts are not always available, and then the researcher has to do the best he can. Furthermore, the research process clarifies concepts nearly as often as the concepts guide research. To return to Merton's words, "the very requirements of empirical research have been instrumental in clarifying received concepts. The process of empirical inquiry raises conceptual issues which may long go undetected in theoretic inquiry."[29] In my case, I began with a set on concepts in the autumn of 1972, learned something about them while doing my interviewing, reorganized them while writing *The Domestic Presidency,* continued to think about them afterward, and began further research in the autumn of 1980 with a considerably modified set of conceptual guidelines. I would expect concepts to guide my research, and research to instruct my concepts as long as I continue.

Finally, research is similar to writing. When I begin a research project, I do not know what I am going to find, how I am going to find it, or how long it will take. When I begin to write, I do not know what I am going to say, how it will all fit together, or how long the manuscript will be. What research and writing have in common is that the discipline imposed by the process tends to solve these problems. The selection of concepts guides the researcher toward certain data. The selection of concepts helps the writer to organize his material. Doubts alert both researcher and writer to particular problems along the way. None of this guarantees quality, but the necessity of choosing moves the scholar from uncertain beginnings to a final product.

Notes

1. Charles O. Jones, "Doing Before Knowing: Concept Development in Political Research," *American Journal of Political Science* 18 (Feb. 1974): 216.

2. Richard Fenno, *Home Style: House Members in their Districts* (Boston: Little, Brown, 1978), 251.

3. Ibid., 281.

4. John H. Kessel, "The Parameters of Presidential Politics," *Social Science Quarterly* 55 (June 1974), 8–24.

5. A full account of what happened during this period would certainly include my contacts with other political scientists whose advice I urgently sought. I emphasize here my own intellectual capital because the research was shaped by the concepts with which I was familiar and my own cognitive style.

6. Donald Matthews, "Patterns of Influence in the U.S. Senate: Five Approaches" (paper presented at the Annual Meeting of the American Political Science Association, New York, Sept. 8-10, 1960), 2.

7. Heinz Eulau, *The Behavioral Persuasion in Politics* (New York: Random House, 1963), 17.

8. Herbert A. Simon, "Comments on the Theory of Organizations," *American Political Science Review* 46 (Dec. 1952): 1030, 1031, 1039.

9. Let me stress that these premises are by no means unique to me. As the quotations suggest, they were introduced by others, and I had simply adopted them. They are important in this context because they suggest the approach that I was likely to follow in my own research.

10. Heinz Eulau and Kenneth Prewitt, *The Labyrinths of Democracy: Adaptations, Linkages, Representation and Policies in Urban Politics* (Indianapolis, Ind.: Bobbs-Merrill, 1973).

11. David Truman, *The Congressional Party* (New York: Wiley, 1959).

12. Thomas E. Cronin, *The State of the Presidency* (Boston: Little, Brown, 1975).

13. Aage A. Clausen, *How Congressmen Decide: A Policy Focus* (New York: St. Martin's, 1973).

14. Thomas E. Cronin, "'Everybody Believes in Democracy until He Gets to the White House . . .': An Examination of White House Departmental Relations," *Law and Contemporary Problems* 35 (1970): 573-625.

15. This research was concept rich, but theory poor. That is, a great many concepts were included, but relationships between the concepts were not specified. This leaves open the possibility that relationships between the concepts may be discovered in the analysis, but it also means that one does not begin with much theory. I have a hunch that a lot of exploratory research is of this character.

16. For an extended discussion of interviewing as such, the reader should consult Chapters 10 and 11.

17. The break-in had taken place, but the extent of White House involvement was not known at the time. Only one of my respondents turned out to be involved in any way. Many of my respondents were worried about their futures but for another reason. All had been ordered to resign immediately after Nixon's reelection, and they did not know what jobs, if any, they would get during Nixon's second term.

18. Jones, "Doing Before Knowing," 217.

19. There was other material in chs. 1, 5, and 6. This material was, of course, germane to the book but not to my purpose here of illustrating how concepts are rearrayed for more efficient communication.

20. David Truman, *The Governmental Process* (New York: Knopf, 1950).

21. John G. Kemeny, J. Laurie Snell, and Gerald L. Thompson, *Introduction to Finite Mathematics* (Englewood Cliffs, N.J.: Prentice-Hall, 1956), ch. 7.

22. This was an instance that illustrates borrowing measures from other investigators (Eulau and Prewitt) but then using a different form of analysis.

23. Jacob Bronowski, *The Ascent of Man* (Boston: Little, Brown, 1973).

24. This question arose not because of a close relationship between the Bronowski discussion and my conceptual problem but because I had been wondering how to conceptualize environmental constraint, and the mention of time in the book triggered a possible answer in my mind. I mention this here because I usually cannot remember how I got an idea. I am conscious of being perplexed about a problem: then I know I am inclined to handle it in a given way. I do not know how I got from the first state to the second.

25. The principal reason for this difference was that neither Richard Allen nor any other members of Allen's NSC staff were willing to be interviewed. With this exception, 85 percent of the Reagan staff members contacted agreed to interviews.

26. Richard Fenno handled this problem differently in his fieldwork for *Home Style*. He distinguished between "good" interviews, with persons comfortable with academics, and "bad" interviews, with persons who were not. "In the end, seven of the eighteen members [whom Fenno accompanied in their districts] were people who were used to and comfortable with academics, six were neither accustomed to nor comfortable with academics, and five were somewhere in between on this version of the 'at-homeness' index" (1978, p. 255). Because of his awareness of this problem, Fenno is in a better position to assume that his sample is representative.

27. I should like to thank Professor Milton Lodge for making these results available to me.

28. Robert K. Merton, *Social Theory and Social Structure,* rev. ed. (New York: Free Press), 115.

29. Ibid., 117.

4

Quantitative Analysis

GEORGE C. EDWARDS III

THE AMERICAN PRESIDENCY has been a prime topic of research
interest to political scientists from the time political science
emerged as a discipline. Despite this interest our progress in understanding the presidency has been very slow. One reason for
this is that scholars have generally relied upon modes of analysis
that are either irrelevant or inappropriate for examining analytical questions on basic relationships of the presidency. In this
chapter I argue that we need to make greater use of quantitative
analysis in our studies of the presidency, and I demonstrate both
the utility of this type of analysis and the possibilities for overcoming constraints on the use of quantitative methods. I also stress
the importance of theory in using quantitative analysis and the
types of questions unlikely to be susceptible to quantitative
research.

THE NEED FOR QUANTITATIVE ANALYSIS

PERHAPS the most striking fact about most literature on the presidency written by political scientists is the low regard with which
it has been held by the discipline. Of course, the discipline might

be incorrect in its evaluation of scholarship on the presidency, but I do not think so. Research on the presidency too often fails to meet the standards of contemporary political science, including the careful definition and measurement of concepts, the rigorous specification and testing of propositions, the employment of appropriate quantitative methods, and the use of empirical theory to develop hypotheses and explain findings.

This point should not be exaggerated. There *is* high quality research being done on the presidency. Moreover, I am not condemning all traditional scholarship on the presidency. Research focusing on the legal setting of the presidency in the tradition of Edward S. Corwin has had a deservedly honored place in political science. Answers to questions about the legal powers of the presidency and related institutions and constraints on the actions of each of these institutions are significant in our constitution-based democracy. Similarly, the institutional approach to studying the presidency, describing its organizations and processes, has important contributions to make. Whereas at one time this literature concentrated on formal descriptions of the institution, that is, its organizational structure and rules, much of it has now turned to the more important topic of describing the behavior of the actors who compose the presidency (see Chapter 1). Obviously, we must know what the political actors relevant to the presidency are doing before we can analyze the causes and consequences of their behavior.

Nevertheless, research on the presidency, taken as a whole, has not advanced our understanding of the institution very far. Although we have innumerable descriptions of it and its occupants, we have a fundamental lack of understanding of why things happen as they do. We have generally not focused on explanations, that is, the relationships between two or more variables. Instead, we have usually examined only one side of an equation. This presents a striking paradox: the single most important institution in American politics is the one that political scientists understand the least.

I propose that we add some questions for examination. We want to know not only the boundaries of constitutionally acceptable behavior and what behavior occurs, but also *why* the public, the Congress, the White House staff, and the bureaucracy behave in the ways they do toward the president and what difference the president's behavior makes. Reconceptualizing the study of the presidency into a set of relationships leads us to develop and test hypotheses that attempt to explain the causes and consequences of the behavior of those who compose the presidency and those with whom they interact.

To increase our understanding of the presidency we must move beyond the description of the institution and its occupants and attempt to explain the behavior we observe. In addition, we must seek to reach generalizations rather than being satisfied with discrete, ad hoc analyses. To explain we must examine relationships, and to generalize we must look at these relationships under many circumstances. Quantitative analysis can be an extremely useful tool in these endeavors.

Of course some scholars of the presidency have employed traditional methods and have attempted to explain as well as describe, but we should be skeptical of conclusions reached with this approach. Often the data base is composed of a small number of examples or only one. There is usually little or no possibility of controlling for alternative explanations. Naturally, generalizations based upon such data must be viewed as tentative at best.

Let me illustrate the problem with a few examples. One of the crucial decision points in America's involvement in fighting in Vietnam was July 1965 when President Johnson committed the U.S. to large-scale combat operations. In his memoirs the president describes his process of decision on this issue, and he goes to considerable lengths to show that he considered all the options available at this time very carefully.[1] One of his aides later provided a detailed account of the dialogue between Johnson and some of his advisers.[2] It shows the president probing deeply for answers, challenging the premises and factual bases of options, and playing the devil's advocate. Yet in a recent book a presidency scholar has argued persuasively that this "debate" was a charade, staged by the president to lend legitimacy to the decision he had already made.[3]

Another useful example is President Johnson's efforts at obtaining the support or at least the neutrality of Senate Finance

Committee chairman Harry Byrd of Virginia on the 1964 tax cut. Hubert Humphrey reported in his memoirs that Johnson cajoled Byrd into letting the tax bill out of committee, relying on Lady Bird's charm, liquor, and his own famous "treatment."[4] Presidential aide Jack Valenti tells a different story, however. He writes that the president obtained the senator's cooperation by promising to hold the budget under $100 billion.[5] Thus, we have two eye witnesses reporting on two different tactics employed by the president and each attributing Senator Byrd's response to the presidential behavior that he observed.

To confuse matters further, Henry Hall Wilson, one of the president's congressional liaison aides, indicates that both eye witnesses were wrong. According to Wilson, when the president proudly told his chief congressional liaison aide, Lawrence O'Brien, about his obtaining Byrd's agreement to begin hearings on the tax cut on December 7, O'Brien replied, "You didn't get a thing. I already had a commitment for the 7th."[6] In other words, Johnson's efforts were irrelevant. Both eyewitnesses were wrong in attributing influence to him.

Even tapes of conversations in the Oval Office may be misleading. As Henry Kissinger explains regarding the Watergate tapes,

> Anyone familiar with Nixon's way of talking could have no doubt he was sitting on a time bomb. His random, elliptical, occasionally emotional manner of conversation was bound to shock, and mislead, the historian. Nixon's indirect style of operation simply could not be gauged by an outsider. There was no way of telling what Nixon had put forward to test his interlocutor and what he meant to be taken seriously; and no outsider could distinguish a command that was to be followed from an emotional outburst that one was at liberty to ignore — perhaps was even expected to ignore. . . .
>
> The significance of every exchange turns on its context and an appreciation of Nixon's shifting moods and wayward tactics. Remove these and you have but random musings — fascinating, entertaining, perhaps, but irrelevant for the most part as the basis for the President's actions.

One of Nixon's favorite maneuvers, for example, was to call a meeting for which everybody's view except one recalcitrant's was either known to him or prearranged by him. He would then initially seem to accept the position with which he disagreed and permit himself to be persuaded to his real views by associates, some of whom had been rehearsed in their positions, leaving the potential holdout totally isolated.[7]

Advantages of Quantitative Analysis

THE advantage of quantitative analysis of the presidency can be seen in the quantitative studies that have been done already. For example, one of the most crucial relationships of the presidency is the president's standing in the public. Why are presidents as popular (or unpopular) as they are? We are just beginning to make some headway in the investigation of this question.[8] Related to these studies are those of the attitudes and beliefs of children toward the presidency and the president.[9] This research has come out of the subfield of political socialization. Substantial progress in understanding public support for the president, a factor that I believe to be of great significance to the operation of the presidency, would simply be impossible without the use of quantitative analysis and the technique of survey research.

The other side of this relationship is the president's leadership of public opinion. We know presidents devote considerable efforts to this task, but without quantitative analyses our understanding of the impact of presidential efforts to lead or manipulate public opinion will remain almost completely conjectural. Fortunately, a few scholars have begun to explore this area with quantitative techniques, including experimentation. Some have focused on the public's response to presidential leadership,[10] while others are concerned with variance in the content of what the president presents to the public.[11] Other efforts have focused on the important questions of the nature of media coverage[12] and its effect on public approval and expectations of the president.[13]

The study of presidential-congressional relations has also been advanced through the use of quantitative analysis. We have been able empirically to test propositions about the extent of presidential coattails,[14] the pull of the president's party affiliation,[15] the influence of the level of the president's public approval[16] and electoral support,[17] and the significance of presidential legislative skills.[18] Many of our findings have been counterintuitive, and none of them would have been possible without the use of quantitative analysis. As in the case of the president's public support, we have only scratched the surface of the utility of quantitative techniques.

Even more exciting is the prospect of applying quantitative analysis to entirely new areas of presidency research. One such area in which quantitative analysis would be useful is that of presidential decision making, including presidential advisory systems. Nearly every student of the presidency has at one time or another discussed in lectures, writings, or both, how the organization of the White House staff influences presidential decisions, probably illustrating the point with examples like Richard Nixon's infamous "Berlin Wall." Yet it is difficult to show that the organization of the White House staff has any influence whatsoever on presidential decisions. This is not to say that it has no effect; it is to point out, however, that we cannot have confidence in conclusions based on our present understanding of presidential decision making. We need to measure information flow, including the options, information, and analyses placed before the president, in different organizational structures and in different organizational structures with different personalities at the top. Only then will we be able to state with confidence how organizational structure affects the options and information received by the president.

We are also interested in other influences on presidential decision making. Who influences the president? An article by Cole and Wayne illustrates the utility of applying quantitative analysis to such questions.[19] How do external constraints and pressures, such as public opinion, the state of the economy, and international events, affect presidential decisions and decision making? Some progress is being made. Studies have examined the effect of a crisis situation on decision-making processes;[20] the influence of the public's approval of the president on the scheduling and conduct of press conferences;[21] and staff attitudes and communication and influence patterns in domestic policymaking.[22]

Another area inviting quantitative analysis is that of policy implementation. Scholars have generally given the president's role as "executor" of the law limited attention, and most of what attention it has received has been of an anecdotal or case-study nature. First, we must identify the variables critical to successful implementation, such as communications, resources, implementors' dispositions, bureaucratic structure, and follow-up mechanisms.[23] Then we need to develop measures of them as well of implementation itself. Some very interesting survey work has been done on dispositions.[24] Finally, to make much headway toward understanding presidential policy implementation, we should employ quantitative methods to relate, systematically and empirically, possible causes with possible effects.

Overcoming Constraints on Quantitative Analysis

There have been three principal constraints on using quantitative analysis to study the presidency. The first, the frequent failure to pose analytical questions, has already been discussed. The second constraint has been the small number of cases, that is, presidents. Viewing the presidency as a set of relationships, however, helps to overcome this problem. Although there may be few presidents, many persons are involved in relationships with each president, including the entire public, the membership of Congress, the federal bureaucracy, world leaders, and so on. By focusing on these relationships, which include many people interacting with the president in one form or another, we are no longer inhibited by the small universe of presidents.

This leads us to the third perceived constraint on the quantitative study of the presidency: lack of data. Since scholars of the presidency have typically been more interested in description than analysis, they have often been primarily concerned with "inside" data on the president and the presidency. As we have seen, however, this usually is only one side of a relationship, and we ought to be looking at both sides in order to develop reliable explanations.

When we pose analytical questions, we are naturally led to search for data on the causes and consequences of presidential behavior. For example, we may ask what the president wants from other political actors, what he is trying to get people to do. Among other things, the president wants support from the public, positive coverage from the media, votes for his programs from Congress, options, information, and analyses from his advisers, and faithful policy implementation from the bureaucracy. Thus, we ought to look for data on these political actors, whose behavior is usually the dependent variable in our hypotheses, that is, what we are trying to explain. Similarly, we ought to seek data on independent variables, on causes of behavior toward the president, such as the determinants of public opinion, congressional support, and bureaucratic faithfulness.

With a little imagination we can find a substantial amount of relevant data, some of which is discussed in later chapters. Extensive collections of public opinion polls with questions dealing with the presidency and individual presidents are in archives at the Roper Center at the University of Connecticut and the Louis Harris Data Center at the University of North Carolina at Chapel Hill. Measures of presidential approval and numerous personal characteristics and attitudes of respondents are available in the election studies from 1968 to the present at the University of Michigan's Center for Political Studies. New samples for socialization studies can be easily drawn. Congressional Quarterly continues to provide us with presidential election results for each state and congressional district. The Television Archive at Vanderbilt University is a data source largely untapped by those interested in the effect of the media on presidential politics. All of the president's public statements and press conferences are available from a number of sources, including the Government Printing Office. Broader presidential efforts at influencing public opinion are beginning to be well documented. What we need to do now is to correlate the measures of the independent variables that are now available with their potential results, that is, popular support for the president, always controlling for alternative explanations.

The availability of data on Congress is overwhelming. Virtually all roll-call votes on the floor plus an increasingly large number of committee votes are made public, and the former can be obtained in machine-usable form. These votes can be aggregated into indexes fashioned for the researcher's special purpose, and Congressional Quarterly calculates a yearly overall Presidential Support Score for each member of Congress. Debates, hearings, bills, amendments, and other potential indicators of congressional relations with the presidency are widely available, and congressional staff members are generally accessible for interviews. Some members of Congress and the White House staff are as well, but access will remain difficult to achieve on a systematic basis.

Access is part of the reason there are few quantitative studies of presidential decision making. It is almost impossible to monitor on-going White House decision making systematically without being there. Until recently, presidential papers have not been convenient for most of us to use. The improved physical facilities of presidential libraries and our increasing familiarity with them should alleviate at least some of this problem (see Chapters 8 and 9), as should improved theory, which will help us to sift relevant data from the abundance of information in the libraries. Naturally, interviews will remain an invaluable tool.

The problem regarding studies of policy implementation is not access, I am convinced, but simply one of lack of attention to this crucial area. The large number of case studies on the bureaucracy provide ample evidence that there is little bureaucratic behavior that is hidden from scholars.

THE IMPORTANCE OF THEORY

THUS far I have shown that quantitative analysis is both necessary and feasible for answering many fundamental questions about the presidency. In this section, however, I want to raise a red flag of warning: methods and models must be appropriate for the questions under investigation. If this seemingly obvious rule is not followed, the conclusions that authors reach are likely to be inaccurate. The fact that they are produced through the use of impressive looking, and therefore seemingly authoritative, statistics only makes matters worse. Unfortunately, this simple rule is often ignored.

The primary causes for using inappropriate methods and models in studies of the presidency are the weak theoretical underpinnings for the hypotheses being tested and attempts to push data on the presidency into the most sophisticated mode of analysis possible. We often possess more methodological sophistication than is applicable to the research question at hand and are anxious to exploit our skills. At the same time we are often insufficiently sensitive to the implications of the hypotheses or models we are testing. In other words, we often fail to employ theory satisfactorily.

As a result of this combination of methodological skill and theoretical weakness, statistics and models that are not appropriate to testing the hypotheses under study are sometimes employed. The conclusions such studies reach are unreliable and, often, uninterpretable. To illustrate my point I will rely on two subjects of my own recent research: presidential approval and presidential influence in Congress. For each area I will explain why I chose the methods and approaches I did and contrast them with some other methods and approaches used by other researchers examining the same topics. I will show how a lack of attention to theory may result in the use of inappropriate methods, ranging from statistical tests to variable measurement.

PRESIDENTIAL APPROVAL

MOST studies of presidential approval have relied upon time-series analysis.[25] In essence, scholars have compared the rise and fall in presidential approval (treated as a dependent variable) over time with the rise and fall of possible explanatory variables, such as unemployment and inflation. The greater the change in presidential approval that is associated with changes in the independent variables, so the argument goes, the greater our ability to explain presidential approval.

Although the scholars who have done such studies have been talented professionals and have made a major contribution by focusing our attention on presidential approval and possible explanations of it, I chose not to employ time-series analysis in my attempt to explain presidential approval for several reasons. The first is technical in nature. In the words of Lee Sigelman, a close student of studies of presidential approval,

> Time-series analysis is a statistical minefield, where a single misstep can cause the entire analysis to blow up in the face of the unwary researcher. Virtually every conceivable statistical problem shows up in its most virulent form in time-series analysis, and the technical fixes not infrequently surpass the understanding of reader and researcher alike. The complexity of these problems and solutions means that substantive conclusions about presidential popularity are often based on inappropriate statistical procedures and that these conclusions have gained broad currency because readers who are unable to judge for themselves whether a statistical analysis is competent have accepted them at face value.[26]

In time-series analysis, "technical" problems include autocorrelation (the correlation of variables with themselves over time, which distort findings); gaps in data sets (that many researchers either ignore or complete through interpolation without alerting the reader); the selection of time units of months, quarters, or years; and the use of changes in levels or absolute levels of presidential approval as the dependent variable. There is also the problem of the coding of independent variables occurring in some previous month. How long should we assume they have an impact? How fast should we discount their impact over time? Do people blame the president for conditions, such as the state of the economy, that were determined before he took office? Do people compare the present with the past or just consider current conditions as absolutes? Finally, small fluctuations in presidential approval between two points in time may be due to sampling error or other polling limitations.

Despite the confusion and uncertainty that generally pervade time-series analyses of presidential approval, this is not the heart of their limitations. Their biggest drawback is in the area of theory. The implicit theory behind correlating variables such as economic conditions with presidential approval in time-series analyses is that as the environment and circumstances of individuals change, their level of support for the president will also change. If unemployment and presidential approval vary together, for example, then researchers conclude that unemployment levels are part of the explanation for presidential approval.

The careful reader will note that in time-series analyses, scholars have used aggregate data—the national Consumer Price Index, for example—because they lack individual-level data. Yet they often make direct or implied inferences to the individual level. Conclusions as to who decrease their support of the president—the unemployed, those worried about unemployment more generally, or some other group—must be speculative, however. Aggregate time-series data do not allow us to answer such questions.

The best way to test such propositions is to obtain individual-level data and then examine it to see what, if any, circumstances or perceptions of persons are related to differences in presidential approval. This is what I did.[27] In this way I could make reasonable inferences about the impact of various factors, such as the economy and war, on presidential approval and see whether the direct impact of such factors on individuals causes approval levels to rise and fall or whether persons react to other considerations.

Individual-level data is very useful in another way. In time-series analyses it is often unclear just what certain variables measure. "Dummy" variables representing Watergate, international crises, and individual presidents cannot contribute much to our understanding of the causes of presidential approval. They are too imprecise, and we have no idea how people perceive them. Moreover, arbitrary judgments must be made on how to weight each factor and how long its impact lasts. Dramatic, sharply focused international crises, for example, often referred to as "rally" variables, are generally all weighted the same, and the researcher must make a decision as to the duration of their possible impact on public opinion *prior* to testing for any impact.

No more theoretically illuminating are conclusions based upon variables measuring the public's level of approval of the president in the previous month or over time. Even if strong correlations result from the use of such variables, we do not know how to interpret them. We do not know what the variables really measure or why they affect the president's standing in the public.

Another problem inherent in time-series analyses is that the meaning we attribute to variables may change over time, although the theories underlying their use hold that their meaning is constant. For example, although reports of the unemployment rate continue to count the percentage of the population that is unemployed, the composition of the unemployed has changed over time and the hardship caused by unemployment has been reduced. Women and youths now compose a larger percentage of the unemployed than in the 1950s. Since many of these women and youths are not the primary wage earners in their families, the correspondence between hardship and unemployment is probably less now than in earlier decades. More liberal eligibility requirements for unemployment insurance and welfare programs and increased payments over time buttress the argument that unemployment has a different impact on people's lives today than in the past. The extent to which this difference translates into impact on presidential approval is, of course, an open question. The point is that a variable may have different meaning over time, further reducing the reliability of findings. Cross-sectional analysis allows us to compare the effect, if any, of a variable at different points in time to see if it has changed over time and if it is greater when the values of the variable are extreme, such as in the case of high unemployment.

A final difficulty with aggregate social indicators is that they are often poor measures of what they purport to represent. Statistics concerning the Vietnam War are notoriously suspect. Numerous articles on the limitations of economic indicators such as the Consumer Price Index and the unemployment rate appear in scholarly journals. Even to the extent that the latter is an accurate measure at any one time, the figures that are employed in time-series analyses may not reflect the total percentage of the population that is unemployed in a year. The rate may be stable while newly unemployed people replace those who found employment. Thus, many more people may be unemployed in a year than the official rate indicates. Rather than relying on measures of doubtful validity and that do not match our theorizing, it is preferable to find out how individuals perceive their circumstances and the degree to which their circumstances have changed.

PRESIDENTIAL INFLUENCE IN CONGRESS

In the last few years a substantial number of research papers have been written on presidential-congressional relations regarding legislation. Many have followed the basic format of using time-series analysis, with some measure of presidential success in Congress each year as the dependent variable in an equation with several independent variables. The goal is to learn to what degree the latter influence legislative success. If such an analysis could be done properly, it would have several advantages, including gauging the relative effect of each variable, controlling for the influence of all other variables, and providing us with a comprehensive explanation of presidential success in Congress. This is indeed an attractive prospect.

Despite these potential advantages, such studies are inherently unable to tell us much about presidential influence in Congress or even explain bottom-line presidential success in Congress. The dependent variables in the studies are yearly aggregates, masking variability in support for the president among individual members of Congress or groups of members. Some statistics even average aggregate figures for the House and Senate! This, of course, makes no theoretical sense at all. This overaggregation makes inferences about the causes of behavior of individual members of Congress toward the president impossible.

For this reason I chose to use Presidential Support Scores, calculated separately for each member of Congress.[28] Starting with individual-level data, I could disaggregate as much as my independent variables would allow and compute aggregate figures for groups of representatives and senators when it was appropriate to do so. Beginning with one aggregate figure to represent behavior, on the other hand, makes it impossible to disaggregate it to the individual level.

It is also important that we be clear about what we are trying to explain and choose a dependent variable that is a valid measure of the concept. I was interested in explaining presidential influence in Congress and not success in passing the president's program per se. Although "success" seems at least as important as "influence," we learn much less by studying the former. The results of such an analysis do not allow us to make reasonable inferences about the causes of congressional behavior. (One of the greatest errors of the aggregate studies is that they generally end up making such inferences.) What such analyses do provide is conclusions such as presidents have greater success in obtaining congressional passage of their programs when they have a cohesive majority in Congress. Such a conclusion is, of course, correct, but it is also virtually a truism and unrevealing about the causes of behavior.

Aggregate independent variables are just as limited as aggregate dependent variables. Using only one figure to represent a concept for each year inevitably leads one to miss or distort important relationships. For example, I found that presidential electoral performance in each congressional district is sometimes a source of White House influence in Congress and that presidential popularity is a source of presidential influence but affects Democrats and Republicans differently. These findings have not been disputed. Yet, aggregate studies have not been able to include such measures. The reason is straightforward: they require disaggregation. Similarly, presidential legislative skills are basically ignored as possible sources of influence because we have no one indicator to represent this variable.

Political party affiliation is quite naturally included in all studies of presidential-congressional relations. In aggregate studies it is usually represented by some measure of party strength in Congress. No matter how party is measured in such a study, findings based on it cannot serve as the basis for inferences about the effect of party affiliation on congressional voting on presidential requests. Making such inferences requires examining the changes in the voting behavior of party groups on the same issues when the party occupying the White House changes. That Democrats and Republicans vote differently tells us nothing about why they do so. Thus, it is *not* sufficient to correlate party membership figures with measures of legislative success. This only produces truisms. Unfortunately, some authors forget this and end up stating uninterpretable conclusions about the importance of party affiliation.

Another seemingly obvious but often forgotten point in quantitative studies of the presidency is that the statistics one employs must be appropriate to the hypotheses being tested. In testing for the importance of presidential prestige as a source of presidential power, I used two measures of the independent variable: the president's vote in each congressional district and the president's standing in the Gallup poll. To test for the impact of the first variable, I found it necessary and appropriate to employ path analysis, which requires the use of unstandardized regression coefficients as the measures of association.

Gallup poll data, on the other hand, are not available for individual constituencies, so I had to use a time-series model. More important to our discussion here, I used the standard correlation coefficient (r) as the measure of association I chose to report. I selected this measure instead of the often more appealing unstandardized regression coefficient (which is produced by the same calculations) because of theory. The latter measure is interpreted as a unit change in the independent variable producing a certain change in the dependent variable. This naturally implies a direct relationship between the variables. I chose to rely on the correlation coefficient because neither I nor anyone else has ever been able to provide a theoretical foundation for such an interpretation. Presidential popularity is more reasonably viewed as a background variable and the r is a better representation of such an influence, since it simply represents covariance. Unfortunately, in the rush to be scientific, many researchers overlook the critical link between theory and methods and choose inappropriate statistics to test their hypotheses.

Methods must also be appropriate to the data being used to test hypotheses. Interval-level data is the most highly prized because it allows us to employ regression analysis, but not all data can be reasonably coded into an interval scale. For example, no one has yet developed a comprehensive measure of presidential legislative skills, much less one' on an interval scale. Until that can be done, the impact of legislative skills will not be appropriately tested by regression models. In this case we can either ignore them, which is typically done in aggregate studies, or employ a less sophisticated mode of analysis. In the case of legislative skills, which I could describe but not calculate, I chose to compare the presidential support of several subgroups in Congress to see if they varied at all, and if so, if the presidents who had "greater" legislative skills received more support in Congress. Since there was little variance, I concluded that overall, presidential legislative skills were not a significant systematic influence on congressional support for the president.

To summarize this section, the proper use of quantitative analysis, like any other type of analysis, is predicated upon a close linkage between the methods selected and the theoretical arguments underlying the hypotheses being tested. Too often, theory is either ignored or treated cavalierly. As assertion that something causes something else to happen is not a theoretical argument, it is only an assertion. A theoretical argument requires an emphasis on explanation, that is, *why* two variables are related. If closer attention is given to the use of theory in research on the presidency, our understanding of the institution will increase more rapidly than it has in the past.

LIMITATIONS OF QUANTITATIVE ANALYSIS

DESPITE its utility for investigating a wide range of questions dealing with the presidency, quantitative analysis is not equally useful for studying all areas of the presidency. In this section I will discuss these limitations while, at the same time, pointing out that often they are less restrictive than some scholars may think.

LACK OF VARIANCE IN INDEPENDENT VARIABLES

THE research situations in which quantitative analysis is least likely to be useful are those in which there is a lack of variance in the variables under study. If the focus of research is just one president and the researcher is concerned not with the president's interactions with others but with how factors such as the president's personality, ideas, values, attitudes, and ideology influence his decisions, quantitative analysis will be of little help. The independent variables are unlikely to vary much during a term in office. Similarly, factors in the president's environment, such as the federal structure of U.S. government or the basic capitalist structure of our economy, vary little over considerable periods of time, and it is therefore difficult to employ quantitative analysis to gauge their impact on the presidency.

Ideally we should move beyond case studies, whether of a single president or a single country, and make comparisons across different presidents and different nations. Such studies would provide us a firmer basis for confidence in our conclusions. Whether all the necessary factors can be controlled to make such comparisons useful is an open question, however.

LEGAL AND INSTITUTIONAL STUDIES

QUANTITATIVE analysis is also unlikely to be useful for what I earlier termed the legal and institutional approaches to studying the presidency. Both approaches are valuable and both will continue to rely on more traditional methods. I certainly would not argue that I would abandon an area of study just because it is not susceptible to quantitative analysis. I advocate only the necessity of moving beyond these approaches if we are to understand and explain the causes and consequences of the behavior of those who compose the presidency and those with whom they interact.

NORMATIVE QUESTIONS

NORMATIVE questions and arguments have always occupied a substantial percentage of the presidency literature, and rightly so. Can quantitative analysis aid scholars in addressing these concerns? The answer is, "partially." Let me illustrate this with the example of what has probably been the central normative concern regarding the presidency: its power.

To reach conclusions about whether the presidency is too powerful or not powerful enough requires a three-part analysis. The first is an estimation of just how powerful the presidency is. As I have shown in earlier portions of this chapter, quantitative analysis can be of great utility in measuring and explaining the power in the presidency in a large range of relationships. The significance of quantitative studies for the first part of this normative analysis, then, is clear.

The second step in answering the question of whether the presidency is too powerful or not powerful enough requires an analysis of the consequences of the power of the presidency. In other words, given the power of the presidency, as determined in part one, what difference does it make? Are poor people likely to fare better under a weak or a powerful president, for example? Are civil rights and civil liberties more likely or less likely to be abused? Or is the power of the presidency irrelevant? Or is it only important when it interacts with other crucial variables? To answer these and similar questions rigorously requires that we correlate levels of power with policy consequences. This does not have to be done quantitatively, of course, but such analyses will be more convincing if we have measurements of economic welfare, school integration, wiretapping, military interventions, and other possible consequences of presidential power as well as measures of mediating variables.

Quantitative analyses will be of much less utility in arriving at conclusions in the third part of the analysis concerning presidential power: do we evaluate the consequences of power levels determined in part two of the analysis positively or negatively? Our like or dislike of the consequences will determine our ultimate answer to the question of how powerful the presidency should be. Our evaluation of these consequences will, of course, be determined by our values. Nevertheless, it is important to remember that quantitative analysis can be very useful in helping us to arrive at the point where our values dominate our conclusions.

THEORY BUILDING

WE have seen that quantitative analysis leads us to examine theoretical relationships and that it has considerable utility in testing and refining them. The question remains, however, of whether quantitative analysis is useful in developing theories themselves, the basic conceptions of the relationships between variables.

Our first response must be that quantitative analysis is a mode of inquiry, it is *not* a substitute for conceptual frameworks or theories. Indeed, quantitative analysis should be useful for testing propositions derived from many theories and frameworks.

This is not to say, however, that quantitative analysis has no role in theory building. We have no inclusive, elaborate theories of the presidency, and none looms on the horizon. In the absence of such theories, it is better to focus on more limited sets of relationships than to lament our lack of general theory. Much of this effort will involve what has been termed "pre-theory," formulating lists of factors considered significant for understanding a set of relationships and attempting to evaluate their significance.[29] Quantitative analysis should prove useful in this process.

Earlier in this chapter, I discussed some of my research on presidential-congressional and presidential-public relationships, two areas in which I have been able to apply quantitative analysis. Each of these topics had received considerable attention by other scholars before I began my own investigations of them. Let me now turn to another area of my research to illustrate how I suggest that theory building about the presidency is likely to take place.

I wrote an entire book on a topic crucial to the presidency, policy implementation, without employing quantitative analysis at all.[30] This is not because I concluded that quantitative analysis was inappropriate for the study of implementation but because my theoretical understanding of implementation had not reached the point at which I had propositions to test. Thus, my task was to identify crucial factors that influence implementation and flesh out their relationships to it.

To accomplish this I began deductively and asked what was necessary for implementation to succeed. Having arrived at some general categories, I proceeded to read all that I could that was relevant to the topic (much of which did not fall under the heading of "implementation"). The categories I had previously derived helped me organize information, but my reading about policy-making, mostly case studies, caused me continuously to elaborate, revise, and refine my original categorizations and notions about relationships. There was continuous interaction between deductive and inductive thinking.

That is as far as I got. The next step, it seems to me, is to develop measures of the variables affecting implementation and of implementation itself. Then we should systematically test the hypothesized relationships, discarding those that turn out to be false and focus on those in which we have more confidence. It is through such a process that we are most likely to reach more complete understanding of the presidency.

Quantitative analysis cannot replace the sparks of creativity that lie behind conceptualizations, but quantitative studies may produce findings upon which syntheses may be built. Conversely, they may produce findings contrary to the conventional wisdom and thus prod scholars into challenging dominant viewpoints. To the extent they do this, they will be useful in theory building.

METHODOLOGICAL CHALLENGES

No one should be under the illusion that quantitative analysis is easy to do or that there is consensus on either appropriate methods or indicators. Our discussion of the importance of theory has shown this in some detail. Some indicators lack validity and reliability, and some tests are inappropriate. Conclusions based on them are likely to be incorrect.

In addition, findings can and should be refined as our indicators and tests are refined. For example, I earlier referred to examining the importance of presidential legislative skills as a source of influence in Congress. My goal at the time was to take a first cut at the question, and I concluded that on a broad scale they were not a systematic source of influence. This does not mean, however, that studies of presidential influence in Congress that focus on narrower indicators of presidential success and presidential legislative skills may not find that under certain conditions legislative skills are important. I expect that they will.

In essence, quantitative analysis poses methodological problems precisely because it attempts carefully to measure concepts and test for relationships. Studies that do not involve such concerns are able to avoid methodological questions, but, of course, most of them also lack the analytical potential of quantitative studies. No one ever said that quantitative analysis is easy or that it will not experience growing pains. It is not, and it will.

CONCLUSIONS

THE time is ripe for the application of quantitative analysis to the study of the presidency. Professional standards call for it, our desire to explain relationships demands it, and relevant data await to be exploited. At the same time, researchers must carefully examine the assumptions underlying their quantitative techniques to see that they correspond to the theoretical arguments they have made in deriving their hypotheses. Although quantitative analyses are inappropriate to answer all the important questions and although they must be continuously refined, they can do much to increase our understanding of the presidency.

NOTES

1. Lyndon Baines Johnson, *The Vantage Point: Perspectives of the Presidency, 1963–1969* (New York: Popular Library, 1971), 144–53.

2. Jack Valenti, *A Very Human President* (New York: Norton, 1975), 317–19.

3. Larry Berman, *Planning a Tragedy: The Americanization of the War in Vietnam* (New York: Norton, 1982), 105–21.

4. Hubert H. Humphrey, *The Education of a Public Man: My Life and Politics* (New York: Doubleday, 1976), 290–93.

5. Valenti, *A Very Human President,* 196–97. See also Russell D. Renka, "Bargaining with Legislative Whales in the Kennedy and Johnson Administrations" (paper presented at the Annual Meeting of the American Political Science Association, Washington, D.C., Aug. 27–30, 1980), 20.

6. Transcript, Henry Hall Wilson Oral History Interview, April 11, 1973, by Joe B. Frantz, 16, LBJ Library.

7. Henry Kissinger, *Years of Upheaval* (Boston: Little, Brown, 1982), 11–12, 1182.

8. The literature on this question is vast. See, for example, Samuel Kernell, "Explaining Presidential Popularity," *American Political Science Review* 72 (June 1978): 506–522; Stephen J. Wayne, "Great Expectations: Contemporary Views of the President," in Thomas Cronin, ed., *Rethinking the Presidency,* (Boston: Little, Brown, 1982); and George C. Edwards III, *The Public Presidency* (New York: St. Martin's, 1983), ch. 6; and sources cited therein.

9. This literature is also very extensive. See, for example, Fred I. Greenstein, "The Benevolent Leader Revisited: Children's Images of Political Leaders in Three Democracies," *American Political Science Review* 69 (Dec. 1975): 1371–98; Jack Dennis and Carol Webster, "Children's Images of the President and of Government in 1962 and 1974," *American Politics Quarterly* 3 (Oct. 1975): 386–405; and sources cited therein.

10. Lee Sigelman, "Gauging the Public Response to Presidential Leadership," *Presidential Studies Quarterly* 10 (Summer 1980): 427–33; Carey Rosen, "A Test of Presidential Leadership of Public Opinion: The Split-Ballot Technique," *Polity* 6 (Winter 1973): 282–90; Lee Sigelman and Carol K. Sigelman, "Presidential Leadership of Public Opinion: From 'Benevolent Leader' to Kiss of Death?" *Experimental Study of Politics* 7, no. 3 (1981):1–22.

11. Lawrence C. Miller and Lee Sigelman, "Is the Audience the Message? A Note on LBJ's Vietnam Statements," *Public Opinion Quarterly* 42 (Spring 1978): 71–80; John H. Kessel, "The Parameters of Presidential Politics," *Social Sciences Quarterly* 55 (June 1974): 8–24, and "The Seasons of Presidential Politics," *Social Science Quarterly* 58 (Dec. 1977); 418–35.

12. Michael Baruch Grossman and Martha Joynt Kumar, *Portraying the President: The White House and the News Media* (Baltimore: Johns Hopkins Univ. Press, 1981), ch. 10.

13. David L. Paletz and Richard I. Vinegar, "Presidents on Television: The Effects of Instant Analysis," *Public Opinion Quarterly* 41 (Winter 1977–78): 488–97; Dwight F. Davis, Lynda L. Kaid, and Donald L. Singleton, "Information Effects of Political Commentary," *Experimental Study of Politics* 6 (June 1978): 45–68, and "Instant Analysis of Televised Political Addresses: The Speaker Versus the Commentator," Brent D. Ruben, ed., *Communication Yearbook I,* (New Brunswick, N.J.: Transaction Books, 1977), 453–64; Thomas A. Kazee, "Television Exposure and Attitude Change: The Impact of Political Interest," *Public Opinion Quarterly* 45 (Winter 1981): 507–18.

14. George C. Edwards III, "The Impact of Presidential Coattails on Outcomes of Congressional Elections," *American Politics Quarterly* 7 (Jan. 1979): 94–108, and *Public Presidency,* 83–93.

15. Mark Kesselman, "Presidential Leadership in Foreign Policy," *Midwest Journal of Political Science* 5 (Aug. 1961): 284–89, and "Presidential Leadership in Congress on Foreign Policy: A Replication of a Hypothesis," *Midwest Journal of Political Science* 9 (Nov. 1965): 401–06; Charles M. Tidmarch and Charles M. Sabatt, "Presidential Leadership Change and Foreign Policy Roll-Call Voting in the U.S. Senate," *Western Political Quarterly* 25 (Dec. 1971): 613–25; Aage R. Clausen, *How Congressmen Decide: A Policy Focus* (New York: St. Martin's, 1973), ch. 8; Aage R. Clausen and Carl E. Van Horn, "The Congressional Response to a Decade of Change: 1963–1972," *Journal of Politics* 39 (Aug. 1977): 624–66; Herbert B. Asher and Herbert F. Weisberg, "Voting Change in Congress: Some Dynamic Perspectives on an Evolutionary Process," *American Journal of Political Science* 22 (May 1978): 409–16; George C. Edwards III, *Presidential Influence in Congress* (San Francisco: Freeman, 1980), ch. 4.

16. Edwards, *Presidential Influence in Congress,* ch. 4; George C. Edwards III, "Presidential Influence in the House: Presidential Prestige as a Source of Presidential Power," *American Political Science Review* 70 (Mar. 1976): 101–13, and "Presidential Influence in the Senate: Presidential Prestige as a Source of Presidential Power," *American Politics Quarterly*

5 (Oct. 1977); 481–500; Jon R. Bond and Richard Fleisher, "The Limits of Presidential Popularity as a Source of Influence in the U.S. House," *Legislative Studies Quarterly* 5 (Feb. 1980): 69–78.

17. George C. Edwards III, "Presidential Electoral Performance as a Source of Presidential Power," *American Journal of Political Science* 22 (Feb. 1978): 152–68; Loren Waldman, "Liberalism of Congressmen and the Presidential Vote in Their Districts," *Midwest Journal of Political Science* 11 (Feb. 1976): 73–85; Milton Cummings, *Congressmen and the Electorate* (New York: Free Press, 1966); Marvin Weinbaum and Dennis Judd, "In Search of a Mandated Congress," *Midwest Journal of Political Science* 14 (May 1970): 276–302; J. Vincent Buck, "Presidential Coattails and Congressional Loyalty," *Midwest Journal of Political Science* 16 (Aug. 1972): 460–72; Jeanne Martin, "Presidential Elections and Administrative Support Among Congressmen," *American Journal of Political Science* 20 (Aug. 1976): 483–90; Katheryn Newcomer Harmon and Marsha L. Brauen, "Joint Electoral Outcomes as Cues for Congressional Support of U.S. Presidents," *Legislative Studies Quarterly* 4 (May 1979): 281–99; Edwards, *Presidential Influence in Congress,* ch. 4.

18. Edwards, *Presidential Influence in Congress,* ch. 5–7; Joseph Cooper and Gary Bombardier, "Presidential Leadership and Party Success," *Journal of Politics* 30 (Nov. 1968): 1012–27.

19. Richard L. Cole and Stephen J. Wayne, "Predicting Presidential Decisions on Enrolled Bills: A Computer Simulation," *Simulation and Games* 11 (Sept. 1980): 313–25.

20. Lee Sigelman and Dixie Mercer McNeil, "White House Decision-Making Under Stress: A Case Analysis," *American Journal of Political Science* 24 (Nov. 1980): 652–73.

21. Jarol B. Mannheim and William W. Lammers, "The News Conference and Presidential Leadership of Public Opinion: Does the Tail Wag the Dog?" *Presidential Studies Quarterly* 11 (Spring 1981): 177–88.

22. John H. Kessel, *The Domestic Presidency: Decision-Making in the White House* (North Scituate, Mass.: Duxbury, 1975).

23. For one attempt to do this, see George C. Edwards III, *Implementing Public Policy* (Washington, D.C.: Congressional Quarterly, 1980).

24. Joel D. Aberbach and Bert A. Rockman, "Clashing Beliefs Within the Executive Branch: The Nixon Administration Bureaucracy," *American Political Science Review* 70 (June 1976): 456–68; Richard L. Cole and David A. Caputo, "Presidential Control of the Senior Civil Service: Assessing the Strategies of the Nixon Years," *American Political Science Review* 73 (June 1979): 399–413.

25. See note 3.

26. Lee Sigelman, "Presidential Popularity: Some Unresolved Issues," *Presidency Research Group Newsletter* 3 (Apr. 1981): 9.

27. See Edwards, *Public Presidency,* ch. 6.

28. For this discussion generally, see Edwards, *Presidential Influence in Congress.*

29. James H. Rosenau, "Pre-Theories and Theories of Foreign Policy," in R. Barry Farrell, ed., *Approaches to Comparative and International Politics,* (Evanston, Ill.: Northwestern Univ. Press, 1966), 27–92.

30. See Edwards, *Implementing Public Policy.*

II

DATA SOURCES

AND TECHNIQUES

5

A Guide to Information Sources

JENNIFER DeTORO

THE INFORMATION SOURCES available for the study of the presidency are plentiful. One need only review Fred I. Greenstein and colleagues' bibliographical compilation of citations and abstracts on the subject in order to be impressed with the myriad of resources available.[1]

This chapter will not provide another review of the classic monographs. Rather, it will focus first on primary sources of information and the means of accessing those sources. Second, it will identify and describe indexes of both primary and secondary sources, including nontraditional computerized indexes, useful for locating pertinent information on the presidency.

RECORDS OF ADMINISTRATIVE ACTIVITY

PRESS RELEASES

A CLEAR record of all administrative and presidential activity is found in the White House press releases, issued by the White

House Office of the Press Secretary. These releases, issued daily with few exceptions, record the president's major addresses and remarks, proclamations, executive orders, communications to heads of departments and agencies, messages to Congress, and letters to foreign heads of state; fact sheets on various presidential initiatives, programs, and legislative proposals; names and biographies accompanying nominations and appointments; communiques; statements by the president, his press secretary, or senior advisors; and memorandums. Also as commonly available as White House press releases are unedited transcripts of presidential press conferences and interviews with writers, editors, and broadcast news commentators. Press releases are the official statements of fact, policy, and opinion. They are indispensable sources of information regarding presidential initiatives, goals, and policy. These releases, together with the daily press briefings constitute a primary source for White House correspondents' reports. [2]

From 1936 to 1977 a small staff in the White House press release office indexed the releases, answered questions regarding them, and provided copies upon request. The indexes were handprinted on a series of three-by-five-inch index cards. Often, quotes from the releases were entered in the index and multiple cross-references were made. These cards were the single source of access to the press releases from 1936 to 1965 and the best index to presidential materials for the time period that they cover.

This valuable indexing service was terminated in 1977, and the index cards, spanning forty-four years and seven administrations, were all dispersed to the respective presidential libraries and are available at those libraries. In its place, two automated indexes to the press releases were created for the Carter administration. One system provides an index to the releases through the use of a thesaurus of terms that was adapted from a 1941 archival list of subject headings. References are made in this printed index both to the citations in the *Weekly Compilation of Presidential Documents,* when available, and to the frame number of a microfiched set of press releases. A chronological list of press releases was also created. The second index references key words and dates taken from the press releases and provides access through an online computer information-retrieval system. These indexes are currently housed with the materials for President Carter's library in Atlanta, Georgia. Beginning with the Reagan administration, press releases are again being indexed in detail on three-by-five-inch index cards by the staff of the press release office. The indexing procedures are also being reviewed for possible automation.

WEEKLY COMPILATION OF PRESIDENTIAL DOCUMENTS

EACH administration determines the distribution policy for its White House press releases and press briefings. The method by which the releases are most widely distributed is through the publication of the *Weekly Compilation of Presidential Documents (Weekly Comp.)*. This summary, published by the Office of the Federal Register, National Archives and Records Service, and printed by the Government Printing Office (GPO), is available by subscription to individuals, institutions, and, at no cost, to depository libraries.[3] Most academic and government libraries arrange for the receipt of the *Weekly Comp.*

The first *Weekly Comp.* was published on August 2, 1965. It is printed each Monday for the week ending the previous Saturday. Each issue contains a cumulative index of press releases for the current quarter; however, it excludes those for the issue in which it is published. Semiannual and annual indexes are published separately.

The *Weekly Comp.* is a selective compilation of press releases and generally contains presidential proclamations, executive orders, addresses, remarks, letters, messages and telegrams, memorandums to federal agencies, communications to Congress, bill-signing statements, presidential press conferences, communiques to foreign heads of state, appointments, and nominations. Items omitted are fact sheets; biographical information on appointees and nominees for U.S. attorneys, U.S. marshals, and U.S. circuit and district court judges; news conferences with senior administration officials; and transcripts of press briefings.

In the back of each issue of the *Weekly Comp.* is a section that makes references to specific activities or events announced by the Office of the Press Secretary. These lists of press releases not contained in the *Weekly Comp.* include the president's schedule, nominations, and acts approved by him.

One problem in using the *Weekly Comp.* index is that there is no standard controlled vocabulary. As a consequence, subject headings may not be consistently applied to the same concept. The researcher, armed with this knowledge and searching for all references made by the president on one subject, must be thoroughly imaginative and examine all possible synonyms for the topic of research.

PRESIDENTIAL PAPERS

THE official compilation of presidential papers, called *Public Papers of the President,* is published by the Office of the Federal Register, National Archives and Records Service. It is an annual cumulation of the *Weekly Comps.* Official compilations have been published for Presidents Hoover, Truman, Eisenhower, Kennedy, Johnson, Nixon, Ford, and Carter.

A little-known fact regarding the presidential papers from 1965 to 1976 is that they contain only a selective compilation of press releases originally collected and published in the *Weekly Compilation of Presidential Documents.* Beginning with President Carter, the presidential papers were not edited and contain the full contents of the *Weekly Comps.* This explains why most libraries maintain copies of the *Weekly Comp.* from 1965 to 1976 in addition to the volumes of presidential papers, and thereafter maintain the *Weekly Comps.* only until the next annual volume of the presidential papers becomes available. Each volume contains an annual index; however, there is no cumulative index for the multiple volumes published by the National Archives for each president. A commercial publisher, KTO Press, had addressed this need, providing cumulative indexes to the public papers of each administration from Truman through Nixon.[4]

Privately published compilations of presidential documents supplement the official series. Scholarly publishers have made significant contributions to collections on the presidency, such as the University of Chicago Press, which published *The Papers of James Madison.*[5] Other notable university publishers include the University of North Carolina Press (*The Adams-Jefferson Letters: The Complete Correspondence Between Thomas Jefferson and Abigail and John Adams*), Princeton University Press (*The Papers of Woodrow Wilson*), and the Johns Hopkins University Press (*The Papers of Dwight David Eisenhower*).[6] Historical societies and commissions have also served as publishers, collating and publishing hitherto inaccessible presidential documents. Most notable is the George Washington Bicentennial Commission, publisher of the thirty-nine volumes constituting *The Writings of George Washington From the Original Manuscript Sources, 1745-1799.*[7]

In addition to the *Weekly Compilation of Presidential Documents* and the *Public Papers of the Presidents,* compiled by the National Archives and Records Service, and the privately published collections of presidential papers, the working papers for each contemporary administration are available in the presidential libraries. The presidential papers prior to Hoover are located in the Manuscript Division of the Library of Congress.

PRESIDENTIAL LIBRARIES

EACH of the presidential libraries contains those documents donated directly to the library by the individual or his heirs, often called "papers," and the White House office files, often called "central files." Subject name and numerical indexes guide the researcher's approach to these materials. Shelf lists are provided to smaller series and are guides to the folder titles listed in the order that the folders are filed in the document containers. In addition, there are registration sheets indicating content, quality, and dates for the manuscript collection.

Political science students and researchers wishing to use the historical materials in the presidential libraries are encouraged to make their request in writing, in advance of their planned trip, to the director of the library. Users are aided by archivists, who will provide copies, at cost, of library resource materials. Access is defined by the guidelines of each of the presidential libraries housing the materials.

All archival records in the presidential libraries of Presidents Hoover through Johnson are available for research. Records of President Ford's pre-presidential career have been processed and are currently available for research. To access the presidential papers of Presidents Ford, Nixon, and Carter, special approval is required. Chapters 8 and 9 provide more detailed information on the collections and the use of presidential libraries.

EXECUTIVE ORDERS AND PROCLAMATIONS

In addition to the publicly released statements and archival records of each administration, presidential communications and directives can provide insight into the exercise of presidential authority. Forms of presidential communications and directives include executive orders, proclamations, presidential determinations, memoranda, designations, messages transmitting budget rescissions and deferrals, letters to other nations, trade agreements, and executive agreements. Of these, executive orders and proclamations have been most frequently used.

The areas encompassed by executive orders and proclamations have never been clearly stated,[8] although attempts have been made to define the form and procedure of writing and filing of executive orders.[9] Nevertheless, general observations can be made regarding their traditional uses.

Proclamations are addressed to the public at large. The word "proclaim" usually means to give wide publicity; to make known by public announcement. Proclamations are generally ceremonial and often celebratory in nature. They are issued to commemorate holidays, special occasions, and events.[10]

An executive order (EO) is a written document, signed by the president, communicating a decision. An executive order generally cites statutory authority as the basis for its issuance, but reference may also be made to the president's constitutional powers as the source of authority. Rarely, however, will no authority be noted.[11] It is generally accepted that there is no legal difference between a proclamation and an executive order,[12] and that either, when issued pursuant to authority delegated by the Congress, has the same effect as a statute.[13]

Executive orders have had a multitude of applications. In the early days of the Republic, executive orders were commonly used in the disposition of public lands and natural resources. Their use greatly increased during periods of natural emergencies and wars. Franklin D. Roosevelt issued 3,723 executive orders. The total number of all numbered executive orders issued prior to that date was 5,494. In comparison, Woodrow Wilson issued 1,791 EOs, Hoover issued 1,004, Truman issued 905, Dwight D. Eisenhower issued 482, and Lyndon B. Johnson issued 377.

More recently, the use of executive orders continues to be a cause for review and scrutiny.[14] In 1981, President Reagan issued an EO that dramatically affected the regulatory roles and authorities of the federal departments and agencies and independent commissions concerning the president's regulatory relief efforts.[15]

The study of presidential executive orders and proclamations is a significant means of assessing presidential power and authority. A description and explanation of the means to access them follows.

Access to Orders and Proclamations Before 1936.   The earliest executive orders did not have any numbers ascribed to them nor was there any uniform system of organizing, distributing, or maintaining them. Valiant efforts have been made to collect, collate, and make these elusive documents accessible. One such effort is the *List of Presidential Executive Orders Unnumbered Series, 1789–1941.* These previously uncollated executive orders were edited by Clifford Lord, prepared by the Historical Records Survey of the Works Progress Administration, and published in 1943 in two volumes.[16] This list records the date of the first executive order as October 20, 1789, and reveals the subject: "A clear account of affairs connected with their Departments." The last executive order cited in this work was dated January 11, 1941. Volume 1 is a chronological listing of titles, and volume 2 is a subject index. Frequently cited sources of the full text of these early orders are the *Annals of Congress* and the *Congressional Globe,* predecessors of the *Congressional Record,* and Richardson's *A Compilation of the Messages and Papers of the Presidents, 1789-1902.* [17] Although Richardson's work is not comprehensive, it lists numerous executive orders and can be used as an index to the executive orders microfilmed by the Library of Congress. Eleven reels of microfilm contain the full texts of the numbered executive orders, from 1 to 7,403 and dated 1845 through 1936. [18] The executive orders of this early time period can also be identified by the noteworthy work entitled *Presidential Executive Orders, Numbered 1-8030, 1862-1938.* This series was edited by Clifford Lord, prepared by the Historical Records Survey of New York City, and published in 1944. Volume 1 is a chronological list of executive orders (*The List*), and volume 2 is a subject index (*The Index*). [19]

Access to Orders and Proclamations Since 1936. Since the beginning of the Republic, the federal government has issued orders, directives, and proclamations. There was no systematic publication or distribution of executive orders, rules, and regulations or any published table to define the status of such administrative directives until 1936. In fact, before 1936 the only systematic organization and numbering of executive orders was instituted by the Department of State. The State Department, however, could not force the other departments and agencies to file their executive orders with them. It took a highly embarrassing but humorous situation in 1934 to change this situation. The Supreme Court was considering a case that involved regulation of the oil industry when it was discovered that the regulations upon which the case was supposed to have been based had been revoked, without the knowledge of the parties or their attorneys. [20] To avoid a recurrence of this situation, Congress passed the *Federal Register* Act in 1935 (49 Stat. 500 [1935]). The act required the publication of presidential proclamations, executive orders (of general applicability and legal effect), rules, regulations, licenses, proposed rules, policy statements, and documents in a daily *Federal Register* beginning March 14, 1936. [21]

The subject matter of the *Federal Register* is codified into fifty titles of subject classes similar to the fifty titles of the *U.S. Code.*

Each of the fifty titles is published annually in pamphlet form. Containing all regulations in force at the time of the printing, it is entitled the *Code of Federal Regulations* (CFR). All of the contents of the daily *Federal Register* are not included in the CFR.[22] Therefore, numerous libraries maintain copies of the daily registers on microfiche.

The presidential documents section in the *Federal Register* is codified in Title 3. It is usually located at the beginning of the *Federal Register* and notes recently issued executive orders and proclamations. Other presidential communications including memorandums, presidential determinations, letters, directives, reorganization plans, designations, and a list of messages transmitting budget rescissions and deferrals also appear in the *Federal Register*.

In the CFR, presidential documents from 1936 through 1970 are located in *Title 3 — The President*. From 1971 through 1975, all presidential materials were published in the appendix to Title 3, referred to as *Title 3A — The President*. From the 1976 annual cumulation to the present, all presidential papers have again been codified in *Title 3 — The President*.[23]

To review the status of an executive order and to determine if it has been revised, rescinded, or revoked, the indexes to consult are Title 3, 1936–65, Consolidated Subject Index; and Title 3, 1936–65, Consolidated Tables. Thereafter, consult Title 3, 1970–75, Consolidated Tables, updated by Table IV in each annual volume of Title 3, 1976 through 1980. The annuals are updated by the *List of Sections Affected* (LSA), published monthly and updated by the daily cumulation for a month in the *Federal Register*.

Additional research tools are provided in the *Finding Aids* volume of the CFR. In a research project investigating presidential authorities and responsibilities the following tables from Title 3 may prove useful:

Table I lists presidential proclamations and cites the *Federal Register* in which they were originally published.

Table II lists the number and date of the executive orders and refers to its *Federal Register* citation.

Table III lists the *Federal Register* citation for presidential documents other than executive orders and proclamations.

Table IV lists which presidential documents issued in earlier editions have been affected (amended, revoked, etc.) by documents published in this edition.

Table V displays the statutes that have been noted and cited as the president's authority to issue an executive order or other presidential document.

ADMINISTRATIVE ORDERS
(OTHER THAN EXECUTIVE ORDERS AND PROCLAMATIONS)

Types of administrative orders other than executive orders and proclamations include presidential memorandums, various types of presidential directives, and presidential determinations. In general, memorandums are the customary means for communicating information among and within government agencies. They may request action, information, concurrence, or clearance, or they may convey policy decisions or guidance. Discussion of the types of memorandums and other presidential directives follows.

Presidential Directives. Memoranda in the form of directives are official statements of presidential policy or interest. They are used to communicate official instructions from the White House to the executive departments and agencies for the conduct of governmental affairs. For example, the president issued a memorandum on May 11, 1978, to the heads of executive departments and agencies requesting their cooperation with his reorganization project staff in its review and evaluation of the government's statistical programs.[24] In other cases, memoranda accompany "determinations" that are not formally numbered as "presidential determinations" (PD) and are indexed in Table III of the CFR as "memoranda." Thus, the memorandum of September 8, 1978, "Determination Extending the Exercise of Certain Authorities under the Trading with the Enemy Act," is noted as a memorandum, not a presidential determination.[25]

Presidential Determinations. Presidential determinations are issued pursuant to statutory authority. They are sequentially numbered by fiscal year; PD 81-1, PD 81-2, PD 81-3, and so on. Presidential determinations frequently concern the transfer of funds from the United States to foreign governments for specific purposes. For example, Presidential Determination no. 78-12 authorized financial assistance to refugees in Somalia and Djibouti.[26] A presidential determination may also authorize the sale of defense weapons and services to other countries. For example, Presidential Determination no. 78-8 permitted the sale of specified defense articles to Turkey.[27] Other types of presidential determinations may concern trade matters. Presidential Determination no. 78-13 renewed the U.S.-Romanian Agreement on Trade Relations.[28]

Other forms of presidential directives include recommendations, for example, "Recommendations approved by the President concerning Radiation Protection Guidance to Federal Agencies for Diagnostic X-Rays."[29] Infrequently codified in Title 5 of CFR are letters. An example is a letter from the president to the chairman of a regulatory commission disapproving of a determination issued by the commission.[30]

Just as executive orders and proclamations are filed chronologically, so too are published memoranda. Presidential determinations, recommendations, and letters are filed chronologically within Subchapter B of Title 3, containing administrative orders.

National Security Memoranda. Memoranda describing national security communications are formally numbered documents setting forth official U.S. policy on a specific subject or country. Each presidential administration since Truman has used the National Security Council System as the standard mechanism for communicating policy decisions and guidance to the departments and agencies of the government. These National Security Council policy documents are:

National Security Council Policy Papers (NSC), (Truman)
National Security Action Memoranda (NSAM), (JFK and LBJ)
National Security Decision Memorandum (NSDM) and National Security Study Memorandum (NSSM), (Nixon and Ford)
Presidential Directive (PD/NCS) and Presidential Review Memorandum (PRM/NSC), (Carter)

National Security Decision Directive (NSDD) and National Security Study Directive (NSSD), (Reagan).

Most of these documents as well as many presidential determinations are classified and are not available to the general public. On occasion, classified documents are declassified. Sometimes, though very rarely, the declassified document will be issued as a White House press release. An example is President Reagan's policy on nuclear nonproliferation and peaceful nuclear cooperation.[31] All requests for information on or for copies of these documents should be referred to the Staff Secretary, National Security Council, Washington, D.C. 20500. Other classified materials may become available to historical researchers according to the provisions of Section 4 of Executive Order 12065.[32]

DESIGNATIONS AND BUDGETARY MESSAGES

Following reorganization plans in the CFR are designations, located in Subchapter 2 of Title 3. Designations are presidential directives delegating certain officials to perform specific functions. For example, specific staff members in specific offices in the Executive Office of the President were designated to classify information as "top secret" by an order dated June 28, 1978.[33]

Lastly, and concisely located in one place (Appendix A to Title 3) is a list of "Messages Transmitting Rescissions and Deferrals." The list of messages is chronologically arranged to indicate the full text source of the message in the *Federal Register*. Such messages are also accessible in the White House press releases, *Weekly Comp.,* and *Congressional Record.*

REORGANIZATION PLANS

Beginning in 1939 and for most of the time since, the president has been given authority to reorganize the executive branch, subject to congressional veto. The procedure is for the president to submit reorganization plans to the Congress, which has sixty days to disapprove the plan. If neither house disapproves, the plan takes effect. The reorganization authority, last granted for a four-year period, expired on April 4, 1981 (5 USC, sec., 905b). President Reagan has requested an extension of that authority.

At the time that the president submits a reorganization plan to the Congress, it is entered into the *Congressional Record* and is printed in the House and Senate document series. These materials become the sources to consult for those plans failing to win congressional approval. The approved reorganization plans are published in the *Federal Register,* and in Title 3 of the CFR, Subchapter C. In the CFR, reorganization plans are included with other administrative orders, chronologically listed with references to their statutory authority. Reorganization plans are also located in the *Statutes at Large* and in the appendix to Title 5 of the *United States Code* (commercial publishers specializing in updating the official series also print the reorganization plans). The best single source to review enacted reorganization plans is the *U.S. Code,* in which the reorganization plans are published following the specific reorganization acts by which they are authorized, together with associated presidential messages and executive orders.

TREATIES AND EXECUTIVE AGREEMENTS

By virtue of his constitutional authority, the president may negotiate treaties on behalf of the United States with the advice and consent of two-thirds of the Senate (Art. II, Sec. 2). He may also enter into an executive agreement with a foreign government without prior or subsequent legislative or treaty authority.

The sources for treaties and other international agreements from 1873 through 1950–51 are the *United States Statutes at Large,* volumes 1–64. The *Statutes* contain treaties, executive proclamations, conventions, and protocols. All the treaties published in the *Statutes* prior to 1950 have also been compiled in a single work: *Treaties and other International Agreements of the United States of America, 1776–1949.*[34] Compiled by Charles I. Bevans, it is thought to be the definitive edition of U.S. treaties and international agreements for this time period.

The *United States Treaties and Other International Agreements* (UST) is a chronological arrangement of treaties from 1950 to the present, comprising thirty-one volumes to date. Each volume has a country and subject index. Subject headings are generally taken strictly from the title of the treaty and thus are not standardized.

The UST is the bound version of treaties that are initially compiled in a binder with a slightly different title: "Treaties and Other International Acts Series" (TIAS). This numbered series of the full text of the treaties is indexed by the *Department of State Bulletin, Monthly Catalog,* and the *Treaties in Force* and is compiled by the Treaty Affairs staff, Office of the Assistant Legal Advisor to Treaty Affairs, U.S. Department of State. It lists all treaties and international agreements to which the United States is a party as of the date of the compilation.

Current developments on treaty negotiations can be found in the *Department of State Bulletin.* The *Bulletin* began in 1939 as a weekly publication with semiannual indexes. Since January 1978, it has been issued monthly with annual indexes. The *Bulletin* contains the texts of all major foreign policy speeches and news conferences by the president, secretary of state, and other senior government officials.

Unofficial compilations of indexes to treaties are *United States Treaties and Other International Agreements, Cumulative Index 1776–1949,* compiled by Kavass and Michael, and *UST Cumulative Index, 1950–1970,* compiled by Kavass and Sprudzs. A useful source of nonratified treaties is *Unperfected Treaties of the United States of America, 1776–1976,* edited by Christian Wikter.[35]

INDEXES

THERE are two types of general indexes to information sources on the presidency. They are the traditional printed sources and the automated on-line sources.

SELECTED TRADITIONAL PRINTED INDEXES

THE traditional printed sources continue to be the standard indexes and have not significantly changed over the years. Many daily newspapers continue to publish periodic indexes recording presidential activities. They differ in clarity of format and ease of use. The *Wall Street Journal Index* separates the corporate news citations from those referring to the general news. The *Washington Post Index* is time efficient with its columnar page references and succinct descriptions. The *New York Times Index* continues to be more an efficient yearbook or narrative of annual events than an easily used index tool.

Periodical guides have also not changed greatly in recent years. The Public Affairs Information Services (PAIS) consistently presents a useful guide to scholarly books, journals, and government reports emphasizing economic and social conditions, public administration, and international relations.[36]

The indexes to legal information sources have expanded. The standard legal index has been *Index to Legal Periodicals* (ILP), published since 1908, which indexes approximately 360 legal journals and newspapers. Since 1980 a new legal index has been published, entitled *Current Law Index* (CLI), which indexes approximately 660 periodicals with a more refined and specific subject approach than the ILP, and unlike the ILP, it contains an index by the popular names of laws. The popular names index is extremely valuable, allowing the researcher to look up articles that discuss specific laws. One could thus look under the name "War Powers Act" rather than being limited to the generic and commonly used subject heading "presidential powers."[37]

Since 1895, the *Monthly Catalog of United States Government Publications* has been the basic bibliography of U.S. government publications. While it is a helpful index and is the official government publication, it is not a comprehensive index to all government publications. The best single source of access to government reports continues to be those published by Congressional Information Services. This private firm publishes two indexes. The first is entitled *CIS/Index*. This is the sole source of comprehensive information regarding all congressional publications and legislative histories. The second index is entitled *American Statistics Index* (ASI). Despite its name, the ASI is the best source of comprehensive information regarding all publications published by the executive branch. Both indexes use a standard controlled thesaurus and provide lengthy annotations of each monograph, enabling a researcher to conduct a thorough review on any subject.[38]

Another noteworthy index to valuable primary documents is the *Federal Index*.[39] Indexing a diversity of sources, public and privately published documents, it covers the *Congressional Record, Federal Register, Weekly Compilation of Presidential Documents,* and *Washington Post,* with citations to the *Code of Federal Regulations,* the *U.S. Code,* House and Senate bills, and other federal documents. The *Federal Index* is currently published monthly by a private firm, Capitol Services, Inc.

ON-LINE INDEXES AND INFORMATION SOURCES

On-line information systems are a relatively new form of information resource. There are a small number of very large and widely used commercial suppliers of automated indexes subscribed to by many public libraries as well as university, government, and other specialized libraries. Three of these large commercial suppliers are Systems Development Corporation (SDC), Lockheed, and Bibliographic Retrieval Service (BRS). Each of these suppliers has hundreds of individual data bases in their systems covering extensive subject areas. Often numbered, these data bases, or files, contain citations to articles, reports, and documents published from about 1970 to the present. A library may subscribe to the data bases of these suppliers just as they would to journals. The suppliers charge on a connect-hour fee basis that ranges from $6 to $140 an hour.

Other suppliers of on-line information systems are government agencies. JURIS, a legal data base provided by the Department of Justice, and LABSTAT, a statistical data base provided by the Department of Labor, are two examples of government-sponsored systems.

A political science student's primary access to automated systems is the academic library. Policies and procedures for accessing systems at public and other libraries and information centers can usually be supplied by the university reference librarian. Access to government-sponsored systems vary. It is best to consult the issuing agency for policies regarding access to their information systems. The Library of Congress maintains access for the public, from its main reading room, to its own information system, called SCORPIO.

On-line sources for information retrieval are fast becoming the dominant source for finding recently published literature. There are two types of on-line information systems. The first is the on-line index that refers to sources of information in the form of bibliographic citations. Some bibliographic citations contain annotated abstracts and/or lengthy digests of the information cited. The second type contains the full text of documents. Descriptions and examples of each type will more adequately explain the usefulness of these resources.

On-line computerized indexes are extremely valuable for three reasons. They provide access to vast amounts of information in extremely short periods of time. For example, one can elicit from a computerized information data base in less than thirty seconds references to all articles on the presidency published during the previous six months in the more than 100 political science journals. Second, on-line information sources can combine terms, using Boolean logic, to enable a researcher to perform a refined subject search with ease. For example, using a printed index to identify articles on the president's regulatory relief initiatives, one must first look under the index term "president" and then under "administrative procedures, rules, and regulations." However, when a researcher queries a data base on line, the two-step procedure is accomplished as one. The computer retrieves only those documents concerning both the president and regulatory reform issues. Finally, the need to copy citations by hand from a printed index is eliminated, since the printer accompanying the computer terminal can automatically print the citations.

Information-retrieval systems containing the full text of documents, as well as bibliographic citations, are as valuable as they are few in number. Examples of such systems are NEXIS, LEXIS, WESTLAW, and JURIS. The value of having the full text can be illustrated with JURIS, which in one file contains the full text of the *U.S. Code*. Using it, one can review the citations and full text of selected statutes. In a brief period of time the system can identify and print all of the presidential authorities in a specific area — such as the president's emergency powers or war-making powers. It can also print all of the presidential authorities noted throughout the *U.S. Code*.

A selection of on-line indexes containing bibliographic citations as well as full text of documents useful for the study of the presidency follows.

Newspaper Indexes. NEXIS provides access to the full text of selected newspapers, wire stories, and magazines, including the *Washington Post,* Associated Press (AP), United Press International (UPI), foreign national and state wires, Reuters, *Facts on File, World News Digest, Newsweek,* and the *National Journal.* It is supplied by Mead Data Central.

The New York Times Information Bank I indexes and abstracts sixty-two publications, including the *New York Times, Wall Street Journal, Washington Post, Financial Times of London,* and *Business Week.* Items are indexed according to a controlled list of terms. Coverage begins in 1969 for the *New York Times;* for the others, it begins in 1971. Information Bank II provides access to the complete textual material from the late city edition of the *New York Times,* from June 1980 to the present. The supplier is the New York Times Information Service, Inc.

Newspaper Index (*NDEX*) provides bibliographic citations to news articles published in the *San Francisco Chronicle, Chicago Tribune, Los Angeles Times, Washington Post,* and other newspapers from 1976 to the present. NDEX is prepared by Bell and Howell and supplied by SDC.

Newsearch provides bibliographic citations to the *New York Times, Christian Science Monitor,* and *Wall Street Journal.* It is updated daily, and each month the file contents are transferred to the National Newspaper Index, which contains references back to 1979. Newsearch is prepared by Information Access Corporation and supplied by Lockheed; Newsearch is File 211, and National Newspaper Index is File 111.

Political Science Sources. *PAIS* provides international coverage of all fields of political and social science, indexing more than 800 English-language journals and 6,000 monographs from federal, state, and local sources. It includes the *Foreign Language Index* (1972–present) and *PAIS Bulletin* (1976–present). Updated monthly, bibliographic citations are provided. It is prepared by Public Affairs Information Service, Inc. The supplier is BRS and Lockheed, File 49.

United States Political Science Documents (USPSD) provides abstracts to more than 150 of the most widely circulated political science journals published in the U.S. Special emphasis is placed on the areas of electoral behavior, public opinion and attitude, political parties, public policy, comparative politics, and international relations. Economics, law, and world politics as well as theory and methodology are included. USPSD is prepared by the University of Pittsburgh, University Center for International Studies. Coverage begins in 1975 and is supposed to be updated quarterly, but in practice it is closer to semiannually. Suppliers are SDC and Lockheed, File 93.

American Bibliographic Center provides bibliographic citations, the majority with abstracts or annotations to articles from 300 journals covering political science and government from 1963 to present. (More extensive coverage is given to American history and sociology.) It is prepared by American Bibliographic Center-CLIO Press, Inc. The supplier is Lockheed, File 38.

The Federal Index, available in hard copy and on-line, indexes official and commercial publications covering government activity, including the *Congressional Record, Federal Register, Law Week, Washington Post,* and the *Weekly Compilation of Presidential Documents.* Coverage is October 1976–80 on-line, and October 1976 to the present in hard copy. Prepared by Capitol Services, Inc., the supplier is SDC and Lockheed, File 20.

The Comprehensive Dissertation Index provides biblio-graphic citations to all doctoral dissertations from accredited universities in the United States and Canada from 1861 to the present and is updated monthly. It is prepared by University Micro-films International, supplied by FRS, Lockheed (File 35), and SDC.

The Inter-university Consortium for Political and Social Research (ICPSR) is a partnership between the Center for Political Studies, located at the Institute for Social Research at the University of Michigan, and more than 220 member universities and colleges. Their information holdings are referred to as a "Data Archives" in the form of machine-readable tapes. The data are generally statistical in nature, unlike the narrative data bases described earlier. The political science student can gain access to these files by consulting the political science or social science department of institutions belonging to the consortium. The archival holdings of interest to the political science student include the following:

Measures of Political Attitudes
1. CBS/NYT Election Surveys 1976. Provides results of surveys designed to monitor the public's changing perceptions of the candidates, the issues, and the candidates' position on the issues.
2. Election Study Series-American National Election Study. Covers the years 1948–80. Provides national survey results including:
    respondents' expectation about outcome of elections
    respondents' party identification and political history
    respondents' interest in politics, issue positions, and assessments of major national problems
    sources of political information
    measures of political efficacy, ideology, and trust in government

Election Returns
    United States Historical Election Returns, 1788–1979. Contains county-level returns for more than 90 percent of all elections to the offices of president, governor, U.S. senator, and congressman from 1788 through 1979. (ICPSR 0001)

Political Participation

Political Participation in America, 1967. Contains a national cross-section survey of more than 2,500 respondents conducted in 1967 concerning numerous aspects of political participation at the national and local levels. (ICPSR 7015)

Public Opinion on Political Matters

1. Media Center and Analysis Study, 1974. Provides newspaper content and readers' perceptions before and immediately after the November 1974 congressional election. (ICPSR 7586)

2. Perceptions of the 1963 Presidential Transition. Contains respondents' perceptions of the presidential transition and state of the nation in December 1963. (ICPSR 7231)

Congressional Voting Records

1. Voting Scores for members of the U.S. Congress, 1945–1978. Data taken from *Congressional Quarterly Almanac* contains scores for voting participation, partisan voting, bipartisan voting, conservative coalition support, and presidential support. For the years 1960–78 voting scores were calculated by the Americans for Democratic Action (ADA), Citizens for Political Education (COPE), the National Farmers Union (NFU), and the Americans for Constitutional Action (ACA).

2. U.S. Congressional Roll-Call Voting Records, 1789–1980. Includes complete roll-call records for House and Senate from the First Congress through the First Session of the Ninety-sixth Congress. (ICPSR 0004)

The National Opinion Research Center, affiliated with the University of Chicago, provides public opinion surveys taken in the United States from 1941 to the present in numerous subject areas, including social and political science.

Legislative Sources. House LEGIS is a legislative information and status system maintained by House Information Systems, Committee on House Administration, U.S. Congress. It contains digests, sponsors, chronology of actions, and related information on all bills, resolutions, and amendments from the Ninety-sixth Congress to the present and on all bills in the Ninety-fourth and Ninety-fifth Congresses that became public law. Summaries of executive communications, presidential messages, and petitions and memorials to Congress are additional files available on LEGIS. The summary of proceedings and debate (SOPAD) is another system maintained by House Information Systems available to LEGIS users. It lists the House schedule for the day and the week and gives an account of debate, roll calls, and amendments on the House floor for the current day.

Senate LEGIS is the legislative information system designed by the Senate Computer Center of the U.S. Congress. It provides information on all bills, resolutions, and amendments from the Ninety-fifth to the present Congress. The communication files include presidential messages, executive communications, petitions, and memorials beginning with the Ninety-sixth Congress. Information concerning nominations received in the Senate are available beginning with the Ninety-seventh Congress.

LEGI-SLATE is a computerized bill, vote, and committee tracking system. It provides access to legislative actions as well as votes on all bills and resolutions, indicating whether they are voice votes, division (or standing) votes, teller votes, or recorded votes by individual names of members. It also provides recorded committee votes and can profile the voting performance of any member or group of members of a party or caucus, including identifying member profiles on votes selected by specific rating groups, such as ADA and ACA. Computer searches can be stored on line. Coverage is from the Ninety-sixth Congress to the present. LEGI-SLATE is both the provider and supplier.

VOTES contains the voting records of congressmen and senators on all roll-call votes of the U.S. Congress on bills, resolutions, treaties, and nominations. Individual member profile tracking is possible via this system. Coverage extends from 1979 to the present. Citations include the title, number, sponsor, date introduced, actions taken, and other data. VOTES is prepared by the Policy Review Associates and supplied by SDC.

The Electronic Legislature Search System provides descriptions of bills and resolutions, including short titles, sponsors, dates of introduction and committee referrals, committee and floor actions, bill status, and legislative histories for all current bills for the fifty states and the U.S. Congress. It also contains roll-call votes for the current Congress. It is prepared and supplied by Commerce Clearinghouse.

Congressional Record Abstracts contains abstracts of the *Congressional Record* from 1976 to the present, covering roll-call votes, executive communications and ·speeches, floor debates, and congressional activities regarding bills and resolutions. It is provided by Capitol Services, Inc., and is supplied by Lockheed, File 135.

CIS/Index (CIS) is the machine-readable form of the *CIS/Index* to Publications of the United States Congress. It provides access to all congressional documents from 1970 to the present. (If available, the printed index is preferable to use.) It is provided by Congressional Information Services, Inc., and is supplied by Lockheed, File 101.

Calliope System (Computer Assisted Legislative Liaison; Interactive On-Line Political Evaluation) is a very large congressional data base with sophisticated statistical analysis capabilities. The data files include:

Roll-call votes, Ninety-seventh Congress
Congressional committee votes
Biographical characteristics of members of both houses
Presidential support levels of legislation
Measures of party loyalty
Primary and general election returns, 1972 to present by congressional district
Congressional district demographics
Campaign contributions
Candidate characteristics
Congressional committee assignments: standing, special, joint, and party committees for both houses, 1972 to present
Interest group ratings 1977 to present

Calliope was developed by Polimetric Associates of Burlington, Vermont. Calliope provides more than simple information retrieval of a fact, vote, sponsor, or status of a bill. It enables the user to apply statistical analysis techniques to the study of congressional activities. Multiple factors can be correlated to produce an insightful picture of the legislating process. Correlating roll-call votes with political party and geographic representation reveals more than a unidimensional statement of a roll-call vote.

Voting behavior patterns can be better understood and analyzed if one knows group patterns of behavior. Congressmen may vote with one group of colleagues on one issue and with a different block on another issue. Reviewing voting patterns correlated with presidential support indicates, in part, the president's ability to persuade congressmen to support his initiatives. Understanding voting habits and behavior may lead to greater ability to forecast congressional activities and events. This is the only system currently available with sophisticated analysis techniques applied to the study of the Congress. The supplier is expected to be Capitol Services, Inc., Washington, D.C.

Legal Sources. JURIS, made available to federal agencies through the Department of Justice, provides complete texts of the briefs presented and the decisions of the Supreme Court since 1900, district courts since 1970, Court of Claims since 1956, and Court of Appeals since 1962. It also covers *Federal Rules Decisions* and the *Military Justice Reporter* from 1975 to the present. JURIS provides digest material obtained from West Publishing Company. The system contains complete texts of public laws from January 1973 to the present. In addition, one can shepardize court cases and statutes using JURIS, and it is frequently used as a source of the decisions of the comptroller general and the attorney general.

LEXIS (and NEXIS) provides on-line access to the Federal Register File. Beginning with the issue of July 1, 1980, the full text of every *Federal Register* is available for full text retrieval, including proclamations and executive orders, within seventy-two hours after publication. The General Federal File is also available on LEXIS. It contains the full text of the *U.S. Code,* U.S. Supreme Court decisions beginning in 1925, and the other resources covering federal and state court decisions. The supplier is Mead Data Central.

WESTLAW is a file providing summaries and full texts of federal court cases (1961 through the present) and state court cases (starting dates vary greatly) reported in the National Reporter System. The supplier is West Publishing Company, St. Paul, Minnesota.

Federal Register provides citations to the *Federal Register* from March 25, 1977, to the present. Prepared by Capitol Services, Inc., the suppliers are Lockheed (File 136) and SDC. Other suppliers providing citations to the *Federal Register* are LEXIS; Commerce Clearinghouse, Chicago, Illinois; and REG-ULATE, Washington, D.C.

The Legal Resources Index system indexes 660 law journals and four legal newspapers as well as the *Christian Science Monitor, New York Times,* and *Wall Street Journal* and general, government, and academic publications, covering January 1980 to the present. It is prepared by Information Access Corporation, and the supplier is Lockheed, File 150.

Miscellaneous.   The Library of Congress Card Catalog (LCCC) contains bibliographic citations for books catalogued and housed in the Library of Congress, chiefly consisting of English language monographs for the years 1968 to the present.

The Bibliographic Citation File contains bibliographic citations and abstracts of journal articles, law reviews, and selected congressional and executive publications from 1976 to the present in all areas of political science and public policy. It is prepared by the Congressional Research Service of the Library of Congress.

For additional information concerning on-line sources of information, consult the *Encyclopedia of Information Systems and Services.*[40]

NOTES

1. Fred I. Greenstein, Larry Berman, Alvin S. Felzenberg, with Doris Lidtke, *Evolution of the Modern Presidency* (Washington, D.C.: American Enterprise Institute, 1977).

2. Press briefings, generally conducted on a daily basis, allow the press secretary and/or deputy press secretary together with (often anonymous) administration spokespersons to brief reporters on current and planned activities, frequently on an "off the record" basis. Reporters are dependent upon their memories and note-taking skills, since the transcripts of the press briefings are not publicly released.

3. Depository libraries receive numerous documents published by the federal government. According to guidelines governing the depository libraries program, libraries can select specific types or series of documents to receive as they are issued; they are then obliged to make them publicly available. Laws governing designated depository libraries as well as a list of those libraries by state and city can be found in a committee print, entitled *Government Depository Libraries,* published by the U.S. Congress, Joint Committee on Printing, 96th Cong., 1st sess., 1979, 109 pp.

4. *The Cumulated Indexes to the Public Papers of the Presidents of the United States — Harry S. Truman, 1945-1953* (Millwood, N.Y.: KTO Press, 1979); *The Cumulated Indexes to the Public Papers of the Presidents of the United States — Dwight D. Eisenhower, 1953-1961* (Millwood, N.Y.: KTO Press, 1979); *The Cumulated Indexes to the Public Papers of the Presidents of the United States — John F. Kennedy, 1961-1963* (Millwood, N.Y.: KTO Press, 1979); *The Cumulated Index to the Public Papers of the Presidents of the United States — Lyndon B. Johnson, 1963-1968* (Millwood, N.Y.: KTO Press, 1979); *The Cumulated Index to the Public Papers of the Presidents of the United States — Richard M. Nixon, 1969-1974* (Millwood, N.Y.: KTO Press, 1979).

5. William T. Hutchinson, et al., eds., *The Papers of James Madison,* 13 vols. to date (Chicago: Univ. of Chicago Press, 1962-).

6. Lester J. Cappon, ed., *The Adams-Jefferson Letters: The Complete Correspondence Between Thomas Jefferson and Abigail and John Adams,* 2 vols. (Chapel Hill: Univ. of North Carolina Press, Institute of Early American History and Culture at Williamsburg, Va., 1959); Arthur S. Link, ed., *The Papers of Woodrow Wilson,* 36 vols. (Princeton: Princeton Univ. Press, 1966-81); Alfred D. Chandler, Jr., et al., eds., *The Papers of Dwight David Eisenhower,* 9 vols. (Baltimore: Johns Hopkins Univ. Press, 1970-78).

7. John C. Fitzpatrick, et al., eds., *The Writings of George Washington from the Original Manuscript Sources, 1745-1799,* 39 vols., prepared by the George Washington Bicentennial Commission (Washington, D.C.: U.S. Government Printing Office, 1931-44).

8. Arthur Miller, *Presidential Power in a Nutshell* (St. Paul, Minn.: West Publishing, 1977), 86.

9. Initially defined by Executive Order (EO) no. 7298, Feb. 18, 1936. Superseded by EO no. 10006, Oct. 11, 1948; superseded by EO no. 11030, June 19, 1962.

10. Contrary to its general use, the proclamation was used as the means by which President Ford pardoned President Nixon (Proclamation 4311, Sept. 8, 1974, 3 CFR, 1971–75 Comp., 385; 39 Fed. Reg. 32601). In similar fashion, President Lincoln freed the slaves by the "Emancipation Proclamation," not an executive order.

11. EO no. 10,671, 3 CFR 81 (1956 supp.). Also, EO no. 12044, Mar. 23, 1978, simply states, "As President, I direct . . ."

12. Miles O. Price and Harry Bitner, *Effective Legal Research* (Boston: Little, Brown, 1979), 98.

13. *Jenkins* v. *Collard,* 145 U.S. 546; 36. L.Ed. 812; 12 S.Ct. 868 (1892).

14. A good overview of the uses of executive orders can be found in *Executive Orders: A Brief History of Their Use and the President's Power to Issue Them,* by Grover S. Williams, revised by Walter Albano (Library of Congress, Washington, D.C.: Congressional Research Service, 1977).

15. EO no. 12,291, 46 Fed. Reg. 13193 (1981).

16. Clifford Lord, ed., *List of Presidential Executive Orders Unnumbered Series, 1789–1941,* prepared by the Historical Records Survey of the Works Progress Administration, Newark, New Jersey, 1943.

17. James D. Richardson, ed., *A Compilation of the Messages and Papers of the Presidents, 1789–1902,* 10 vols. (Washington, D.C.: Bureau of National Literature and Art, 1904).

18. Library of Congress, *Presidential Executive Orders, 1–7403, 1845–1936,* 11 reels (Washington, D.C.: Library of Congress, Photoduplication Service, n.d.).

19. Clifford Lord, ed., *Presidential Executive Orders, Numbered 1–8030, 1862–1938,* 2 vols., prepared by Historical Records Survey, New York, and sponsored by the city of New York and Columbia University (New York: Archives Publishing, 1944). (Reprint edition: Dennis & Co., Buffalo, N.Y., 1953; microfiche: Princeton Data Film, Princeton, N.J.).

20. "Oilsuit dismissed in Supreme Court." *New York Times,* Oct. 2, 1934, p. 1. *Panama Refining Co.* v. *Ryan,* 293 U.S. 388; 55 S.Ct. 241; 79 L.Ed. 446 (1935).

21. Published daily save Saturday, Sunday, and official federal holidays. A complete list of the regulations governing the form and content of the *Federal Register* is listed in Title 1 CFR.

22. Items not entered into the codified version include proposed rules and regulations; agency policy statements in regard to proposed

rules; repealed rules; and descriptive statements on agency organization.

23. Every four or five years there are periodic cumulations to Title 3, which greatly enhance the ease of access. They have been issued as follows: 1936–38; 1939–42; 1943–48; 1949–53; 1954–58; 1959–63; 1964–65; 1966–70; 1970–75.

24. Memorandum of May 11, 1978,"Review of the Federal Statistical System," 3 CFR 303 (1979).

25. Memorandum of Sept. 8, 1978, "Determination Extending the Exercise of Certain Authorities under the Trading with the Enemy Act," 3 CFR 309 (1979).

26. Memorandum of May 23, 1978, "Determination Pursuant to Section 2 (c) (1) of the Migration and Refugee Assistance Act of 1962, as Amended (the 'Act'), Authorizing the Obligation of $750,000 of Funds made Available Under the United States Emergency Refugee and Migration Assistance Fund," PD no. 78–12, 3 CFR 304 (1979).

27. Memorandum of Mar. 24, 1978, "Determination Under Section 620 (x) of the Foreign Assistance Act of 1961, as Amended, to Permit the Sale of Certain Specified Defense Articles to the Government of Turkey," PD no. 78–8, 3 CFR 296 (1979).

28. Memorandum of June 2, 1978, "Renewal of the U.S.-Romanian Agreement on Trade Relations—Finding and Determination Under Subsection 405(b) (1) of the Trade Act of 1947," PD no. 78–13, 3 CFR 305 (1979).

29. Memorandum of Jan. 26, 1978, "Recommendations approved by the President concerning Radiation Protection Guidance to Federal Agencies for Diagnostic X-Rays," 3 CFR 280 (1979).

30. Letter of Apr. 22, 1978, Welded Stainless Steel Pipe and Tube Industry, 3 CFR 301 (1978).

31. Presidential Statement on United States non-Proliferation and Peaceful Nuclear Cooperation Policy, released Thursday, July 16, 1981, by the White House Office of the Press Secretary.

32. EO no. 12065, 3 CFR 190 (1979). This EO was later revoked by Reagan by EO 12356, 47 Fed. Reg. 14874 (1982).

33. EO no. 12065, 3 CFR 190 (1979).

34. Charles I. Bevans, ed., *Treaties and Other International Agreements of the United States of America, 1776-1949,* 13 vols. (Washington, D.C.: Department of State, U.S. Government Printing Office, 1968–76).

35. Igor I. Kavass and Mark A. Michael, eds., *United States Treaties and Other International Agreements, Cumulative Index 1776-1949,* 4 vols. (Buffalo, N.Y.: W.S. Hein, 1975); Igor I. Kavass and A. Sprudzs, eds.

UST Cumulative Index: 1950–1970, 4 vols. (Buffalo, N.Y.: W.S. Hein, 1973); Christian L. Wikter, ed., *Unperfected Treaties of the United States of America, 1776–1976,* 3 vols. to date (Dobbs Ferry, N.Y.: Oceana Publications, 1976–).

36. *Public Affairs Information Services Bulletin* (New York: Public Affairs Information Services, 1914–).

37. *Index to Legal Periodicals* (New York: H. W. Wilson, 1908–); *Current Law Index* (Menlo Park, Calif.: Information Access Corp., 1980–).

38. *Monthly Catalog of United States Government Publications* (Washington, D.C.: U.S. Government Printing Office, 1951–); *CIS/Index* (Washington, D.C.: Congressional Information Service, 1970–); *American Statistics Index* (Washington, D.C.: Congressional Information Service, 1973–).

39. *Federal Index* (Washington, D.C.: Capitol Services, 1975–).

40. Anthony Kruzas, ed., *Encyclopedia of Information Systems and Services,* 3d ed. (Detroit: Gale Research, 1978).

6

Research in Executive-Legislative Relations

G. CALVIN MACKENZIE

White House Seeks Hill Approval of Radar Plane Sale to Saudis
White House Quickly Squelches Talk of Tax Compromise
Survey Finds Senate Ready to Confirm Judge O'Connor
House Democrats Challenge Reagan on Budget Voting

THESE HEADLINES appeared in the *Washington Post* in the summer of 1981. Like their daily echoes in newspapers all over the country, they testify to the kinship between the presidency and the Congress, to the important constitutional and political relationship that these institutions share. The simple fact is that one cannot fully comprehend the shape and character of the American presidency without examining the nature of its perennial partnership with the American Congress.

Presidential footprints almost inevitably lead to Capitol Hill, for there is little that a modern president does that does not somehow involve the Congress. A new president selects his cabinet; the Senate must confirm his selections. A president proposes a sweeping national energy policy; most of its components require legislative enactment. A president wants to restructure the Executive Office of the President; the Congress has to review his reorganization plan. And so it goes. The Congress is the nation's sounding board. The most important of the tones and timbres it must test are those that emanate from the White House.

The political significance of the interactions between president and Congress is not, however, the only reason why students of the presidency will find it valuable to do some occasional reconnaissance in congressional information sources. What they will discover is that the Congress is a researcher's wonderland. No other political institution in the world can compare with the American Congress in the breadth of the topics it explores or in the depth of the analyses it sponsors; and no other public institution can begin to match the Congress in the dazzling variety of its publications. Congressional documents are superb source material for the study of many topics, among the most important of which is the presidency. There are few more reliable sources of data about the composition of the White House office than the annual appropriations hearings conducted by the House and Senate Appropriations subcommittees that oversee its budget. An interest in the state of American relations with Latin America can be fruitfully pursued in oversight hearings held by the House Foreign Affairs Committee or in ambassadorial confirmation hearings before the Senate Foreign Relations Committee. Or what better way to discern journalistic reaction to a major presidential speech than by perusing the newspaper editorials inserted in the *Congressional Record* by sympathetic and antipathetic members of Congress?

There is a problem, however, for those who choose to undertake serious research in the resources provided by the Congress: those resources are so ample and their variety is so broad that the novice researcher is often overwhelmed. Without appropriate guidance or forethought, one can wander aimlessly for days on end through the Capitol building itself or in the congressional documents wing of a library without ever stumbling across the specific information that is most essential to a particular project. The best ways to begin such research are to develop a sensitivity to the peculiar nature of the congressional research environment and to acquire a cognizance of the guides and research aids that are available to assist in unveiling its mysteries. The aims of this chapter are to identify the most significant of the congressional information sources and to suggest some efficient and effective ways of using them.

Documentary Sources

Congressional documentation has a style and a nomenclature all its own. One simply cannot be effective in using this abundant resource without first learning at least the rudiments of the congressional document organization and numbering system. What follows here is a list of the major types of documents published by the Congress and an indication of the manner in which they are numbered and commonly cited.

BILLS AND RESOLUTIONS

Bills and resolutions, the focus of the legislative activities of the Congress, fall into four principal categories:

1. *Bills.* Bills are the means by which most legislation is introduced. To become law, bills require the approval of majorities in each house of Congress and the signature of the president (or a congressional override of his veto). Bills introduced in the House are numbered sequentially in each Congress and are given the prefix "H.R." Bills introduced in the Senate are also numbered sequentially and are given the prefix "S." For example, H.R. 1091 would be the number for House Bill 1091; S. 1091 would designate Senate Bill 1091.[1] Because each house has an independent numbering system, there is no reason to suspect that bills with the same number deal with the same topic.

2. *Joint Resolutions.* Like bills, joint resolutions require passage in both houses and a presidential signature to become law. This form, used infrequently, is primarily for limited purpose appropriations

and constitutional amendments. When a joint resolution proposes a constitutional amendment, and only then, passage requires a two-thirds majority in each house but does not require the president's signature. Joint resolutions may be introduced in either house. They are numbered sequentially in each house and bear the prefix "H.R.J. Res." if introduced in the House of Representatives and "S.J. Res." if introduced in the Senate. For example, H.R.J. Res. 96 would be read House Joint Resolution 96.

3. *Concurrent Resolutions.* Although concurrent resolutions need majority support in both houses for enactment, they do not require the signature of the president. They are used primarily for "sense of the Congress" resolutions and for such actions as congressional rules changes, setting annual budget targets and ceilings, and legislative vetoes. They may be introduced in either house, they are numbered sequentially in each house, and they bear the prefix "H.R. Con. Res." (if introduced in the House) or "S. Con. Res." (if introduced in the Senate). H.R. Con. Res. 17 would be read House Concurrent Resolution 17. Concurrent resolutions do not have the force of law.

4. *Resolutions.* Simple resolutions require only a majority in the house in which they are introduced for enactment; no concurrence in the other house or presidential signature is necessary. They are used for internal housekeeping matters in each house (e.g., rules changes, creation of new committees) and for enactment of "sense of the House" or "sense of the Senate" resolutions. They are numbered sequentially in each house and bear the prefix "H.R. Res." in the House and "S. Res." in the Senate. S. Res. 60, for instance, would be read Senate Resolution 60.

COMMITTEE HEARINGS

Congressional committee hearings are a cornucopia of information. Hearings on an issue will contain statements from administration officials, from members of Congress, and from other witnesses with a wide range of viewpoints. Published hearing transcripts may also include research reports from one of the congressional support agencies or from some independent organization, copies of relevant articles from newspapers, magazines, law reviews, and so on, and reproductions of official documents and memoranda that would otherwise be difficult to procure. Although published hearings are inconsistent in the kinds of information they provide, a researcher's interests are usually well served by taking the time to pore through them. Anyone, for instance, who had an interest in the president's war powers would have found in the transcript of hearings held in 1973 by a subcommittee of the House Committee on Foreign Affairs an uncommonly rich array of testimony, statements, and articles dealing with that issue.[2] It is doubtful that one could have acquired all of this information in any other way.

Hearings, although often the most useful congressional documents, are also the most difficult to use. They lack the sequential numbering systems that are used for bills and reports, they are inconsistent in breadth and in the materials they include, and they are poorly indexed. Unless one knows of the existence and contents of a specific hearing volume, it is best to approach these documents through use of one of the research aids described later in this chapter. The Congressional Information Service (CIS) *Indexes* and *Abstracts* are especially useful for this purpose.

COMMITTEE REPORTS

Once a committee has completed action on a bill, it "reports" it to the floor for debate. In so doing, it issues a written report, which accompanies the bill. The principal purpose of the report is to explain the bill and to justify the committee's support for it. Committee reports are generally rather short and typically include the following: a title-by-title review of the bill, a statement of the reasons for the committee's approval of it, signed statements by committee members who oppose the bill or who support it for reasons other than those stated by the committee majority, and, in many cases since 1970, a record of the positions taken by members when the bill was voted upon in committee. Use of committee reports is often the quickest and most efficient way to examine the treatment of a bill by a committee and to identify the range of attitudes held by committee members toward that bill.

Committee reports are numbered sequentially within each

house as they are issued. In the House, they bear the prefix "House Report," or "H.R. Rep."; in the Senate they are prefixed "Senate Report," or "S. Rep." In both houses, the sequence number is preceded by the number of the Congress in which they are issued. Hence H.R. Rep. 97–113 would identify the 113th House report in the Ninety-seventh Congress.

HOUSE AND SENATE DOCUMENTS

HOUSE and Senate documents are a collection of miscellaneous, but often valuable, materials. They include monographs on a variety of topics, investigative reports of congressional committees, presidential messages, reports from executive agencies and from independent organizations chartered by the government, and background information prepared for the use of congressional committees. A good example is H.R. Doc. 93–7, entitled *Impeachment: Selected Materials.* This is a 700-page volume prepared by the staff of the House Judiciary Committee and published on the eve of its deliberations on the impeachment of Richard Nixon. It includes a complete history of the establishment and use of the impeachment power and a number of articles by constitutional scholars on the scope of that power. It is the single best source ever produced on impeachment.

House and Senate documents are numbered sequentially in each house. They bear the prefix "House Document" (H.R. Doc.) or "Senate Document" (S. Doc.), identifying the house that produces them. The sequential number is preceded by the number of the Congress during which the document appeared. Hence, H.R. Doc. 93–7 is the seventh House document produced in the Ninety-third Congress.

CONGRESSIONAL RECORD

THE debates and proceedings of the Congress have been published since it first met in the spring of 1789. From 1789 to 1824, this was accomplished, albeit inconsistently, in a set of volumes entitled *Annals of Congress.* From 1824 to 1837, the *Register of Debates* served this purpose. The *Register* was replaced by the *Congressional Globe,* which was published from 1833 to 1873. These serials were all produced by commercial publishers, and it was only in 1851 that the *Globe* began to reproduce verbatim transcripts of congressional debates. Most of the material published before that year was abstracted from those debates.

In 1873, the U.S. Government Printing Office began to publish the *Congressional Record,* which has been the official record of congressional debates and proceedings ever since. The *Record* appears every day that either house is in session. The daily edition is printed at night and is available within twenty-four hours of the session it covers. The principal purposes of the *Record* are to provide a verbatim transcript of everything said on the floor of both houses and to indicate all of the official actions of the Congress. Simply saying that, however, does not begin to describe the complete functions — or charms — of the *Congressional Record.*

In its own way, the *Record* is a daily surprise package. One who wants to explore the issues in a congressional debate, to identify amendments offered on the floor, and to examine the votes of individual members will, of course, find it most useful for all of those purposes. Students of the presidency will find that it provides other benefits as well. Members of Congress have the freedom to insert for publication in the *Record* almost anything they choose. Among the materials that one commonly runs across in perusing its pages are presidential messages and transcripts of presidential speeches, copies of newspaper editorials and magazine articles dealing with specific presidential actions, reports and information produced by executive agencies, and printed attacks of all kinds on the incumbent administration and its programs. Although the president is not a member of Congress, he is very much a concern of Congress. Nowhere is that more fully reflected than in the pages of the *Congressional Record.*

The *Congressional Record* is published in a daily and a bound edition. The latter is by far the more useful unless, of course, one needs very recent information. The bound edition comprises about thirty hard-cover volumes a year, each covering approximately a dozen legislative days. Since 1946, it has included a "Daily

Digest," which is a very useful condensation of congressional activity. It includes concise descriptions of important congressional actions (e.g., presidential messages received, nominations received and confirmed, action on treaties, and final action on bills). Equally valuable is the chart that appears in the "Daily Digest" entitled "History of Bills Enacted into Public Law." This is a detailed but easy to read legislative history of all public laws enacted in that session of Congress.

An important aid to using the *Record* is the *Congressional Record Index*. This is published every two weeks in the daily editions; in the bound edition, the final volume contains a single cumulative index for the entire session. It is remarkably thorough and easy to use.

Two words of caution about using the *Congressional Record.* One is that valuable material will turn up at all sorts of odd times in the *Record*. One should never assume that information relevant to a particular bill or appointment or treaty will only appear on the days when those are debated. Make use of the *Index;* it is indispensable for getting full value from the *Record.* The other caution is to be careful to try to distinguish that which was actually spoken on the floor from that which was merely inserted for publication. The *Record* includes some helpful keys for making that distinction, but none of these is fully reliable.

PUBLIC LAWS

WHEN a bill becomes a public law it is assigned a number and published. Public laws are numbered sequentially in order of enactment; the sequential number is preceded by the prefix "PL" (for Public Law) and the number of the Congress that enacted it. Hence, PL 93-344 would be the 344th public law enacted by the Ninety-third Congress.

When first enacted, new laws are published in an unbound format called "slip laws." These are superseded at the end of each year by the publication of a bound volume entitled *United States Statutes at Large,* which contains the full text of every public law enacted in that session of Congress.

New laws, however, are often designed to amend old laws, and trying to use *Statutes at Large* to determine the current state of federal law in a particular policy area would be difficult indeed. For that purpose one would want to refer to the *United States Code,* a multivolume set published every six years. It is organized into fifty subject titles and has an excellent index.

References to the *Statutes at Large* are normally in this format: 81 Stat. 142. This would be read as volume 81, *U.S. Statutes at Large,* page 142. The *U.S. Code* is normally cited in this fashion: 18 *USC* 12. This would be read as Title 18, *United States Code,* section 12.

RESEARCH AIDS

A research aid can serve two purposes for people studying the interaction between the president and Congress. It can, of course, serve as a gateway to a rich variety of original congressional sources, indicating what is available and helping to point the researcher in the desired direction. Let us suppose, for instance, a researcher is interested in determining why the Nixon administration sought to establish a program of guaranteed minimum incomes, the Family Assistance Plan, in 1969 and 1970. A research aid would be invaluable. It would help to identify the specific bills that composed this program, the committees that considered them, the groups who testified in support and opposition, the timing and sequence of congresssional consideration, and the nature of final congressional action. The research aid would indicate that the Senate Finance Committee was the real congressional battleground for this program and that the best explanation of the Nixon position might well be found in the testimony of administration officials in hearings held by this committee. The research aid would further facilitate research by indicating the dates on which administration officials testified. All that would then be necessary for the researcher to do is to pull the published transcripts of the Finance Committee hearings from those dates and read their testimony.

In some cases, however, a research aid can eliminate the need even for that final step. Several of the best of those aids also provide abstracts, summaries, and analyses of events that obviate the need to use original sources at all. In this specific example, for instance, the investigator may well find that questions about the administration's support for the Family Assistance Plan are answered adequately by the summary of administration testimony that is included in the research aid. In this sense, a good research aid can serve as more than just a catalog of original sources; under the right circumstances it can be a very effective shortcut as well. The most reliable and readily available of the congressional research aids are described below.

CONGRESSIONAL QUARTERLY (CQ) SERVICE

SINCE it was first published in 1945, Congressional Quarterly has provided an indispensable service to all of those who actively engage in congressional research. The CQ service is provided to subscribers by a private, independent corporation, Congressional Quarterly, Inc.; it is *not* produced by the federal government. The scope of the service has expanded considerably over the years and now provides several different kinds of assistance for congressional researchers.

For those who are interested in current interactions between the president and the Congress, the key publication is the *CQ Weekly Report,* a magazine that appears every week in the year and contains, in addition to stories on important political and governmental activities in the previous week, a number of feature articles, many of them dealing specifically with the presidency. In the first six months of 1981, for example, there were feature stories on President Reagan's highway program, on his approach to the selection of federal judges, on the likely shape of his defense policies, on his congressional liaison operation, and on a number of other topics of direct relevance to students of his presidency.

The CQ approach is objective, it is heavily based on interviews with participants in the governing process, and it relies to a substantial degree on quantitative data. The last point is particularly noteworthy. CQ is an invaluable source of statistical data on a wide range of presidential concerns: executive vetoes, the size of the White House staff, treaties and executive agreements, to name just a few.

At the end of each year, CQ publishes the annual *Almanac.* This exceeds a thousand pages in length and contains reviews of the important political and governmental events of the year organized by substantive policy area (transportation, agriculture, economic affairs, etc.). The *Almanacs* are better indexed than the *Weekly Reports,* and they provide a more comprehensive picture of events. In most research pursuits that extend back beyond the beginning of the current year, the *Almanacs* are a better starting point than the *Weekly Reports.*

The CQ service also provides some other publications of note to congressional researchers with a special interest in the presidency. The set of volumes entitled *Congress and the Nation* is similar to the *Almanacs,* except that each volume covers a four-year period coterminous with a presidential term. They are especially useful for those who wish to explore the development of public policies over the course of an administration, because they are organized chronologically within substantive policy areas. CQ also publishes an annual paperback review of important presidential activities (e.g., *President Carter 1980*). This includes transcripts of important presidential addresses and news conferences and articles on such things as congressional action on presidential proposals, new policy developments, and executive-branch organization.

The CQ Guide to Congress, another enormous volume, has a constitutional and historical orientation, and is full of information and data on the development of the relationship between the president and the Congress. The *CQ Guide to U.S. Elections* and its biennial supplements are the single best source of presidential election statistics available anywhere. They include details on all presidential nominating conventions, biographies of every significant presidential candidate, vote totals from every state presidential primary ever held, and popular and electoral vote totals by state for every presidential election.

I have waxed on at some length here because it is hard to imagine life without CQ. It is a substantial guide to original congressional sources, but it has also become a compelling resource in its own right. The congressional researcher who overlooks it does so at his or her peril.

CONGRESSIONAL INFORMATION SERVICE (CIS)

THE critical task of anyone who does research in congressional documents is to get to the "best" source in the least time. Since 1970, the use of CIS has been the most efficient way to do that.

The *CIS U. S. Serial Set Index, 1789–1969* is the only complete index to the materials published in the Serial Set of congressional documents. It is composed of twelve chronological units, each containing several volumes. In each unit there is one volume with a finding list arranged by report and document numbers and several other volumes arranged by subject.

The *CIS Index to Congressional Publications and Public Laws* is the source most likely to facilitate the location of particular congressional documents. The *Index* has two parts. One is an annual volume that includes a subject and name index, a title index, and indexes by bill number, document number, and report number for all significant congressional documents published that year. (Cumulative indexes are published every four or five years.) Also published each year is an abstract volume in which the publications of all congressional committees are described in detail. This volume contains quite specific descriptions of the contents of these documents, including quotations from the testimony of witnesses at hearings, statements from committee reports, lists of individuals who appeared at hearings, and so on. The abstracts are particularly useful for researchers who want to get a sense of the substance and direction of a congressional hearing or the principal arguments in a committee report but who lack the time to read these documents carefully. At the end of each abstract volume, there are detailed legislative histories listing all of the documents that relate to each bill enacted into law during the year.

commerce clearing house (cch) congressional index

The *CCH Index* is most useful for those who need information on legislation in the current Congress. It is more up to date than the publications of CIS and more systematic than those of CQ. The *CCH Index* is a loose-leaf volume to which new information is added each week. Legislation is indexed by subject, sponsor, and bill number and cross-referenced with numbers of companion and identical bills.

monthly catalog of government publications

Published by the Government Printing Office since 1895, this is the most complete record of the publications of all branches and agencies of the federal government. Each issue lists all government publications for that month, organized by the issuing agency; congressional publications are organized by committee. There is an index at the end of each issue. Indexes are cumulated semiannually, annually, and every five years. Before 1976, the *Monthly Catalog* was indexed only by subject; since then it has been indexed by author, title, subject, and series.

digest of public general bills and resolutions

Prepared by the Congressional Research Service of the Library of Congress, the *Digest* is issued monthly while Congress is in session. It provides detailed summaries of every bill introduced in each Congress, summaries that are far easier to read and comprehend than the texts of the bills themselves. The *Digest* also tracks every bill, indicating the timing and character of all action taken on each (e.g., date of introduction, dates of committee hearings, final actions in committee, and date reported to House or Senate floor). For those who wish to trace the fate of bills that fail to become law, the *Digest* is an indispensable source. It is amply indexed by bill number, sponsor, title, and subject.

Beyond the Documents

Congressional documents and research aids alone are often not sufficient for an understanding of specific interactions between the president and the Congress. The political dramas that lead to government actions are frequently played out in private, in terms and for reasons quite different from those suggested in official sources. Thus, penetration beyond documentary sources is often necessary to uncover the genuine dimensions of executive-legislative interaction. Several useful resources are readily available to researchers seeking information beyond that provided in official congressional documents.

journalistic sources

Several hundred reporters, many of them with significant talent, spend their working days on Capitol Hill. Their job is to determine what goes on "behind the scenes," to identify the real reasons for the actions of congressional committees and individual members. To do this, they conduct interviews with members, with staff, with lobbyists, and with that group of wise old Washington hands usually referred to in the press as "veteran observers." The stories they write are thus a potentially rich source of inside information on the motives and activities that affect legislative-executive relationships.

The rub here is that journalists are not always accurate. The Congress is a large and complex institution, which makes it a difficult place for a reporter to cover. A big story usually has so many pieces that even the best journalists can overlook or misinterpret some that are critical to its outcome. Decision makers spend a good deal of time trying to manipulate journalists, and sometimes they succeed. All of this produces an inconsistency in reliability that may be tolerable for daily journalism but not for good scholarship.

The problem of reliability should not prevent scholars from taking advantage of journalistic sources, but it should impel care and skepticism in their use. Their accuracy needs to be tested against original documents, other journalistic reports, and the accounts of participants in the decision-making process. A comprehensive research strategy on a matter involving presidential-congressional relations ought to take advantage of journalistic sources; it should not rely on them solely.

Congressional researchers will find several categories of useful journalistic material. The first is the major national newspapers, which maintain a stable of full-time reporters on Capitol Hill. For the most thorough coverage of the Congress, one can usually count on the *Washington Post* and the *New York Times*. The *Post* and the *Times* are of particular value to researchers because they have regularly published indexes that facilitate the location of important stories. The *Wall Street Journal* also has a good track record in congressional coverage, though it leans heavily toward financial stories. It too has a published index.

Syndicated columnists are a surprisingly useful source of information about relations between the executive branch and the Congress. Because their readership is vast, many of them have the clout to get them ready access to the very best sources in the Congress and in the White House. Hence, they can often generate insights about a decision that a researcher cannot glean from official documents or from daily reporting. Again, one must be sensitive to the reliability problem, for columnists are rarely perfectly accurate. If the columns of David Broder, James Reston, Joseph Kraft, James J. Kilpatrick, Evans and Novak, and so on, are used to supplement other sources, they may well help to explain decisions and actions that might otherwise seem to defy logic.

One other helpful but often overlooked set of journalistic sources is what is commonly referred to as the "trade press." This includes a number of specialized journals with such names as *Air Transport World, International Trade Forum, Public Utilities Fortnightly,* and *Social Security Bulletin* and a number of "house organs" published by trade associations and special interest groups. Though most of these are narrowly focused, they often cover stories in their realm of interest in great depth. Their Washington correspondents usually have excellent sources in the congressional committees and member offices that deal with the issues that concern them. Legislative activities that may be too obscure or too technical to attract the attention of journals with a national audience are often covered only in the trade press. For one who is doing research on such an issue, this may well become an invaluable source of information and insight.

Access to many of the sources mentioned here is often exceedingly difficult. Most newspapers do not publish an index of their own; some are indexed collectively in NEXIS and NDEX (see p. 144). Magazines and similar periodicals are inconsistent about indexes. A few publish their own; the vast majority do not. For this reason, the *Reader's Guide to Periodical Literature* and the *Public Affairs Information Service Bulletin (PAIS)* are enormously helpful. As the most thorough and widely available collective indexes, they are an important source of access to hundreds of general and specialized periodicals.

SCHOLARLY LITERATURE

BECAUSE of its openness and internal diversity, the Congress has been an appealing subject for political scientists for several generations. The literature they have produced is rich and deep. For anyone attempting to understand congressional reaction to presidential initiatives, it is a literature usually well worth consulting.

To identify and locate scholarly books on legislative-executive relations, one is unlikely to find any guide more useful than the card catalog of a good library. This is a literature that grows rapidly, and a good part of it becomes dated rather quickly. Hence, published bibliographies tend to be of limited value. The best of the recent bibliographies are those listed here, which have been published by congressional committees and the Congressional Research Service:

The United States Senate: A Historical Bibliography (January 1977; available from the U.S. Senate Historical Office or from the Government Printing Office)

Commission on the Operation of the Senate, *A Select Annotated Bibliography on the Senate* (January 1977; prepared by the Congressional Research Service and available from the Government Printing Office)

Congressional Research Service, *The United States House of Representatives: A Select Annotated Bibliography* (March 1977; available through members of Congress)

U.S. House of Representatives, *House Report No. 96–866: Final Report of Select Committee on Committees,* pp. 605–69 (April 1980; available from the Government Printing Office or members of Congress)

Articles on legislative-executive relations that appear in scholarly journals are indexed in several places. Law review articles are indexed in the *Index to Legal Periodicals,* which is published monthly and cumulated every three years. Most of the relevant articles in social science journals are indexed in the *Public Affairs Information Service Bulletin,* which appears bimonthly with quarterly cumulations and an annual bound volume.

DIRECT CONTACT

THERE are some research questions that no written source can answer satisfactorily. Why was Senator X out of town on a day when his vote would have prevented the confirmation of a nominee to the Supreme Court? Why did Congressman Y vote for the president's foreign aid proposals after speaking against them on the floor of the House? Those intrigues that make legislative-executive relations so interesting are frequently the most difficult to penetrate and explain. Often there is no substitute for direct contact with the participants in critical decision-making processes. When this is the case, the personal interview becomes a research technique of great importance.

There are several general guides to elite interviewing that are worth perusing as preparation for interviewing on Capitol Hill, including Chapters 10 and 11 in this book.[3] A couple of special characteristics of congressional interviewing, however, are worth noting here.

The first deals with logistics. For most members of Congress, a "schedule" is a concept that is honored mostly in the breach. When members are in Washington their days are full of activities, a good many of which run longer than anticipated. Anyone who has interviewed any substantial number of members of Congress will have spent a good deal of time waiting for those members to return from the floor, from a committee session, or from a meeting in someone else's office. Often the member must run off immediately for another appointment and must cancel the scheduled interview entirely.

A researcher can do little to prevent this, but there are several ways to cope with it. One is simply to anticipate these logistical problems and to prepare for them. A tight schedule of interviews with several members should not be attempted; interviews should be well spaced and spread out over several days or weeks. The researcher from out of town should allow several extra days for interviewing so that abandoned appointments can be rearranged. In fact, one is often better off not to interview members in their Washington offices, but to ask permission to ride with them on a plane trip to their district or while motoring to the Capitol from home or after a speech downtown. If convenient, it is perferable to interview members in their own district than in Washington because they have greater control over their time and are thus more faithful to appointments arranged in advance.

Interview procedures will, of course, vary considerably from one member to the next. If there is a key to getting a good interview, it is to put the member at ease and to engage him or her in the subject and the purpose of the interview. The researcher should try to explain what he or she is doing in a way that will seem worthwhile to the member and should make a special effort to indicate why the particular interview was thought to be essential. Questions should be as specific and direct as possible (e.g., "Before you voted on this bill, did you get any advice from union leaders in your district?" rather than "Does labor influence the way you vote?").

In elite interviewing, there is no substitute for thorough preparation. Interviews should come at the end of the research process, not at the outset. If the researcher is not fully familiar with the issues the interview will cover, it will not be very productive, nor, in all likelihood, will it prove very interesting for the interviewee.

No single format is likely to be appropriate for all interviewers of members of Congress on all topics. Experience suggests, however, that members of Congress are often uncomfortable when asked to give definite responses to a long list of close-ended questions. They deal with great complexity in their jobs, and they find it hard to simplify what they do or what they think into the brief responses that close-ended questions require. It is often far more effective to go into an interview with a short list of questions or topics to be covered and to attempt to engage the member in a conversation that works its way through all of them. Most members are excellent conversationalists. The principal task of the interviewer is to provide direction to their conversation.

A question that all researchers should pose to themselves before they begin to make direct contacts on Capitol Hill is whether they need to interview members of Congress at all. On many projects, essential information can be procured just as effectively without going through the logistical hassles of scheduling and conducting interviews with very busy members of Congress. Surrogates are often much easier to contact, much less circumspect in their responses, and much more knowledgeable on the issues that are most important to the researcher.

Among the surrogates most likely to be productive interviewees are members' personal staff assistants, committee staff, representatives of interest groups, and Capitol Hill journalists. Granted anonymity, most of the people who fall into these categories will speak openly, and often incisively, about decisions or events on which they have detailed or inside knowledge. As a general rule, they are more readily available than members of Congress and less burdened by the fear of having their words come back to haunt them when they appear in print.

ELEMENTS OF A RESEARCH STRATEGY: TWO ILLUSTRATIONS

THIS chapter will conclude with an examination of two specific research questions involving congressional responses to presidential initiatives. The first involves a presidential appointment, the second a legislative proposal. Use of these cases should help to illustrate ways in which one might formulate a research strategy for determining valid answers to questions like those posed here. There is never a single right way to do this, of course; this discussion is designed simply to suggest some significant and appropriate avenues of exploration.

ILLUSTRATION ONE:

How did Lyndon Johnson Win Congressional Support for the Economic Opportunity Act of 1964?
There are both advantages and disadvantages in researching legislative-executive interactions that occurred many years before the research is conducted. The principal disadvantages are that some of the significant participants in those interactions will have died, or their memories of specific events will have hazed over with the passage of time. Nevertheless, there are compensating benefits. The written record will be more ample with the addition of memoirs and historical analyses. Private papers and internal documents will be more readily available in presidential libraries and other collections. And those participants who are still about and whose memories of the appropriate events are still vivid will be more free and open in talking about them than they would have been at the time they occurred.

As in almost all research involving the Congress, one is best advised to begin with Congressional Quarterly, in this case with the *CQ Almanac* for 1964. This will provide a review of the events that led to the passage of the Economic Opportunity Act and of the critical points at which the White House had to confront determined opposition. The *Almanac* will also guide the researcher to important congressional documents like committee hearings and reports and indicate the days on which floor debate occurred in each house.

One might also find it helpful at the outset to read the accounts of consideration of this legislation that are contained in the memoirs of those who had a hand in it. Lyndon Johnson, many of his aides and appointees, and several members of Congress have written books that discuss this bill and their role in its enactment. Though the accounts they provide are sometimes sanitized and always self-justifying, they are nevertheless a helpful tool for assessing the concerns and tactics of various participants at the time of an important decision.

Once the researcher has a pretty clear mental picture of the sequence of events that led to the passage of the Equal Opportunity Act, then it is time to focus specifically on the role that Lyndon Johnson played in bringing it to fruit. To do that, one must first determine the substance and size of the opposition and then look for indications of the ways in which Johnson sought to overcome or mollify that opposition. This is where congressional documents can be especially helpful. In committee hearings, opposition to an administration bill is often reflected in the testimony of witnesses and in the questions and statements of committee members. If the committees report some version of the president's bill, as occurred in this case, the report that accompanies it to the floor will usually contain a direct statement of the views of committee members who oppose it. In debate on the floor itself, the opposition will take advantage of the time allotted them to state their case against the bill.

Determining the shape and scope of the opposition is the easy part. The hard part is to find out what the president did to cope with that opposition. Much of the bargaining and compromising that occurs on complex legislation is substantive in nature: the text of the bill is changed to obtain the support of those who opposed some of the language in the original version. Those kinds of presidential actions are easy enough to track down because they usually occur in the form of amendments in committee or on the floor. The amendments will have the support, or at least the acquiescence, of the congressional managers of the administration's bill.

Other presidential influence, however, comes in the form of presidential persuasion of individual members, of administration lobbying, or of bargains that are struck between the White House and opposing members of Congress, bargains in which the currency of exchange is something other than the language of the bill. To track down this kind of evidence of presidential influence, one must again depart from the public record for slipperier research grounds. The behind-the-scenes activities that compose much of what we often refer to as presidential influence must be reconstructed by the researcher from contemporary journalistic accounts, from the memoirs of participants, and, where possible, from interviews and oral histories.

For access to the relevant journalism of the time, one would be best served by the *Readers' Guide to Periodical Literature* and the *New York Times Index* (none of the other "national" newspapers published indexes in 1964). Memoirs could be located in a library card catalog or appropriate bibliography under the names of those individuals known to have participated in the creation of the Economic Opportunity Act of 1964 or to have had access to the thinking of those who did. To identify relevant oral histories, one could check several sources. Presidential libraries generally have transcripts of oral histories with most of the important White House aides in an administration and often also with leading members of Congress. The Former Members of Congress, an association of defeated and retired members, has been sponsoring an oral history project for some time as well. To locate and determine the availability of potential interview subjects, one might first check the *Congressional Directory* to find out which of the members actively involved in debate on the Economic Opportunity Act is still serving in Congress. Those congressional members and executive officials no longer serving in government, but still alive, can be located by using *Who's Who in America, Who's Who in American Politics,* or even (since "Potomac fever" is generally incurable) the telephone book of the District of Columbia or neighboring Maryland and Virginia.

The story of Lyndon Johnson's effort to secure passage of the Economic Opportunity Act must ultimately be pieced together. The researcher will find that with the passage of time much evidence will have accumulated from which this can be done wisely and insightfully.

Who Slew Ted Sorensen?

In late December of 1976, word began to trickle through Washington that President-elect Jimmy Carter intended to nominate Theodore C. Sorensen to the sensitive and important position of director of the Central Intelligence Agency. Sorensen had served as a high-level White House aide in the Kennedy and Johnson administrations, and he had been one of Carter's earliest supporters and fund-raisers in his quest for the presidency. On December 23, Carter made a public announcement of his intention to nominate Sorensen to the CIA. In the three and a half weeks that followed, the Sorensen nomination became a source of great controversy and — for the president-elect — of great dismay. On January 17, 1977, at the start of televised Senate confirmation hearings, Sorensen withdrew his name from nomination. This was a striking and highly unusual setback for a president who had not yet even taken the oath of office.

What happened? Why did Carter choose Sorensen? Why did Sorensen withdraw? And what does this suggest about Jimmy Carter's management of the presidency?

What makes this a particularly challenging research question is that so little of what transpired between December 23, 1976, and January 17, 1977, appears in any public record. There was no debate on this nomination on the floor of the Senate nor any discussion of it in a committee hearing. Nor are there committee reports or other documents that help explain its failure. The researcher must navigate by the seat of his pants.

A sensible first stop is the *Congressional Quarterly Weekly Report* for the weeks during which the Sorensen nomination was under discussion. This will give an outline of the issues involved and indicate the dates of critical turning points in this decision. One might then turn to the *New York Times Index* and to the *Times* itself to read articles that follow the daily flow of the decision and that suggest some of the reasons for the nomination's failure. Similar inquiries in other newspapers — the *Washington Post* and *Washington Star,* for instance — might further help to flesh out this tale. Careful attention to the op-ed pages is especially useful in a case like this, for they are often full of insights about the real reasons for opposition to presidential initiatives. A perusal of the *Readers' Guide to Periodical Literature* might also identify some periodical sources of information.

By consulting widely in journalistic sources, one ought to be able to reconstruct a detailed sequence of events, to identify critical participants, and to catalog some likely reasons for Sorensen's decision to withdraw. Still, two concerns remain. One is that this information from journalistic sources is likely to include some contradictions and inconsistencies. The other is that it is difficult to vouchsafe its reliability.

The only genuinely effective way to resolve the contradictions and inconsistencies and to verify the explanations provided in the press is to conduct interviews with some of those who were actively involved in or who directly observed the events that led to the withdrawal of the Sorensen nomination. The press accounts ought to identify most of these people. For this particular case, interview subjects might include Sorensen himself, the members and staff of the Senate Select Committee on Intelligence, other senators (or their aides) who were active in supporting and opposing the nomination, members of Carter's legislative liaison team, and perhaps representatives from those interest groups who tried to influence the outcome of these events. In this particular case, for instance, the AFL-CIO took an active interest. Its top leaders opposed Sorensen, in substantial part because he had earlier been active in supporting an insurgent faction within the union.

Even ambitious interviewing is not likely to resolve fully all the inconsistencies in the way this story has been told or to fix any sure consensus on why Sorensen ultimately withdrew. Different people will see the events through different perspectives and thus attribute to them different explanations. Inevitably, analysis has to rely on a weighing and marshaling of the evidence and the thoughtful exercise of informed judgment. For these, there is no substitute.

Conclusion

The "truth" is elusive. That is the frustration, yet also the challenge, of most research into the relations between the president and the Congress. What usually emerges, even from the most intelligent of research designs, is a composite sketch, not a photograph. The frustrated researcher is well reminded of John F. Kennedy's warning, "The essence of ultimate decision remains impenetrable to the observer — often, indeed, to the decider himself. . . . There will always be the dark and tangled stretches in the decision-making process — mysterious even to those who may be most intimately involved."[4]

A realistic set of objectives is essential. The task of the researcher is not to impose a single vision where no single vision exists, nor to reduce complex events to a simplified equation. The task instead is to provide an accurate portrait of events in all their complexity, and then to enlighten those with reasonable interpretations of their meaning and significance. Those who take that responsibility seriously will find a wealth of research tools and techniques appropriate to their needs.

Notes

The author is indebted to Ms. Rita Bouchard for her generous assistance in the preparation of this chapter.

1. Citation forms used in this chapter follow the style of *A Uniform System of Citation: Forms of Citation and Abbreviations,* 12th ed. (Cambridge, Mass.: Harvard Law Review Association, 1976).

2. The reference is to *War Powers:* Hearings on s. 440 and Related Bills before the Subcommittee on National Security Policy and Scientific Developments of the House Committee on Foreign Affairs, 93d Cong. 1st sess., 1973.

3. See, for example, Lewis A. Dexter, *Elite and Specialized Interviewing* (Evanston, Ill.: Northwestern Univ. Press, 1970); Walter Bingham, Bruce Moore, and John Gustad, *How to Interview,* 4th ed. (New York: Harper & Row, 1959); Raymond L. Gorden, *Interviewing: Strategy, Technique, and Tactics* (Homewood, Ill.: Dorsey Press, 1969).

4. Foreword by John F. Kennedy to Theodore C. Sorensen, *Decision-Making in the White House: The Olive Branch or the Arrows* (New York: Columbia Univ. Press, 1963), xi, xii.

7

Making Use of Legal Sources

LOUIS FISHER

THE CONSTITUTIONAL CRISES precipitated by presidential excesses during the Lyndon Johnson and Richard Nixon administrations helped stimulate what Richard Pious in 1974 called a "renaissance of public law."[1] Students of the presidency have indeed taken a quantum leap in understanding and appreciating the separation-of-powers doctrine, war powers, executive privilege, pocket vetoes, impoundment, legislative vetoes, executive agreements, impeachment, and other issues of a constitutional dimension.

The danger is substantial, however, that this interest represents a momentary flowering, a transient reawakening that will be followed by a retreat to indifference and inattention. This kind of relapse is less likely to happen if we keep in mind the heritage of political science and the legal context that permanently and inescapably binds Congress, the president, the courts, and the public.

Public law at one time supplied an essential orientation for political science. No one dreamed of separating law from government. The first graduate school of political science in America, set up at Columbia College in 1880, was grounded in history, law, and philosophy. America's first journal of political science, *Political Science Quarterly,* chose for its subtitle "A Review Devoted to the Historical, Statistical and Comparative Study of Politics, Economics and Public Law." The declared purpose of the American Political Science Association, established in 1903, was the "scientific study of Politics, Public Law, Administration and Diplomacy."

In recent decades we have managed to drive an artificial wedge between the disciplines of political science and law. Large numbers of political scientists, including those who study the presidency, have cut ties with their public law heritage. Contributions in the literature have been limited, for the most part, to constitutional histories of the early years of the United States, the process of selecting judges, and behavioral studies restricted to psychological analyses and quantitative techniques.[2] In a 1963 study of the fields in which the most significant work was being done in political science, general politics and behavioralism headed the list. Next came comparative government and international relations. Public administration, political theory, and American government and politics followed. Stranded at the bottom was public law.[3]

The doctrine of mechanical jurisprudence and the supposed nonpolitical character of the judicial function were convenient excuses that kept most political scientists from thinking about the courts. Law was seen as something remote instead of just one of several outcomes of political activity. As C. Herman Pritchett perceptively noted, politics and law drifted apart because of semantic, philosophical, and practical reasons: "Law is a prestigious symbol, whereas politics tends to be a dirty word. Law is stability; politics is chaos. Law is impersonal; politics is personal. Law is given; politics is free choice. Law is reason; politics is prejudice and self-interest. Law is justice; politics is who gets there first with the most."[4]

Justices of the Supreme Court have contributed to the conceptual confusion. The refusal of courts to decide cases that involve "political questions" has encouraged the belief that there is indeed a gulf between law and politics. Chief Justice Marshall, in *Marbury* v. *Madison* (1803), insisted that "Questions in their nature political . . . can never be made in this court."[5] Yet in that very decision he established a precedent of far-reaching political importance: the right of the judiciary to review and over-turn the actions of Congress and the president.

The Politics of Legal Action

Private organizations regularly conclude that their political interests will be better achieved by turning to the judiciary for assistance. As Justice Brennan remarked in 1963, litigation is "a form of political expression." Groups unable to find satisfaction in the executive or legislative branches will look to the courts: "under the conditions of modern government, litigation may well be the sole practicable avenue open to a minority to peti-tion for redress of grievances."[6] To understand how these politi-cal conflicts are resolved, a student of government must become comfortable with using legal sources as research tools.

Recent decisions by federal courts — in the areas of prison reform, school districting, and improvements in hospitals and mental institutions — have generated complaints that the judici-ary has invaded territory formerly belonging to administrators and legislators. Congress has not lost sight of the political signif-icance of these actions. There are many present efforts to curb the courts, especially the move by Congress to control the ap-pellate jurisdiction of federal courts.[7]

The political significance of court decisions involving the presidency has been too conspicuous to ignore. When the Su-preme Court decided in 1952 that President Truman lacked au-thority to seize steel mills, despite the government's need for steel for the Korean War, the political impact was unmistakable. Newspapers gave front-page coverage to Truman's action, the litigation in the lower courts, and the Supreme Court's dramatic verdict.[8] Also prominent were efforts by private parties and members of Congress to test the constitutional power of Presi-dents Johnson and Nixon to conduct a war in Southeast Asia without explicit authorization from Congress, and the approximately eighty decisions by federal courts that challenged the right of Nixon to impound funds that Congress had appropriated. Judicial review of President Carter's termination of the defense treaty with Taiwan, his settlement of Iranian assets and the hostage question, and Reagan's hiring freeze in 1981 (raising the issue of a breach of contract with newly hired employees), are other prominent issues that commanded the public's attention.

Other important political issues that percolate through the courts include campaign financing, regulatory policy, protection of "whistleblowers" in the federal bureaucracy, the use of affirmative action to increase the numbers of women and minority groups employed by federal agencies, the use of appropriated funds by agencies to lobby Congress, the president's use of executive agreements as a substitute for treaties, and the scope of the president's law-making power when he issues executive orders and proclamations.

When presidential actions threaten legislative interests, members of Congress are quick to defend their institution. In *Myers* v. *United States* (1926), involving the president's power to remove executive officials, the Supreme Court invited Senator George Wharter Pepper to present the case for Congress. His oral argument and extract of his brief, along with those of appellant and the solicitor general, are printed immediately before the Court's opinion.[9] During the impoundment disputes of the Nixon administration, members of Congress submitted an *amicus curiae* brief on behalf of the appellee suing the administration.[10] In the abortion case eventually decided by the Supreme Court in 1980, concerning the constitutional power of Congress to use its power of the purse to restrict federally financed abortions, the district court permitted Senator James L. Buckley, Senator Jesse A. Helms, and Congressman Henry J. Hyde to intervene as defendants.[11] The Ninth Circuit invited both the House and the Senate to submit briefs concerning a legislative veto used by Congress in deportation cases.[12] After losing in the Ninth Circuit, both houses had their attorneys participate in oral argument when the Supreme Court addressed the matter on February 22, 1982.

A striking development of the past decade is the frequency with which members of Congress take issues directly to the courts.

Senator Edward M. Kennedy was successful at both the district court and appellate court levels in challenging Nixon's attempt to use the "pocket veto" during brief recesses of the House and the Senate. As a result of Kennedy's lower-court victories, the Ford administration announced that it would use the pocket veto only during the final adjournment at the end of a Congress.[13]

When members of Congress try to gain political objectives through the courts, there is concern on the part of judges that the controversy is really not Congress against the president but rather one group of legislators against another. Federal judges suspect that members of Congress are turning to the courts because they have been unable to attract sufficient votes from a majority of their colleagues to act through the regular legislative process. If legislators fail to make use of remedies available within Congress, judges are unlikely to grant them standing to resolve the issue in court.[14]

A recent example is the case of *Crockett* v. *Reagan* (1981) in which eleven members of Congress charged that President Reagan had violated the War Powers Resolution of 1973 by sending fifty-six military personnel to El Salvador. Sixteen senators and thirteen members of the House of Representatives promptly intervened, in a separate memorandum, to warn the court not to interfere with a political issue that should be resolved through the regular legislative process.

Although Congress had been represented in court by the Department of Justice and sometimes through appearances by senators, representatives, and attorneys acting as *amicus curiae,* this sporadic activity was not satisfactory to Congress. A Senate committee concluded in 1966 that the effect upon Congress of court decisions "should be a matter of continuous concern for which some agency of the Congress should take responsibility."[15]

The Legislative Reorganization Act of 1970 explicitly recognized the need for a more systematic and continuing review of court decisions that affect legislative prerogatives. The statute created a Joint Committee on Congressional Operations, responsible for identifying "any court proceeding or action which, in the opinion of the Joint Committee, is of vital interest to the Congress, or to either House of the Congress, as a constitutionally established institution of the Federal Government. . . ." The Joint Committee was directed to make periodic reports and recommendations to the Senate and the House.

Starting in 1971, the Joint Committee on Congressional Operations began publishing a series of reports on legal proceedings of interest to Congress. Many of the issues concerned head-on clashes between Congress and the president, especially congressional access to executive-branch information. After the Joint Committee went out of existence in 1977, the responsibility for publishing the report fell initially to a newly created House Select Committee on Congressional Operations, working in concert with the Senate Committee on Rules and Administration. When the House decided to discontinue the Select Committee, the House Committee on the Judiciary inherited the responsibility for producing the reports on legal proceedings.

In recent years, Congress has become concerned about the refusal of the Justice Department to defend the constitutionality of certain provisions of law. Sometimes the department took this position after deciding that a particular statute infringed on presidential powers or was so patently unconstitutional that it could not possibly be defended, as in the bill of attainder case in 1946 (*United States* v. *Lovett*, 328 U.S. 303).[16]

As a result of language placed in authorization acts for the Justice Department over the past few years, the attorney general is required to report to Congress whenever the Justice Department intends to refrain from defending the constitutionality of a law passed by Congress. These reports specify the provision of law at issue and include a detailed statement of the reasons given by the Justice Department for calling a statutory provision unconstitutional.

A Senate committee concluded in 1977 that the institutional interests of Congress made it inappropriate, for reasons both of principle and the constitutional separation of powers, for Congress to depend upon the attorney general to defend its vital constitutional powers.[17] As part of the Ethics in Government Act of 1978, the State established for itself an Office of Senate Legal Counsel. The principal duty of the counsel is to defend the Senate or a committee, subcommittee, officer, or employee of the Senate.

The House of Representatives continues to rely on the Clerk of the House, whose staff (assisted by private attorneys under contract) litigates cases for members, House officers, and staff.

How to Locate the Law

When a bill passes Congress and is signed by the president, or is vetoed by the president and Congress overrides the veto, the bill is printed either as a public law or a private law. The latter series is reserved for legislation intended for the relief of private parties, especially bills dealing with claims against the United States, the waiver of claims by the government against individuals, and exceptions for individuals subject to certain immigration and naturalization requirements.

The enacted bill first appears as a "slip law." The heading indicates the public law number, date of approval, and bill number. For example, the Bankruptcy Tax Act of 1980, which originated as H.R. 5043, was enacted on December 24, 1980, and designated Public Law 96–589 (the 589th public law of the Ninety-sixth Congress). The heading also indicates the volume and page in the *U.S. Statutes at Large,* where the public law will appear. For the Bankruptcy Tax Act of 1980, the citation is 94 Stat. 3389. At the end of the slip law is a convenient legislative history that refers to the House and Senate reports and floor debates that preceded the bill's enactment. Private laws are numbered by a separate series, also prefixed by the Congress. Thus, a bill for the relief of Miriama Jones, enacted October 28, 1978, was called Private Law 95–110.

Bound volumes, called the *U.S. Statutes at Large,* contain public laws, private laws, reorganization plans, joint resolutions, concurrent resolutions, and proclamations issued by the president. There is little practical difference between a bill and a joint resolution. Both forms of legislation must be presented to the president for his signature; both are legally binding. Concurrent resolutions, adopted by the House and the Senate, are not presented to the president and generally do not have the force of law.

Beginning with volume 52 (1938), each volume of the *Statutes at Large* contains the laws enacted during a calendar year. After volume 64, treaties and other international agreements were no longer printed in the *Statutes*. They are printed in a new series of volumes, published by the State Department, called *United States Treaties and Other International Agreements*. The documents first appear in pamphlet form numbered in the "Treaties and Other International Acts Series" (TIAS). Citations are usually given to both the TIAS number and the volume of *United States Treaties and Other International Agreements,* as in 30 UST 617, TIAS 9207 (1978).

Treaties may supersede prior conflicting statutes.[18] By virtue of Article VI, Section 2, the Constitution, statutes, and treaties are collectively called "the supreme Law of the Land." On the other hand, executive agreements cannot be "inconsistent with legislation enacted by Congress in the exercise of its constitutional authority."[19] In cases where executive agreements violate rights secured by the Constitution, they have been struck down by the courts.[20]

As laws are modified or repealed by subsequent enactments of Congress, the need arises for a publication that consolidates the permanent body of law. The first codification of U.S. laws, enacted June 22, 1874, appeared in the *Revised Statutes*. A second edition was published in 1878, followed by supplements. In 1926, Congress passed a law to provide for a code intended to embrace the laws of the United States that are general and permanent in their character. The first volume, reflecting the laws in force as of December 7, 1925, was printed as volume 44, part I, of the *Statutes at Large*. This series is now known as the *United States Code*. New editions of the code appeared in 1934, 1940, 1946, 1952, 1958, 1964, 1970, and 1976. Supplements to the code are issued after each session of Congress. The code consists of fifty titles organized by subject matter (Agriculture, Highways, Money and Finance, etc.). Index references are to title, section, and year, as in 7 USC 443 (1976) and 10 USC 1434 (Supp. II, 1978).

Unless superseded by federal statute or invalidated by the courts, presidential proclamations, executive orders, and regulations are other sources of law. Not until 1935 did Congress pass legislation to provide for the custody and publication of these administrative rules and pronouncements. This publication, the *Federal Register,* includes all presidential proclamations and executive orders that have general applicability and legal effect, as well as agency regulations and orders that prescribe a penalty. Based partly on the statutory authority vested in him by the Federal Register Act, President Franklin D. Roosevelt issued an executive order in 1936 that vested in the Bureau of the Budget (now Office of Management and Budget) the responsibility for reviewing all proposed executive orders and proclamations.[21]

The *Federal Register* is published daily, Monday through Fridays, except for official holidays. A typical citation would be 46 Fed. Reg. 36707 (1981). The rules, regulations, and orders that constitute the current body of administrative regulations are arranged under fifty titles (generally parallel to those of the *United States Code*) and printed as the *Code of Federal Regulations.* Citations are by title and section, as in 50 CFR 17.13 (1980).

There is continuing controversy over the range and legal effect of executive orders and proclamations. Executive orders cannot supersede a statute or override contradictory congressional expressions,[22] but the latitude for presidential lawmaking is still substantial and a source of concern.[23] Proclamations also operate in a twilight zone of legality. When a statute prescribes a specific procedure and the president elects to follow a different course, a proclamation by him is illegal and void.[24] Proclamations have been upheld, however, with only tenuous ties to statutory authority.[25]

Following Interpretations of the Law

As a general guide to the constitutional powers of the president, the student should consult what has become known as the "Annotated Constitution." The actual title is *The Constitution of the United States of America: Analysis and Interpretation,* prepared periodically by the Congressional Research Service of the Library of Congress and printed as a Senate document. Edward S. Corwin wrote the 1952 edition, which has since been substantially revised. Constitutional scholars still turn with profit to Corwin's *The President: Office and Powers, 1787–1957* (New York: New York University Press, 1957). Other basic sources include *The Records of the Federal Convention of 1787,* a four-volume work edited by Max Farrand and published by Yale University Press in 1937, and the *Federalist* papers of Hamilton, Jay, and Madison, the most prominent edition of which was published by Harvard University Press in 1966 under the guidance of Benjamin Fletcher Wright.

Other than brief accounts that appear in daily newspapers announcing major decisions by the Supreme Court, a researcher must rely on more specialized sources to keep track of legal interpretations — especially lower-court decisions. Decisions by federal district and appellate courts are fascinating for two reasons: (1) they are the first step in shaping constitutional and statutory law and (2) often they are the last step, for few of their rulings are reviewed by the Supreme Court.

This huge body of material is conveniently organized by the *United States Law Week,* which appears each Tuesday except the first Tuesday in September and the last Tuesday in December. The *Law Week* consists of four major sections: (1) a summary and analysis of major decisions, with page references to more extended treatment in the *Law Week;* (2) new court decisions and agency rulings (decisions, executive orders, regulations, and administrative interpretations) and a "News in Brief" section that contains book reviews, comments on specialized areas of the law, and lists of executive nominations and confirmations; (3) Supreme Court proceedings, including oral arguments before the Court, reviews granted, summary actions, reviews denied, cases recently filed, and special articles summarizing and analyzing the most significant Supreme Court opinions rendered for each term; and (4) Supreme Court opinions.

The *Law Week* is published by the Bureau of National Affairs, Inc., 1231 Twenty-fifth Street, N.W., Washington, D.C. 20037. Citations are by volume, page, and year, as in *Maher* v. *Roe,* 45 U.S.L.W. [or L.W.] 4787 (1977).

Court Proceedings and Actions of Vital Interest to the Congress, now published by the House Committee on the Judiciary, is another useful guide. These decisions typically cover the constitutional immunity of members of Congress under the Speech or Debate Clause, the investigative power, disputed elections, constitutional qualifications of members of Congress, congressional access to executive-branch information, congressional powers, and efforts by member of Congress to litigate. In addition to providing a history of legal disputes that reach the courts, *Court Proceedings* reprints the full decisions. Many of these decisions are not published ("reported") elsewhere. Short descriptions of these decisions are printed regularly in the "Capitol Cases" section of *Staff,* a congressional staff journal published every other month by the Senate Committee on Rules and Administration, Russell Senate Office Building, Room 305, Washington, D.C. 20510.

Two weekly newspapers, catering to the legal profession, are especially valuable. Both newspapers contain stories on appointments to the federal agencies, personnel actions, departmental politics, budget cutbacks, executive-legislative clashes, regulatory policy, and administrative law. They also regularly review the literature. *The National Law Journal* is published weekly by the New York Law Publishing Company, 233 Broadway, New York, N.Y. 10279. The *Legal Times of Washington* is published weekly by Legal Times of Washington, Inc., 1601 Connecticut Avenue, N.W., Washington, D.C. 20009. These periodicals contain incisive, sophisticated, and well-written accounts on current developments. Additional political background on litigation is available from the *Federal Times,* published every Monday by Army Times Publishing Company, 475 School Street, S.W., Washington, D.C. 20024.

The Supreme Court decisions are printed first in the form of "slip opinions." They may be purchased from the Government Printing Office and are usually available from libraries that serve as depositories for government documents. The full decisions are republished in booklets called "preliminary prints" and finally in bound volumes of the *United States Reports.* Citations take this form: *Ohio* v. *Roberts,* 448 U.S. 56 (1980), which indicates that the decision may be found in volume 448, beginning on page 56.

The first ninety volumes of the *Reports* were named after court reporters. Volumes 1 through 4 (1790–1800) were named after Dallas. Later volumes, 5 through 90, carry the names of Cranch, Wheaton, Peters, Howard, Black, and Wallace. Volumes 91–107 (1875–82) are designated "1 to 17 Otto" as well as "United States Reports 91–107." Reprints of volumes 1 through 90 generally have a dual numbering system to the *Reports* and to court reporters, requiring such citations as *Marbury* v. *Madison,* 5 U.S. (1 Cr.) 137 (1803).

The full text of each Supreme Court decision appears in the *Supreme Court Reporter,* issued semimonthly during the session of the Court by West Publishing Company, 50 W. Kellogg Blvd., P.O. Box 3526, St. Paul, Minnesota 55165. The citations for these decisions are in the form *Maryland* v. *Louisiana,* 101 S.Ct. 2114 (1981).

Another source of Supreme Court decisions is *United States Supreme Court Reports, Lawyers' Edition,* published twice monthly by the Lawyers Co-Operative Publishing Company, 50 Broad Street East, Rochester, N.Y. 14694. A unique feature of the *Lawyers' Edition* is a summary of the arguments in each case for the majority of the Court and for justices who concur and dissent. The first series of the *Lawyers' Edition,* consisting of 100 volumes, covers the period from 1790 to 1956. The second series is now past volume 60. A typical citation is *Steagald* v. *United States,* 68 L.Ed. 2d 38 (1981).

Significant decisions by federal district courts are printed in the *Federal Supplement,* issued first in paper edition and later in bound volumes. The citation shows the volume, page, state, and year, as in *United States* v. *Mandel,* 505 F.Supp. 189 (D. Md. 1981). The "D" in parentheses indicates that the decision occurred at the district court level. For decisions that are not reported in the *Federal Supplement,* or in situations where immediate access to a decision is needed, a researcher may call the judge's chamber and receive a copy of the memorandum decision from a law clerk or filing clerk.

To follow appeals of district court decisions, the source is the *Federal Reporter,* consisting of two series. The first series (F. or Fed.) stopped with volume 300; the second series (F.2d) is now in the

600s. Typical citations would be *Rowe* v. *Drohen*, 262 F. 15 (2d Cir. 1919) and *Romeo* v. *Youngberg*, 644 F.2d 147 (3d Cir. 1980). These decisions are initially available as slip opinions and in memorandum form either from the court or libraries.

The "citator" or citation book tells the student whether a decision is still valid and authoritative. A decision by a lower court may be affirmed, reversed, or modified. *Shepard's Citations,* a widely used sourcebook, has spawned such words as "Shepardize" and "Shepardizing" to describe the process of determining the current state of the law. *Shepard's United States Citations* includes citations to Supreme Court decisions, U.S. statutes, treaties, and court rules for federal courts. *Shepard's Federal Citations,* covering decisions by federal courts below the Supreme Court, is issued in two series. One series covers the *Federal Supplement,* and the other the *Federal Reporter.* For more specific guidance on legal sources, the student can turn to Miles O. Price and colleagues, *Effective Legal Research,* 4th ed. (Boston: Little, Brown, 1979) and *Ervin H. Pollack's Fundamentals of Legal Research,* by J. Myron Jacobstein and Roy M. Mersky, 4th ed. (Mineola, N.Y.: Foundation Press, 1973).

Many of the issues that come before the courts have been first explored by the Justice Department and the General Accounting Office. These analyses are published in *Official Opinions of the Attorneys General* and *Decisions of the Comptroller General.* Among his other duties, the attorney general renders important opinions on legal issues presented to him by presidents and departmental heads. Citations to these opinions are by volume, page, and year, as in 40 Ops. Att'y Gen. [or Op. A.G.] 469 (1946). A new series, called *Opinions of the Office of Legal Counsel,* is now available to record the memorandum opinions from the Office of Legal Counsel, which advises the president, the attorney general, and other executive officers. The first volume, published in 1980, covers the period from January 27, 1977 to December 31, 1977.

The comptroller general determines the legality of payments of appropriated funds by federal officials. This function was vested in the Treasury Department from 1817 to 1921 but passed thereafter to the comptroller general as the head of the newly created General Accounting Office. The decisions are cited as 49 Comp. Gen.

59 (1969). Although the comptroller general maintains that his decisions regarding the legality of government expenditures "are binding on the executive departments and agencies,"[26] ever since 1921 the comptroller general and the attorney general have been locked in vigorous disagreements as to statutory interpretations and jurisdiction.[27] In 1969 the comptroller general and the attorney general disagreed completely about the legality of the Nixon administration's "Philadelphia Plan," designed to increase the number of minority workers in federally assisted contracts.[28] In this dispute the courts sided with the attorney general's interpretation.[29]

An indispensable guide to the literature is the *Index to Legal Periodicals*, published monthly except September by the H. W. Wilson Company, 950 University Avenue, Bronx, N.Y. 10452. Currently covering more than 400 legal periodicals, it indexes the articles under subject and author. Entries of special interest to political scientists include administrative agencies, administrative law, administrative procedure, delegation of powers, discrimination, executive agreements, executive power, federalism, freedom of information, freedom of religion, freedom of speech, freedom of the press, government, judicial review, legislation, political science, politics, public finance, separation of powers, United States: Congress, United States: President, and United States: Supreme Court.

SECONDARY SOURCES

THE literature on the presidency suggests a renewal, however tentative, of interest in constitutional issues. Joseph M. Bessette and Jeffrey Tulis have edited a thoughtful and stimulating collection of essays in *The Presidency in the Constitutional Order* (Baton Rouge: Louisiana State University Press, 1981). Richard Loss edited some seminal essays of Edward S. Corwin, published under the title *Presidential Power and the Constitution* (Ithaca: Cornell University Press, 1976) and has edited the first volume of *Corwin on the Constitution: The Foundations of American Constitutional and Political Thought, The Powers of Congress,* and *the President's Power of Removal,* published by Cornell University Press in 1981. Richard Pious, in his comprehensive *The American Presidency* (New York: Basic Books, 1979), is strongly committed to the public law tradition. Also within this orientation are the writings of Louis Fisher, including *President and Congress* (New York: Free Press, 1972), *Presidential Spending Power* (Princeton, N.J.: Princeton University Press, 1975), *The Constitution Between Friends: Congress, the President, and the Law* (New York: St. Martin's Press, 1978; 2nd ed. to be published by Princeton Univ. Press in 1983), and *The Politics of Shared Power: Congress and the Executive* (Washington, D.C.: Congressional Quarterly Press, 1981). Martin M. Shapiro regularly publishes studies of substantial interest, such as his recent "The Presidency and the Federal Courts" as part of *Politics and the Oval Office: Towards Presidential Governance,* edited by Arnold J. Meltsner (San Francisco: Institute for Contemporary Studies, 1981).

For other recent studies one must turn to the law journals. Of special interest I would suggest articles by R. A. Max, "A Judicial Interpretation of the Nixon Presidency," *Cumberland Law Review,* vol. 6, pp. 213–42 (1975); Stephen L. Wasby, "The Presidency Before the Courts," *Capital University Law Review,* vol. 6, pp. 35–73 (1976); P. Allan Dionisopoulos, "New Patterns in Judicial Control of the Presidency: 1950's to 1970's," *Akron Law Review,* vol. 10, pp. 1–38 (1976); Harold H. Bruff, "Presidential Power and Administrative Rulemaking," *Yale Law Journal,* vol. 88, pp. 452–508 (1979); and Douglas H. Rosenberg, "Delegation and Regulatory Reform: Letting the President Change the Rules," *Yale Law Journal,* vol. 89, pp. 561–85 (1980).

Notes

1. Richard M. Pious, "Is Presidential Power 'Poison'?" *Political Science Quarterly* 89 (1974): 635–37.

2. C. Herman Pritchett, "Public Law and Judicial Behavior," *Journal of Politics* 30 (1968): 480.

3. Albert Somit and Joseph Tanenhaus, "Trends in American Political Science: Some Analytical Notes," *American Political Science Review* 57 (1963): 941–42.

4. C. Herman Pritchett, "The Development of Judicial Research," in Joel B. Grossman and Joseph Tanenhaus, eds., *Frontiers of Judicial Research* (New York: Wiley, 1969), 29.

5. 5 U.S. (1 Cr.) 137, 170.

6. *NAACP* v. *Button*, 371 U.S. 415, 429–30 (1963).

7. U.S., Congress, Senate, Committee on the Judiciary, Hearings, *Constitutional Restraints Upon the Judiciary,* 97th Cong., 1st sess., 1981.

8. Maeva Marcus, *Truman and the Steel Seizure Case: The Limits of Presidential Power* (New York: Columbia Univ. Press, 1977).

9. 272 U.S. 52, 65–88 (1926).

10. *State Highway Commission of Missouri* v. *Volpe,* 479 F.2d 1099, n. 1 (8th Cir. 1973).

11. *Harris* v. *McRae,* 448 U.S. 297, 303 (1980).

12. *Chadha* v. *Immigration and Naturalization Service,* 634 F.2d 408, 411 (9th Cir. 1980).

13. Louis Fisher, *The Constitution Between Friends: Congress, the President, and the Law* (New York: St. Martin's, 1978), 97–98.

14. The Honorable Carl McGowan, "Congressmen in Court: The New Plaintiffs," *Georgia Law Review* 15 (1981): 241.

15. U.S., Congress, Senate, 89th Cong., 2d sess., 1966, S. Rept. 1414, p. 47.

16. U.S., Congress, Senate, Committee on the Judiciary, Hearings, *Representation of Congress and Congressional Interests in Court,* 94th Cong., 2d sess., 1976, p. 6.

17. U.S., Congress, Senate, 95th Cong., 1st sess., 1977, S. Rept. 170, p. 11.

18. *United States* v. *Schooner Peggy,* 5 U.S. (1 Cr.) 103 (1801).

19. 11 Foreign Affairs Manual 721.2 (b) (3) (1974); *United States* v. *Guy W. Capps, Inc.,* 204 F.2d 655, 660 (4th Cir. 1953), aff'd on other grounds, 348 U.S. 296 (1955).

20. *Seery* v. *United States,* 127 F.Supp. 601, 606 (Ct. Cl. 1955); *Reid* v. *Covert,* 354 U.S. 1, 16 (1956).

21. 49 Stat. 500, sec. 5 (1935). Roosevelt's exec. order 7298, February 18, 1936, appeared too early for the first volume of the *Federal Register.* It is reprinted in James Hart, "The Exercise of Rule-Making Power," the President's Committee on Administrative Management (Washington, D.C.: U.S. Government Printing Office, 1937), 355.

22. *Marks* v. *CIA,* 590 F.2d 997, 1003 (D.C. Cir. 1978); *Weber* v.

Kaiser Aluminum & Chemical Corp., 563 F.2d 216, 227 (5th Cir. 1977), rev'd on other grounds, *Steelworkers* v. *Weber,* 443 U.S. 193 (1979). The judiciary has struck down executive orders that exceed presidential authority; e.g., *Youngstown Co.* v. *Sawyer* 343 U.S. 579 (1952), and *Panama Refining Co.* v. *Ryan,* 293 U.S. 388, 433 (1935).

23. Note, "Judicial Review of Executive Action in Domestic Affairs," *Columbia Law Review* 80 (1980): 1535; U.S., Congress, House, *Presidential Control of Agency Rulemaking: An Analysis of Constitutional Issues That May be Raised by Executive Order 12291,* a Report Prepared for the Use of the House Committee on Energy and Commerce, 97th Cong., 1st sess. (committee print), June 15, 1981.

24. *Schmidt Pritchard & Co.,* v. *United States,* 167 F.Supp. 272 (Cust. Ct. 1958); *Carl Zeiss, Inc.* v. *United States,* 76 F.2d 412 (Ct. Cust. & Pat. App. 1935).

25. *United States* v. *Yoshida Intern., Inc.,* 526 F.2d 560 (Ct. Cust. & Pat. App. 1975); Fisher, *The Constitution Between Friends,* 126–27.

26. Elmer B. Staats, "The GAO: Present and Future," *Public Administration Review* 28 (1968): 461.

27. E.g., 33 Ops. Att'y Gen. 383, 385 (1933), and 34 Ops. Att'y Gen. 311 (1924).

28. 49 Comp. Gen. (1969); 42 Ops. Att'y Gen. 405 (1969).

29. *Contractors Ass'n of Eastern Pa.* v. *Secretary of Labor,* 442 F.2d 159 (3d Cir. 1971), cert. denied, 404 U.S. 854 (1971).

8

Presidential Libraries: Gold Mine, Booby Trap, or Both?

MARTHA JOYNT KUMAR

PRESIDENTIAL LIBRARIES are a unique resource for scholars because they touch at the heart of a presidency: its decisions, its activities, its people, and its atmosphere.[1] "The first reading of the papers was an exciting experience for me, and I must confess that this sense of excitement has continued through all the labor involved," noted Robert E. Sherwood about his two and a half years of work with the papers of Harry Hopkins for his book, *Roosevelt and Hopkins*. "For I found here so many answers to so many questions that had been piling up in my mind when I was near to high authority; I found solution of much that I had wondered about in my observation of the moods as well as the words and deeds of Roosevelt and Hopkins."[2] Presidential libraries, with holdings such as the Hopkins papers, are exciting because of the personal and official information found there. They offer the most complete portrait available of the presidents of the United States and those who surround them.

The libraries, most of which were set up as a result of the

Presidential Libraries Act of 1955, have been established for the following purposes: to preserve the papers of the individual presidents and their presidencies; to acquire historical materials including books, articles, and audio-visual materials; and to conduct oral history interviews with people associated with particular presidents. In the twenty-six years since the passage of the act, the Hoover, Truman, Eisenhower, Kennedy, Johnson, and Ford libraries have opened. The Franklin Roosevelt library predates the Presidential Libraries Act.

The sheer volume of the library holdings is staggering. Table 8.1 lists the main acquisitions of each, focusing on *manuscripts,* which comprise the documents in the personal and official presidential files, including the papers of staff members, and federal records; *audio-visual items*; *oral history,* which consists of interviews with those connected with the various administrations; *museum objects,* which include items belonging to the presidents and their administrations, the most significant of which are displayed in the exhibits for visitors to the library; and *printed materials.*

The core of each presidential library is its manuscript collection. Of particular importance are the memorandums written for the president by staff people as well as those sent by him to his aides. These memorandums are the footprints of an administration. The first section of this chapter will follow their trail. By looking at the materials available, we can detect how events were perceived and handled, trace policy, discover the process of decision making in a major governmental institution, and sense the atmosphere, activities, and individuals in the White House. We will also focus on some of the ways that presidential library material may be used, including hypothesis building and corroboration of findings made elsewhere. A discussion of the limits of libraries as a research tool, specifically the incomplete records, the unevenness of material within and between libraries, the restrictions on material, and their weak oral history interviews follows in the second part of this chapter. The final section probes some of the methods researchers can use to make the most profitable use of the presidential libraries.

TABLE 8.1

PRESIDENTIAL LIBRARY HOLDINGS, 1981

	HOOVER	ROOSEVELT	TRUMAN	EISENHOWER	KENNEDY	JOHNSON	NIXON	FORD
Manuscripts (pages)	5,769,492	16,402,774	12,824,047	18,645,343	28,860,592	34,775,043	45,865,312	14,961,627
Audio-visual								
still pictures	24,577	126,663	73,964	104,930	116,270	556,905	435,000	310,026
film	133,464	303,424	301,906	597,775	6,022,281	803,743	2,200,000	700,000
video tape	3	10	175	10	166	4,660	3,900	882
audio tape	199	934	246	804	3,124	10,457	1,490	872
Oral history (pages)	9,578	2,917	36,800	21,923	29,640	35,395	2,200	0
Museum objects	4,168	22,104	18,518	26,630	13,920	37,716	21,750	6,857
Printed materials								
books	22,998	45,109	44,352	20,909	24,883	23,174	9,000	7,371
serials	23,972	32,259	66,939	29,498	23,966	2,427	0	33
other (pamphlets, etc.)	615	86,961	73,243	22,484	5,069	4,585	0	3,117

Source: "FY 1980 Appropriated Funds," a memorandum made available by John Fawcett, assistant to the head of the Office of Presidential Libraries, July 7, 1981.

Presidential Libraries as an Information Resource

WHILE the libraries are an obvious resource for students of the presidency, and the executive branch generally, they are also a significant source for scholars seeking information on national politics. Few crises have not included the White House as a major participant. The library files allow us to see how the events of an administration were perceived, what information was available, what the various recommendations for action were, and who was recommending which plan.

The Penumbra of Events

A presidential library provides materials that make it possible to recreate a portrait of a presidency, capturing both the details of the events and a feel for its people. Robert J. Donovan, in his *Conflict and Crisis: The Presidency of Harry S Truman, 1945–1948,* is able to create such a portrait of the Truman presidency. By relying on memorandums and diaries from the Truman library and materials belonging to Henry L. Stimson deposited at Yale University, for example, Donovan gives us a detailed account of the often frustrating relationships that the United States had with its allies as V-E Day approached. He provides a particularly vivid account of Truman's conflicts with General Charles de Gaulle over the latter's bid to place French troops in areas previously agreed upon as assigned to other allied nations. Stuttgart, for example, was to be in the American sector, but de Gaulle was interested in seeing the French occupy it. "I don't like the son of a bitch," President Truman remarked to his staff about de Gaulle.[3] After Truman threatened to make changes in the command structure, the general backed down. The Americans and British had to thwart the designs of the French in northern Italy and in the Middle East before V-E Day finally came. After a month of battling with the French over occupation plans, President Truman remarked in a staff meeting: "Those French ought to be taken out and castrated."[4]

By sifting through the enormous volume of available information, one can develop an account of the processes used by an administration to handle particular situations. "You find in areas of well-established public record that by going back to the original they have instructive elements that weren't reproduced in published form," observed Fred Greenstein, who has spent four years studying the leadership patterns of President Eisenhower. "I think some of the material might be particularly important for political scientists, since we are interested in aspects of process. We may want to turn to fairly small stylistic features which would be thought of as interoffice junk by historians trying to get the main chronicle of events, but we would be interested in what historians would think of as the penumbra of events."[5] Greenstein used the published records in combination with the library files to develop a portrait of President Eisenhower's leadership style.

The library materials provide a dimension to the record that one might otherwise miss if the published memoirs of presidents and their aides were the only source. Greenstein found in *Waging the Peace 1956–1961,* President Eisenhower's memoirs, a letter written to Governor James Byrnes of South Carolina relating to the enforcement of the nondiscrimination regulations for federal contracts. "Historically you wouldn't know from the one letter reproduced that it was part of a rather intricate dialogue between Byrnes and Eisenhower," Greenstein noted.[6] When he found the full complement of letters in the library, Greenstein also discovered that the letters were to be kept personal and confidential, thus demonstrating Eisenhower's efforts to exercise leadership away from the public eye; "hidden hand leadership," Greenstein has labeled it. What might seem like a small, stylistic feature in an individual letter or memorandum may in the aggregate demonstrate a pattern.

TRACING POLICY

THE presidential libraries are particularly useful in gathering information on policy development because the White House has become the center for the initiation of domestic as well as foreign policy. "There is the official story of what happened in the press releases and behind that is the inside story," noted Clement Vose, political scientist and member of the Advisory Council of the National Archives for the past eleven years. "Presidential libraries capture the inside story," he continued.[7] When culling the library files we can discover the inside story on policy by observing the lines of reasoning used by those developing and advocating particular policies. One can also find out who was involved and what their contributions were.

By piecing together fragments from published sources with presidential library files, one can develop a thorough record of policy development. Richard Immerman, a historian at the University of Colorado, has been gathering information on U.S. policy toward Guatemala in the 1950s. For one episode, he used as a starting point Adolf A. Berle's memoirs of his State Department days, *Navigating the Rapids, 1918–1971.* "In the published version there was a memorandum in which Berle discussed a propaganda campaign against the Guatemalan government," Immerman said. He was told that he should go to the Roosevelt library to see the original document. "What was two and a half pages in the book was sixteen pages in the library," Immerman noted. "But Berle also discussed the possibility of American experts going in to Guatemala, and he discussed it in the context of having talked with Allen Dulles [head of the Central Intelligence Agency] and J.C. King [head of the Western Hemisphere division of the CIA]. He had spoken to C.D. Jackson [head of the president's International Information Activities Committee] about this type of thing before he wrote the memorandum and he discusses that. None of that is in the published version." Immerman followed the trail of Berle memorandums on Guatemala from the Roosevelt library to the archives of the Council on Foreign Relations, where he found related memorandums. He stated, "what I had initially was some bits and pieces that seemed interesting; at the end what I had was explicit proof that someone listened to this type of memorandum; it gave 90 percent more information that I would have gotten by just using the published source."[8]

One can get a fairly clear view of policy disputes through an investigation of library material. Internal administration disputes can be quite important in explaining the ultimate outcomes of policies. Francis Rourke, who has been studying agency politics in the Johnson administration, traced the reasons for the withdrawal of a Labor Department reorganization plan put forward at the end of the Johnson administration to a dispute between the department secretary, Willard Wirtz, and President Johnson. "Wirtz was anxious to reorganize before he left office," explained Rourke. "He had a dispute with Johnson on it because Johnson did not want to do anything to tie the hands of his successor and Wirtz et al. were doing it *for* that reason."[9] Wirtz released an announcement to the press detailing the reorganization. President Johnson ordered him to rescind it. When Johnson felt that Wirtz was dragging his heels on the rescission, he sent the deputy attorney general, Warren Christopher, along with Clark Clifford, to read the law to Wirtz. The plan was withdrawn.

The libraries sporadically hold conferences designed to develop an understanding of specific policies, events, and processes. The conferences, privately funded, deal with topics central to the presidencies of the libraries hosting the meeting. The Johnson library, for example, held a conference on education at which Wilbur Cohen spoke. "He came down to the library and went through the papers himself. In spite of his close involvement with education legislation, he discovered in his documentary research things that he was not aware of at the time. He then talked about what there is in the library on the subject," noted John Fawcett, assistant to the head of the Office of Presidential Libraries and himself an archivist in the Johnson library in the 1970s.[10] The Johnson library has also run conferences dealing with the press secretary (1976) and the presidency and Congress (1977). The Eisenhower library has hosted conferences as well, with one about D-Day (1969) and one dealing with impressions of the West (1975), while the Truman library held one concentrating on the Korean War (1975). The Roosevelt library held a symposium on universal youth service (1976). In 1974 the libraries jointly held a conference on the development of wage-price policy during 1945–71.

INSIDE THE WHITE HOUSE: ITS DECISIONS AND PEOPLE

THE papers in the libraries are the best source we have of how one branch of the national government works. Congressional papers, unsystematically kept and spread around the country, do not offer a comprehensive view of the operations of that branch. Attempts to get records of the process of judicial decision making seems unthinkable to the bar and public. The only branch of government we really can view with any depth and breadth is the executive branch.

Through the papers of presidents, we can see how decisions in one major part of the government have been reached. According to John Fawcett, "You see in the Roosevelt papers how Roosevelt was expanding the presidency tremendously but it was sort of an ad hoc thing. He was giving assignments to individuals and he played his people rather than establishing institutions. What you see during the Eisenhower administration is that he kept much of what had developed with the growth of the presidency and institutionalized them such as formalizing the NSC [National Security Council], formalizing the office of congressional relations."[11] Patterns have developed in which Republicans follow the Eisenhower institutional style of White House organization and Democrats keep the institutions but place heavy emphasis on the roles of individual staff members.

Using the materials available at the libraries, one can get a picture of the president as a political figure, how he operated, and what he wanted. Although all of the libraries contain materials that give a personal dimension to their presidents, the Johnson library is particularly rich in material protraying the "Johnson style." In his oral history interview, staff aide DeVier Pierson, for example, describes Johnson legislative techniques by a story about the president's effort to build credit with some powerful members of Congress. As Pierson tells it, Johnson had him leak a story to the *Washington Post* indicating that the administration was considering a cutback in domestic rice production. The story produced the intended response, an outcry from congressmen from rice-producing states. They demanded and got a meeting with President Johnson. First the congressmen were allowed to present their case. Then, according to Pierson,

> about mid-way during the meeting he called me over and whispered to me that when they finished that he wanted to have me make the strongest case I could make for cutting back production. So they finished, and he said "Well, I'm concerned about this." He said, "What do you think about it DeVier?" And I did make the strongest case I could for cutting back and, you know, to the great loss of friendship of all the Congressmen and Senators in the room.[12]

President Johnson waited before making a decision in spite of the congressional pleas for an immediate response. When he decided that it was time to act, he let Pierson know that they were to get something in return. "So after a couple of days he said, 'You call around to Ellender and the others and tell them that I have decided in view of their personal interest in this that I won't do it, but I'll be needing their help on some other matters.' This is chip-building in the classic sense, and he built some chips with some critical people by making them ask for something that I suspect he intended to do all the way along."[13] Similar examples of Johnson's style and his personal force are found throughout his papers.

USES OF LIBRARY INFORMATION

ONE can make use of the information found in the libraries in several ways. It can influence the direction of work from building hypotheses to preparing for interviews. The knowledge gained at the libraries can also help scholars make the greatest use of other available sources, such as contemporary newspapers and periodicals, books, interviews, and archival records.

HYPOTHESIS BUILDING

PRESIDENTIAL libraries are important at every stage of a research project. At the early stages, consulting library materials can be useful for shaping one's hypotheses. "What strikes me about presidential library research and other kinds of primary research is that your hypotheses and your theoretical interests are enormously important," said Fred Greenstein. "In theory building, when you go back into the data you retool the theory. Perhaps at the risk of studying historically minor phenomenon, you nevertheless find things that lead you to support an analytical interest that you have. Or you may shift it in one direction or another because there is such a remarkable vein of material."[14]

In his own case, Greenstein found that through his library research he deepened his understanding of the interaction of advisers with their presidents. Beginning his work from the viewpoint that policy is a result of "multiple advocacy," Greenstein discovered a variety of viewpoints from which policy is created. As he and his associates described it, "We have gone very minutely into policy decisions and what we have found ourselves shifting to was something a little bit closer to what Graham Allison has described as the third level of governmental politics — of who said what to whom, under what circumstances, with more attention to what people were thinking, feeling, and how much participatory action there was."[15] Having done a great deal of library research early in his project, Greenstein was able to refocus his hypotheses and redirect his interests.

CORROBORATION

PRESIDENTIAL libraries are very important for confirming the theories found in secondary sources. The contemporary account of President Johnson's relations with the press, for example, stressed his monitoring of staff contacts with the press, his many meetings with and telephone calls to journalists, and his strong belief that his administration was treated unfairly by the press. All of these notions were corroborated in the Johnson library. Most of the cabinet secretaries, Henry Fowler at the Treasury Department, for example, and the White House staff members, such as Joseph Califano, submitted to President Johnson, at his request, voluminous weekly reports relating to their press contacts. His appointment log confirms his frequent meetings and calls to journalists, and his memorandums, particularly the marginal notes that are sometimes found on those sent to him, reflect his bitter feelings toward the press.

Library materials often demonstrate that impressions formed at the time have to be modified. James Hagerty, press secretary to President Eisenhower, was seen during the Eisenhower administration, particularly after the president's heart attack, as the designer of the administration's publicity plans with his president playing a minor role in communications activities. Expressing that viewpoint was Richard Strout, correspondent for the *Christian Science Monitor,* who said: "Hagerty made policy in addition to interpreting it. . . . Early [Stephen Early, press secretary to President Roosevelt] had a president who knew where he was going; Hagerty did not have that kind of president."[16] The diary that James Hagerty kept during 1953 and 1954, however, demonstrated that President Eisenhower was very much aware of and involved in decisions about how his administration was to be portrayed.

Hagerty once observed that reporters seemed to think that he was acting on his own when he gave his regular briefings to the press. In truth, he said, "many of the times, the notes or the sentences were written in the personal handwriting of the President, and he said, 'say this.' And I'd get up, and say that. There wasn't any answer I made when I *thought* I was reflecting the President's viewpoint. The only answers I made were when I *knew* I was reflecting the President's viewpoint."[17] Hagerty was lord of the press area, but Eisenhower was the president and dictated for himself what was to be communicated. Hagerty suggested how it was to be done.

PREPARATION AND SUPPORT MATERIAL FOR INTERVIEWS

THE White House files are an important part of the preparation involved in interviewing those advisers within a particular White House. The files provide an excellent background on staff members and their work. The library materials can reveal who the people were in an administration and what they did. Through the identification of the people in the White House and with a knowledge of the tasks they performed, one can decide what interviews to set up and what questions to ask. Francis Rourke comments, "I found the Johnson library materials very revealing on the jurisdiction of particular White House staff members. They were useful in this case because the White House was so loosely organized in those days. Among other things, this enables you to identify the staff members you want to interview if you are interested in a policy area."[18] Secondary sources, such as the contemporary press, may not be a sufficiently reliable guide to who the key people were in an administration.

Many members of the White House staff who prefer anonymity shun the press. This is most often the case with staff involved in operations that do not involve advocating policies or selling the administration. "Most of the time process tends to be secretive," a staff member in the Nixon and Ford administrations indicated. "How you arrive at a decision is not something you want to set out. . . . If somebody knows a process or how a decision is reached, they can change the system on you."[19] Those involved in processing material in the White House, such as the staff secretary, the cabinet secretary, and the schedulers, are people who generally have little press contact. Identifying their place in the White House constellation is something that can best be done in presidential libraries.

A researcher's familiarity with the library files can serve to legitimize his or her work in the eyes of potential interviewees. Often, staff people will tell little until they feel the interviewer has a firm grasp on the subject matter. Roger Brown explains: "it helps to tell them that you have gone through material in the library and are familiar with their activities. It establishes your legitimacy and refreshes their memory."[20]

THE LIMITATIONS OF PRESIDENTIAL LIBRARIES

"IT is easy to get carried away with the notion that the library will tell all," Rourke observed.[21] In fact, the libraries provide only part of the story of an administration, the written account, and some presidents and many White House staff people have left few records behind. Not all advisers are tidy, and all those who were tidy do not prove to be close advisers. John Steelman, for example, left few traces of the large role he played in the Truman administration, whereas Robert Kintner left extensive records of his relatively small role during the Johnson years.

There are few transcripts of small meetings or records of oral advice given to presidents. Some presidents and staff members have written or recorded accounts of such meetings but always from their own viewpoint. President Nixon's complete taping procedure is, as far as we know, not a practice followed by any other president, although there are some tapes of individual conversations involving Presidents Eisenhower and Johnson. Diaries are kept by some staff members in most administrations, but not very many are kept by people who operated across the board and could describe all of the major parts of the White House operation.

MEMORANDUMS AS SELF-SERVING

"You know who that memo was written for, don't you?" asked Pierre Salinger of Michael Grossman, who questioned the former Kennedy press secretary about a possibly large publicity role played by Arthur Schlesinger in that administration, based on indications found in the Schlesinger files in the library. When Grossman said that he did not, Salinger smiled and said, "You."[22] Salinger's observation gets to the heart of one of the basic problems with the library files: staff members sometimes use memorandums to build their own prestige in an administration. It is hard to sift through the records and accurately determine if someone had the major role their memos would indicate and if their opinions and recommendations were endorsed by their colleagues. There are several types of memo writers whose purposes run counter to those of the researcher trying to develop a balanced picture of administration actions: "self-promoters," "survivors," and "steam blowers."

"Self-Promoters." In most administrations there are people whose memorandums almost invariably highlight their own activities with little indication of what happened as a result of them. Robert Kintner, the cabinet and staff secretary, frequently wrote Johnson about his own activities in meeting elite journalists to promote the president. The following is typical of the letters Kintner wrote to Johnson:

Mr. President:
I thought the editorial page of the New York Times today was inexcusable. I am having lunch tomorrow at his request with Scotty Reston and I intend to really go to work on him. I also expect to have lunch today with someone who is very familiar with the operation of the New York Times to try to see exactly how it works in regard to policy.[23]

Another memo along the same lines but by a different author speaks to the same point: efforts at getting the media to change its critical tone on the administration's Vietnam policy. The memo is from Robert Komer, the deputy director of the National Security Council.

Warring with the Press: I took on all twelve (count 'em) of the *NY Times* Washington Bureau at lunch yesterday. My wounds are still bloody, but one direct result was Reston's 22 November column on "Why Westmoreland and Bunker are Optimistic." I'm proud of myself. . . .
    I gave Don Oberdorfer of Knight papers a 15 minute quick fill-in on a series about the VC [Vietcong] he plans to do in Saigon. Spencer Davis of AP sat still for an hour on pacification (mostly on the record). Maybe a story, maybe not. Took 2 hours to beat up Rowland Evans and Stewart Alsop on the theme "I told you so." They (and most of the two dozen or so press types I've backgrounded) have been hit hard by the new documented case that we're at long last on the upgrade in Vietnam.[24]

The contemporary record does not bear out Komer's observations about the course the Vietnam War was to take nor did the press follow his and Kintner's advice. On such a well-reported policy as Vietnam, the researcher is well aware that the letters reflect an unfounded optimism and that the efforts of Kintner and Komer bore little fruit. In other, less visible policy areas, it is more difficult for the researcher to assess the importance of similar activities by staff members.

"Survivors." Survivors are people willing to write memos reflecting what they believe their superiors, including the president, want to see. During the Nixon administration, there were quite a few staff members who dealt rather gingerly with H.R. Haldeman. One generally told him what he wanted to hear, if staff members in their memoirs and testimony at congressional hearings are to be believed. Jeb Magruder, an aide in the Office of Communications, indicated that he was following through on some Haldeman suggestions in dealing with an antiwar senator from New York, Charles Goodell, but it turned out that Magruder had not done what Haldeman had expected. Magruder tried to back off from completing the project and suggested in a memo a milder approach. He received the following marginal comments from Haldeman: "This is pure BS—as excuses. I disagree 100% — and besides, this was an order—not a question—and I was told it was being carried out and so informed the P. Now let's get it carried out—and quickly."[25] It does not take more than a couple of such comments to staff members for all to get the idea that one should do what is asked and recommend actions that will be approved.

In administrations where more diversity of viewpoint is tolerated, some staff member still tend to write what they believe will be beneficial to them or the policies and actions they support. In the Carter administration, for example, staff members knew that the president was not swayed by political considerations. "The way to lose an argument with the president was by saying that it would help him politically," said David Rubenstein of the Domestic Policy Staff.[26] Rubenstein's comments were echoed by several other Carter aides interviewed at the end of the administration. Each volunteered the point that Carter was negatively impressed by political considerations when making policy or deciding courses of action. Staff members took the cue and avoided such recommendations even when improving his electoral prospects was their goal.

"Steam blowers." There are people, particularly presidents, who use memos as a way of letting off steam, as a substitute for action. Lyndon Johnson is a good example of this type of person. At times when he was angry over a story appearing the press, he would cause a flurry of activity with his requests for responses indicating where the errors were. When the *New Republic* published an article by James Deakin, the White House correspondent for the *St. Louis Post-Dispatch,* entitled "LBJ's Credibility; or What Happened to 'No Comment'?" one of Johnson's aides, Fred Danzer, wrote a rebuttal for the president, consisting of ten typed single-spaced pages. Johnson, however, did nothing with it.[27] Several years later, when he was asked how he responded to Johnson's attack on him, Deakin expressed surprise that a rebuttal piece had been prepared.[28] He said he had heard nothing from Johnson about the article. Similarly, President Johnson had staff member Tom Johnson request information from a bevy of other staff members for a point-by-point rebuttal to a *Newsweek* article by White House correspondent Charles Roberts on the president's credibility gap.[29] The flurry of memos was an end rather than a means to an end.

THE PAUCITY OF COMPARABLE INFORMATION

To research a question that spans the presidencies of the twentieth century, one must be prepared to travel to West Branch, Iowa; Austin, Texas; Abilene, Kansas; Independence, Missouri; Hyde Park, New York; Boston, Massachusetts; Washington, D.C.; and Ann Arbor, Michigan. The investigator will find that they are as far apart in the quantity and quality of information as in mileage. Until January 20, 1981, when the Presidential Records Act of 1978 went into effect, there was little systematic record keeping. The act, discussed in a later section, declares the president's official papers to be public property.

The individual manner in which administrations have kept records, however, is only part of the reason that comparable material does not exist among the libraries. Another is the change in White House operations. In the Franklin Roosevelt administration, there were few White House aides. Stephen Early, the press secretary, could talk with the other top aides, such as Louis Howe or Marvin MacIntyre, by phone or just walk down the hall. There was no need then as there is today for formal morning senior staff meetings followed by deputies' meetings. Because of the informal nature of the advisory system, few records were kept.

Within the libraries there are sharp differences because even though comparable information is now kept on the presidents, the files reflect the strengths and weaknesses of the individual staff members. "John Steelman operated out of his hat," noted Fred Greenstein, and the result is that "we probably will never know what his role was."[30] In a more recent presidency, Jody Powell, press secretary to President Carter, was a person who operated on the telephone and made a point of keeping no diary. He said that he had told staff people he would not keep one, because he was interested in having them be as honest with him as possible; he thought a diary might make people think he would assign blame in his personal record.[31] What kind of information is available depends on the preferences of the individuals staffing the White House.

One is frustrated in efforts to trace items such as the president's schedule over time because each administration sets its own policy as to how detailed the schedule should be. The Eisenhower library has a schedule that does reflect the highlights of who the president saw and what he did, but the Kennedy library does not. Starting with the Johnson administration, however, we have schedules that conform to the same system of record keeping. Thus, scholars will find the lack of comparable schedule data to be less of a problem as the number of administrations increases.

In addition to the difference in materials that are available, there are differences in the resourcefulness of library staffs in finding information. Some of the people working for the libraries, such as those in the Truman library, have been there many years and are knowledgeable about the contents of their library. Some types of subjects that were not thought to be important at the time, such as public relations, stump the staffs of the earlier libraries.

In great part, presidential libraries have become a reflection of the interests of a president in building a broad record of his administration's work and having that record opened quickly with as few restrictions as possible. "President Johnson was very involved in getting people to give their papers to the Johnson library and to leave them so that they could be opened up fairly quickly," noted Robert R. Brookhart, assistant to the archivist of the United States. "He pressed hard for it in talking with people to get them to give their material; he used the force of his personality. . . . Kennedy did not have that chance and there was no one else to do it for him."[32] Future libraries will depend less on the involvement of the president, since the Presidential Records Act automatically makes official presidential records public documents.

RESTRICTIONS ON MATERIAL

THE Presidential Records Act of 1978 that took effect in January 1981 will make some changes in the kinds of materials retained for future presidential libraries. Instead of allowing presidents to have control over the papers of their administrations as personal papers, the materials are now divided into two categories: personal papers and presidential papers. The personal papers contain those items that "do not relate to or have an effect upon the carrying out of the constitutional, statutory, or other official or ceremonial duties of the President."[33] A president's diary, for example, that was not used in his business would be classified as personal records. The libraries will continue to court those who have personal papers relevant to an administration, but now the bulk of papers in the libraries will come because the papers belong to the National Archives. The files will be opened fairly quickly, since most material can be closed for no more than five years.[34] The president can declare access to certain types of specified material, such as national defense information and material relating to appointments of federal officeholders, as restricted for a period of up to twelve years.[35] Presidents and staff members will be able to put whatever restrictions they want on their personal records, a privilege they formerly could exercise for all of their papers.

Since the libraries currently open are covered by the earlier rules, researchers will have to deal with several restrictions in their research. The basic restrictions that researchers must deal with are donor restrictions and closures by statute that are applied by archivists at the libraries. Persons who give material to the libraries, including those who are interviewed for oral histories, are able to place restrictions that often create burdens for the researchers. Without such restrictions, the staff would not have given their papers, at least that is what National Archives personnel maintain.[36] In order to get into the files of Pierre Salinger, for example, one had until very recently to get his permission. Salinger has been working in Paris for a decade, and is difficult to track down; furthermore, he must send his permission in writing to the library. We tracked him by telephone to Montreal, and he graciously wrote quickly to the library. We noted that we were the first to use his files, and since he was one of the senior aides to the president, his files are important. The materials in the Roosevelt and Truman libraries are now almost all open, but the later libraries still have a number of closed collections and files.

The ability of donors to place restrictions on their material raises the possibility of their releasing information only to those of whom they approve. Donors can use their power to refuse to allow those who may be writing critical pieces on the staff, the administration, or the president to use their material. One scholar with whom I spoke admitted to seeing some letters between an official and his president that were off limits to other scholars. The donor felt comfortable with the person doing the research work, but the researcher was fairly sure that the donor expects something favorable to come out of the release of the letters. The releasing of papers to one or a few scholars can make it difficult to check the accuracy of their work. Arthur Schlesinger was allowed by the Kennedy family to review Robert Kennedy's files for his book on the late senator. At the time his book was published, no one else could get into the material, not even Kennedy library personnel. One scholar said about the Schlesinger book: "Schlesinger can write a 1,000-plus page book on Bobby Kennedy using documents which there is no way really for people to examine either how accurately they were used or whether there are other documents which contradict or in any way cast a different light on something.'[37] Donors thus can have substantial control over the picture that is painted of them in scholarly works.

One is still not home safely after obtaining access to the files. Then one must deal with the restrictions that the libraries place on material through their interpretation of the donors' deeds and of the statute. Material, for example, is sometimes withheld because of security classifications. Another category of material that is not released is material that might tend to "embarrass, endanger, or harass a living person."[38] If it were clear in a memorandum, for example, that the writer considers someone still living to be a drunkard, that would fall under the restriction. Both classifications can easily be appealed, and often the researcher is successful. Francis Rourke found in his visits to the Johnson library that while there were quite a few instances in which material was classified, he was successful in obtaining release of all the material he questioned.[39]

ORAL HISTORIES AS A RESEARCH TOOL

Available in the Truman, Eisenhower, Kennedy, and Johnson libraries are oral history interviews conducted with persons knowledgeable about the particular administrations, such as White House staff members, members of Congress, interest group leaders, and reporters. The interviews provide some important details about White House operations, some explanations of the handling of events, and a sense of who the staff people were and what the president was like. As with the White House files, the oral histories vary in their quality and their quantity. "When the interviewer is interested in process and did a lot of research in the files, and when the interviewee is reflective and was well-placed in the administration, you can get a fine interview," noted William Moss, chief archivist at the Kennedy library.[40] Unfortunately that combination is not present as often as the researcher would like. The oral histories are critical for scholars, especially in Truman and Eisenhower libraries, where there are few opportunities to interview major staff members.

Many are now dead, and the oral histories often represent their only available reflections on their White House days.

Most often the interviews are aimed at finding out how major events were handled and who the participants were. They are generally focused on the president and the interviewee's connection with him. Most of the oral histories do not deal with how the White House operates as an institution and what kinds of tasks are performed. The interviews reflect an interest in building a body of information, particularly favorable information, on an administration and not across administrations.

The oral history collection at the Johnson library, however, does develop a sense of White House operations in the late 1960s. In addition to interviewing senior aides, those conducting interviews also talked with staff members at the middle level. A real bonus is that they interviewed many staff people in place near the conclusion of President Johnson's term. Their recollections were very fresh, and they talked a great deal about how the offices functioned.

Making the Most of the Libraries

Presidential libraries offer the presidency scholar a rich vein of material, but one must think and plan carefully in order to make the most of what is there. The strength of the libraries is the vast amount of information that exists in them and the rich variety that they hold. As with any primary data, it is necessary to check material with all available sources to develop a full picture of what went on and what it all meant.

Because presidential libraries contain the remnants but not the full reality of an administration, it is the task of the researcher to sift through the material so it can be used to reflect a more accurate image of what a presidency was like. "You get this sense as you go through the libraries of things that have been washed up on the beach after a storm," said Fred Greenstein about the contents of the presidential libraries.[41] "At least when you know the broader context and know the period, you start asking yourself questions." As in any archaeological work, the task is made difficult by missing parts and pieces of material that do not proclaim their relative importance. Often one's search in the libraries leads to material in other archives, to individuals with information, and to privately housed records as well as materials already published. It needs to be blended with information found elsewhere in order for all of the pieces of the puzzle to fit together. In researching a presidential administration or an aspect of the presidency itself, presidential libraries are perhaps the single most important archival tool we have, but it is crucial to realize that it is only one tool of many.

One can begin studying an administration by building a framework of who the people were who were involved in one's particular area of interest. "When dealing with presidential libraries, one has to use the whole study of networking, a fancy name for knowing what you are reading and writing about," observed Robert Brookhart of the archivist's staff.[42] The researcher can build a blueprint of his or her area by going through organization charts and internal phone directories, and by seeking out other traces of who interacted with whom. Routing slips on memorandums indicate who the staff people were who read the memos. One can go to their files and see what they indicate. Books like Patrick Anderson's *The President's Men* can be very helpful in identifying top-level staff people.[43]

Once sets of files that are equally complete are found, they can be used in combination with one another. "If you are working in one library, you can get to know it very well and you can establish sets of papers that are in tension with each other. Get the papers of people who occupy different rings or perspectives," recommends Fred Greenstein.[44] In the Eisenhower administration, for example, the Whitman files are excellent to cross-check with those of most anyone at the senior level, such as James Hagerty. Government documents, such as those discussed by Jennifer DeToro and G. Calvin Mackenzie in chapters 5 and 6 are also useful for cross-checking library files.

Agencies and departments also have materials that are useful in cross-checking White House activities. Such files provide a picture of White House activities from an outside perspective and shape ideas of how the executive branch responds. Depending upon the subject, a fair amount of useful information can be gleaned from the administrative histories of the agencies, found in the Johnson library. One can also find executive papers in the Library of Congress. The library has papers of cabinet officials and most of the papers from the presidents of the nineteenth century and those of many of their top aides.

Private libraries and archives are particularly important for those involved in presidency research, since many White House staff members have given their papers to private collections. Sherman Adams's papers, for example, are at Dartmouth College; many of those of John Foster Dulles are at Princeton University, as are President Woodrow Wilson's papers. Private organizations, such as the National Association of Broadcasters, have interviews in their own files with White House and other executive officials who had responsibilities for policy development and regulatory decisions during the tenure of recent presidents.

It is also worth noting that one can obtain a great deal of information from the libraries without having to go to them. Many of the libraries allow their oral history interviews and finding guides, descriptions of the contents of particular collections, to circulate on interlibrary loan.

Presidential libraries, like other sources of information, have their limitations. Sometimes a subject that was a mystery before a visit to a presidential library remains one afterward. Francis Rourke found that even an exhaustive search of the material in the Johnson library bearing on the president's proposal to merge the Departments of Commerce and Labor in 1967 could not solve the mystery of why so politically adroit a president could make so politically unpopular a proposal.[45]

How useful the libraries prove to be to a researcher will depend in large part upon the questions she or he is asking and how interested the various administrations were in dealing with them. For some people the libraries are the most useful tool they have, whereas for others they are of secondary importance. For questions concerning the conduct of one administration, the library will probably be very useful. The library of the particular administration being studied will have more material in one place than any other source. For questions that cut across administrations, however, the libraries may prove to be less useful.

Some of the best materials in the library are not the files that people kept but the daily records that they built with their personal diaries. Whether there are diaries or some notes of recollections of important meetings in the researcher's area of interest depends in large measure on luck. For an investigation of a question, event, or action that got a fair amount of publicity as it happened, the libraries will probably be more important as a check on the information already gathered rather than as a source of new material. Published sources — newspapers, magazines, books, congressional hearings, among others — should be investigated thoroughly before one goes to the library. Then the library will be a valuable resource whether it is as a primary one providing new information or as a secondary one corroborating what might have been found elsewhere.

Notes

1. My own experience with presidential libraries comes from work done in the preparation of a book, *Portraying the President: The White House and the News Media,* by Michael Baruch Grossman and Martha Joynt Kumar (Baltimore: Johns Hopkins Univ. Press, 1981). We spent several days, in some cases weeks, in each of the libraries except the Hoover.

2. Robert E. Sherwood, *Roosevelt and Hopkins: An Intimate History* (New York: Grosset & Dunlap, 1950), xiv. Sherwood was a speechwriter in the Roosevelt White House.

3. Robert J. Donovan, *Conflict and Crisis: The Presidency of Harry S Truman, 1945–1948* (New York: Norton, 1977), 58.

4. Ibid., 59.

5. Interview with Fred Greenstein, June 10, 1981, Princeton, N.J.

6. Ibid. Dwight D. Eisenhower, *Waging the Peace 1956–1961* (New York: Doubleday, 1965), 149 and 2–3.

7. Telephone interview with Clement Vose, July 2, 1981.

8. Interview with Richard Immerman, June 10, 1981, Princeton,

N.J. See Richard Immerman, "Guatemala as Cold War History," *Political Science Quarterly* 95 (Winter 1980–81), 629–53. See also Beatrice B. Berle and Travers B. Jacobs, eds., *Navigating the Rapids, 1918–1971: From the Papers of Adolf A. Berle* (New York: Harcourt Brace Jovanovich, 1973), 617–19.

9. Interview with Francis Rourke, Feb. 26, 1981, Baltimore.

10. Interview with John Fawcett, July 7, 1981, Washington, D.C.

11. Ibid.

12. Transcript, DeVier Pierson oral history interview, tape 2, Mar. 20, 1969, p. 31, Lyndon B. Johnson Library.

13. Ibid., 31–32.

14. Greenstein interview.

15. Ibid. See Graham T. Allison, *Essence of Decision* (Boston: Little, Brown, 1971).

16. Interview with Richard Strout, *New Republic* columnist and *Christian Science Monitor* correspondent, conducted by Michael B. Grossman and Martha J. Kumar, Jan. 23, 1976, Washington, D.C.

17. Transcript, James Hagerty oral history interview, Jan. 31, 1968, pp. 218–19, Columbia University Oral History Collection, New York.

18. Rourke interview.

19. Background interview, Ford administration official, Dec. 1976.

20. Interview with Roger Brown, Feb. 26, 1981, Baltimore.

21. Rourke interview.

22. Interview with Pierre Salinger, conducted by Michael B. Grossman, Oct. 12, 1976, New York.

23. Robert Kintner to President Johnson, Jan. 12, 1967, Confidential Files, EX PR 18, White House Central Files, LBJ library.

24. Robert Komer to President Johnson, Nov. 22, 1967, EX PR 18, WHCF, LBJ library.

25. Jeb Stuart Magruder, *An American Dream: One Man's Road to Watergate* (New York: Atheneum, 1974), 86.

26. Interview with David Rubenstein, conducted by Martha J. Kumar and Michael B. Grossman, Jan. 6, 1981, Washington, D.C.

27. Fred Panzer to E. Hayes Redmond, April 12, 1966. EX PR 18, WHCF, LBJ library. Attached with buck slip by Bill Moyers for the president's night reading, Apr. 20, 1966. The Deakin article appeared in the Jan. 29, 1966, issue of the *New Republic.*

28. Interview with James Deakin, July 1976, Washington, D.C.

29. Tom Johnson to Walt Rostow, Juanita Roberts, Budget Director Shultz, Constance Gerrard, Joseph Califano, Hal Pachios, Dec. 13, 1966, EX PR 18, WHCF, LBJ library.

30. Greenstein interview.

31. Interview with Jody Powell, conducted by Michael B. Grossman and Martha J. Kumar, May 21, 1981, Washington, D.C.

32. Interview with Robert Brookhart, assistant to the archivist of the United States, July 7, 1981, Washington, D.C.

33. H.R. 13500, sec. 2201. Definitions (3), 1–2.

34. Ibid., sec. 2204 (c) (A), 4.

35. Ibid., sec. 2204 (a), 3.

36. Fawcett, Brookhart, and Moss interviews.

37. Background interview, 1981. See Arthur Schlesinger, *Robert Kennedy and His Times* (Boston: Houghton Mifflin, 1978).

38. Fawcett interview.

39. Rourke interview.

40. Telephone interview with William Moss, July 8, 1981.

41. Greenstein interview.

42. Brookhart interview.

43. Patrick Anderson, *The President's Men* (New York: Doubleday, 1968).

44. Greenstein interview.

45. Rourke interview.

9

Presidential Libraries:

How Not to be a Stranger

in a Strange Land

LARRY BERMAN

THIS CHAPTER is intended to be a researcher's guide to the nation's seven presidential libraries. I have written previously on how scholars can utilize primary source materials in analyzing the institution of the American presidency, and Martha Kumar's contribution in this volume addresses the substantive issues of hypothesis testing and theory development from archival data.[1] My task is somewhat akin to the designer of topographical maps for wilderness trails—providing detailed and specialized information that is not readily available from the more general "tourist" brochures. This information is derived from direct observation and extensive research experience in the presidential library system. No first-time visitor to New York City would venture out without a map and description of key landmarks within that massive city, and the same applies to research trips to Austin, Texas; Abilene, Kansas; Hyde Park, New York; Independence, Missouri; Boston, Massachusetts; West Branch, Iowa; and Ann Arbor, Michigan. My guide, I hope, will enrich as well as facilitate the experience of working with primary source materials.

The Evolution of a Presidential Library System

FIRST, several questions must be answered. Why are there only seven presidential libraries but forty presidents? Where have all the other presidential papers gone? Who owns these papers? What is the mission of a presidential library?

The nation's seven presidential libraries are not really libraries in the traditional sense, but rather they are archival depositories for the personal papers and official records of an administration. The libraries are U.S. government agencies authorized by the Presidential Libraries Act of 1955 and administered by the National Archives and Records Service (NARS) of the General Services Administration (GSA). Except for the recently opened Gerald R. Ford Library, all share space with museum exhibits that depict the career and times of the particular president.[2]

When George Washington retired to Mount Vernon in 1797, he had no presidential library in which to deposit his papers. Washington decided to take all personal and official papers with him, establishing the precedent that a president's papers were personal and not public property. (Washington did leave his successor, John Adams, some official documents relating to pending administrative and policy matters.) At the time, Washington's decision was probably a wise one. Philadelphia, the nation's capital, provided no adequate storage facilities, whereas Mount Vernon guaranteed a relatively safe and supervised environment. Washington even contemplated building a facility on his estate to safeguard the documents, but his death in 1799 preempted such plans. In his will, Washington provided that his nephew, Associate Supreme Court Justice Bushrod Washington, should receive "all the papers in my possession, which relate to my civil and military administration of the affairs of this country . . . [and] also, such of my private papers as are worth preserving."[3] Unfortunately,

Washington's nephew used little discretion in limiting access to his uncle's papers. Supreme Court Justice John Marshall made use of the original papers while writing his *Life of George Washington* (1804–07). When Jared Sparks, editor of the *North American Review* later requested permission to visit Mount Vernon in order to prepare *The Writings of George Washington,*[4] he was permitted to take eight boxes of Washington's personal papers back to Massachusetts — six boxes shipped from Alexandria to Boston, and two of the most important carried personally by Sparks over land — where they remained in Sparks's possession for the next ten years. Bushrod Washington died in 1829, and his nephew and heir, George Corbin Washington, sold the president's official records to the government in 1834 for $25,000. Fifteen years later he completed the transaction by selling Washington's private papers to Congress for $20,000.

Today, largely owing to the efforts of the State Department, the Library of Congress, and congressional appropriations, 95 percent of George Washington's papers are housed in the Library of Congress. Nevertheless, Washington's precedent of claiming his papers as personal property and bequeathing these materials to his heirs created insurmountable obstacles to preserving the historical records of his successors. At one time, for example, the papers of Thomas Jefferson were strewn among the Library of Congress, the Massachusetts Historical Society, the Historical Society of Pennsylvania, the Buffalo Historical Society, the American Philosophical Society, the Missouri Historical Society, the Pierpont Morgan Library, the Yale University Library, and the Virginia State Library.[5] One hundred separate purchases were needed to buy the scattered papers of Andrew Jackson. William Henry Harrison's papers were burned accidentally when fire destroyed the Harrison homestead at North Bend, Ohio. President John Tyler's papers also were destroyed by fire during the burning of Richmond in 1865. President Fillmore's son directed the executors of his will "at the earliest practicable moment . . . [to] burn or otherwise effectively destroy all correspondence or letters to or from my father, mother, sister or me."[6] Fortunately, these instructions were never carried out, and the personal papers, later discovered in an attic in Buffalo, New York, are today part of the Buffalo Historical Society collection. President Frankin Pierce and Ulysses S. Grant willfully destroyed many of their personal papers, and Mrs. Warren Harding admitted destroying virtually all of the president's private correspondence. President Lincoln's son, Robert, destroyed much of his father's Civil War correspondence. Even President Truman, while personally presiding over the construction of the Harry S Truman Library, excluded his most important papers until the completion of his memoirs. The president's daughter, Margaret Truman, consulted such hitherto unavailable records while writing her own memoirs of life with father.[7] Today, the remaining papers of Presidents Washington through Coolidge are located in the Manuscript Division of the Library of Congress owing in large part to Herbert Putnam, librarian of Congress from 1899 to 1939, under whose direction all presidential papers were transferred in 1900 from the State Department's Bureau of Rolls and Library (the National Archives was not established until 1934).

Whereas the existing arrangements were satisfactory for the pre-"modern" presidents, it soon became evident to President Franklin Roosevelt that the sheer mass of documentation from his presidency would overwhelm the existing archival resources. On December 12, 1938, the president sent a "personal and confidential" memorandum to a distinguished group of fifteen historians inviting them to the White House in order to discuss plans for the disposition of his presidential papers.[8] Roosevelt realized that if historians were to make use of his official papers, some degree of advance organizational planning was required. Roosevelt told his guests that he wanted to establish a permanent structure to house and protect the records of his presidency. At a press conference following the meeting, the president announced the concept of a presidential library, "one of the most important and promising developments in all archival history."[9]

The Franklin D. Roosevelt Library soon was established as part of the National Archives by a joint resolution of Congress in 1939 and later became the first of the presidential libraries authorized by the 1955 Presidential Libraries Act. On July 4, 1940, Roosevelt deeded sixteen acres of his family's estate in Hyde Park, New York, for the planned library and museum. Within several months, a small group of supporters had solicited private funds for construction of the facilities. The museum opened to visitors on June 30, 1941, and research activities started on May 1, 1946.[10]

Presidents Truman and Eisenhower followed Roosevelt's procedures in creating depositories for their papers, but there was a need to institutionalize the process of building and maintaining libraries for the future. In 1955, the Presidential Libraries Act provided the legal basis for accepting presidential papers and maintaining presidential libraries. The legislation covered only the acceptance (as gifts) of papers and maintenance of facilities, not ownership (to the extent that *anyone* other than the president had a legitimate claim to the papers). The 1955 act brought all presidential libraries into the National Archives system and guaranteed professional care and preservation for presidential materials. The libraries were to be built with private, not public, dollars and the president could set whatever restrictions he deemed appropriate. The National Archives and National Park Service would maintain the library, museum, and grounds, and professionally trained archivists would care for the papers.

Although Roosevelt was singularly responsible for the precedent-setting decision to build a library for his presidential materials, he did not differ from George Washington on the question of ownership. These were Roosevelt's papers — given as a gift to the United States. On this issue all of Roosevelt's successors readily agreed. Not until the disposition of President Nixon's Watergate materials did this unsatisfactory arrangement "become a threat to the very function of a democratic government."[11]

In September 1975, former president Nixon and Arthur Sampson, administrator of General Services, signed an agreement that allowed Nixon legal title and literary property rights to all papers and files from his administration.[12] The Nixon-Sampson agreement gave Nixon possession of 42 million documents and materials relating to his presidency — including the infamous tapes. "The United States gained from the agreement only the restricted use of the material for a few years and the promise of eventual donation of those portions of the papers so designated by Nixon. Nixon rather than the National Archives would determine the historical record to be preserved of the administration of the

37th President of the United States."[13] The terms of the agreement would have allowed Nixon (or his heirs) to destroy the tapes between September 1, 1979, and September 1, 1984.

This negotiated settlement had the appearance of another cover-up and served to raise public awareness on the issue of "ownership." The controversy subsided with the passage of the Presidential Recordings and Materials Preservation Act of 1974 (88 Stat. 1695), signed by President Ford on November 11, 1974.[14] The legislation nullified the Nixon-Sampson agreement; required former President Nixon to assure complete access of the public to documents from his presidency; and established the National Study Commission on Records and Documents of Federal Officials to explore the question of control, ownership, disposition, and preservation of historical materials.

Following several delays, the commission submitted its report on March 31, 1977. This report "recommended that all documentary materials made or received by public officials in discharge of their official duties should be recognized as the property of the United States; and that officials be given the prerogative to control access to the materials for up to fifteen years after the end of their federal service."[15] Based upon those recommendations, President Carter signed the Presidential Records Act of 1978, effective January 20, 1981. The law finally settled the legal question of ownership — the public, not the president, had legal right of access to and ownership of all official presidential records. The law left great leeway, however, in deciding just what constituted personal rather than official documentation.[16]

BACKGROUND INFORMATION FOR THE FIRST RESEARCH TRIP

BEFORE visiting a library, I strongly suggest that the researcher write in advance to the supervisory archivist about his or her research project or interest (see Appendix A) and request a list of the library's holdings and *all* other available information concerning the library, museum, accommodations, restaurants, reproduction costs, and travel. The list of holdings will usually include four major categories: manuscript collections, microfilm, audiovisual materials, and oral history interviews. These materials will provide only enough information to determine if there are sufficient grounds for visiting a library.

For example, the materials from the Eisenhower library will include an extensive appendix on the recently available Whitman File. According to the library,

the Presidential Papers of Dwight D. Eisenhower (Ann Whitman File) constitute the richest historical collection in the Dwight D. Eisenhower Library. These are the president's office files, maintained during his administration by his personal secretary, Ann Whitman. The documents in this collection, totaling approximately 240,000 pages, include the president's correspondence and memoranda of conversations with heads of state, government officials, friends, and associates, as well as correspondence, memoranda, agenda, press releases, reports, and other materials documenting the foreign and domestic policies of the Eisenhower administration, the political activities of the president and his associates, and the president's personal affairs. Generally, the materials cover the years 1953–61, although there are scattered documents dated earlier.

At the close of the Eisenhower administration, these materials were shipped to Gettysburg, where former President Eisenhower used them in preparing his presidential memoirs, *The White House Years*. Following Eisenhower's death in 1969, the papers were transferred to the Eisenhower Library. Six series, constituting approximately 50 percent of the collection, were made available for research in May 1975; and to date a total of thirteen series have been processed and opened to scholars, although portions are closed in keeping with donor restrictions or government regulations. The processed series, totaling approximately 210,000 pages, are as follows: Administration series (45 boxes); Ann Whitman Diary series (11 boxes); Cabinet series (16 boxes); DDE Diaries series (55 boxes); International series (50 boxes); International Meetings series (4 boxes); Legislative Meetings series (3 boxes); Name series (36 boxes); Presidential Transition series (3 boxes); Press Conference series (10 boxes); Speech series (38 boxes); Stag Dinners series (2 boxes).[17]

In addition to these important substantive materials the researcher will receive from the library a useful list of motels and restaurants in Abilene.[18] He or she will also learn that in contrast to its simple exterior of Kansas limestone, the "lobby and corridors are of book-matched Loredo Chiaro marble from Italy. Floors in the principal public areas are Roman Travertine trimmed with Breche d'Alep and Rouge Fleuri marble from France. Ornamental bronze work in the building reflects the geographic environment of the building through the use of a motif based on buffalo heads and bluestem grass."[19]

After receiving these materials, researchers should consult *Prologue,* a quarterly publication of the National Archives that identifies recently opened materials not identified in the library publication. I strongly recommend then making a phone call to the library in order to speak with an archivist. The archivists possess the best perspective on available material because their primary responsibility is declassification and opening papers. They represent the best finding guide in a library. An exchange of questions will help clarify one's intellectual goals and just what kind of material is available. Some people actually begin this process one or two years in advance of their research project to ensure enough time for declassification of materials.

Upon arrival at the library, researchers are given an orientation session with the supervisory archivist. They are then asked to complete a research application. Researchers learn the rules governing research in the library and receive an informal tour of the research facilities. The Johnson library provides a list of procedures for research in the library. With minor variations it applies to all of the libraries:

1. Please sign the register each day when first entering the reading room.

2. Researchers may take blank sheets of paper, note cards, tablets, and handbags to desks in the reading room. All other personal belongings which could be used to conceal documents, such as briefcases, must be left in the wardrobe in the reading room. Anything taken to the desk must be submitted to the archivist on duty for examination before it leaves the room. Although handbags are permitted at the desks, we strongly encourage researchers to leave them in the wardrobe.

3. Researchers may not smoke, eat, or drink in the reading room. Smoking is permitted in the eighth floor hall.

4. Request all materials by filling out a "request slip" and initial your charge out record when receiving materials.

5. Only one cart of material may be checked out at a time, unless approved by the reading room archivist.

6. Do not use a fountain pen while using the documents; you may use a ballpoint pen, pencil, or felt tip pen.

7. Documents shall not be leaned on, written on, folded anew, traced, fastened with paper clips or rubber bands, or handled in any way likely to cause damage. If a staple needs to be removed to facilitate use of the document, the reading room archivist will do it.

8. It is extremely important to preserve the original order within both folders and boxes. A document must always be replaced in the same position within the folder and box in which it is received. Remove only *one folder* from a container at a time. Using a xerox marker to mark the location of a removed folder will facilitate its replacement in the proper place. Papers should not be left askew and should not be placed upside down or backwards in a folder. If the papers appear disarranged, inform one of the archivists; do not attempt to rearrange them.

9. Do not exchange documents or containers with another researcher. All items must be checked in before another researcher uses them.

10. Trade books and oral histories checked out for overnight use must be returned the following morning.

11. Observance of copyright rights and literary property rights retained by the donor is the responsibility of the researcher. The library staff will provide information on the ownership of such rights.

12. Typewriters and tape recorders may be used in the reading room.

The reading room in most libraries is open from 9:00 A.M. to 5:00 P.M., Monday through Friday, except national holidays, and on Saturdays from 9:00 A.M. to 1:00 P.M., by appointment only (see Appendix A). No new researchers will be accepted on Saturday, and the library requests that a Saturday appointment be made by 5:00 P.M., Thursday, and that materials needed for Saturday be requested before 4:00 P.M., Friday. No new requests for materials will be accepted on Saturday. For this reason I have always traveled to and from a library on Sunday and worked Monday through Saturday. This seven-day schedule also fits conveniently with conditions for most supersaver airline flights, booking two weeks in advance and staying a minimum of seven days.

Following the orientation session, an archivist shows the researcher the voluminous finding guides, which list the total range of processed materials in the library and their availability. (Finding guides are available on interlibrary loan.) Perhaps the most frustrating aspect of archival research is to know of the substantive wealth of holdings, only to face the frustration of "closed" materials. Obviously there is much variation in availability *between* libraries. The older, more established libraries — Roosevelt, Hoover, Truman, and Eisenhower — have made much of their holdings available, except for classified materials. For the Kennedy, Johnson, and Ford libraries it will be a matter of time and patience before materials can even be processed.[20] According to Harry Middleton, director of the LBJ library:

The LBJ Library has in its collections some 31 million papers: 21 million are the papers of Lyndon Johnson; of these, two-thirds are from his presidency, the documents, correspondence, memoranda, all the myriad paperwork which accumulated in the White House in the course of his administration. Following the practice of all his predecessors, Johnson took with him into retirement the entire White House files, and they became the nucleus of the Library's collections. The other one-third of the LBJ papers are those he collected in the other stages of his life: early youth, in the Congress, in the Senate, as Vice President, and in retirement.

Of the remaining 10 million papers: 4 million are the personal papers of the 160 persons who were associated with Johnson in the course of his public life — White House aides, Congressional colleagues, journalists who reported on his times. The remaining 6 million are composed of the records of government agencies and advisory boards.

Finally, an estimated 35,000 pages represent the Library's Oral History program. They are transcripts of interviews with more than 800 men and women who supplement and flesh out the stories imbedded in the written record with their recollections of how programs were developed and legislation passed, of the play of personalities on the moving history of the times.

The volume of Johnson papers, of course, is fixed and finite. But the other parts of the collections will continue to grow through the years. We are still acquiring the papers of persons connected in some way with LBJ, and we are still conducting interviews for the Oral History program.

Basically, the mission of the Library archivists is to open the papers, a process that involves arrangement and review of each document. Why review? When President Johnson turned over his papers to the Library, he signed a deed of gift stipulating that all his papers, except those classified for security purposes, should be made available for study unless they contained materials which might embarrass or harass living persons. To this point, about 80 percent of the Johnson materials, mainly the nonclassified presidential papers and those of the early Congressional years, have been reviewed. Less than 1 percent of the papers reviewed so far have been closed; and material that *is* closed is periodically reviewed and opened when the conditions for closing it are removed — which usually, but not always, means the death of the person or persons involved.

Classified papers — they total about 1 million — are another matter. This is the one body of records over which the Library does not have complete control. Generally speaking, this material has to be declassified before it can be made available, and the declassification has to be accomplished either by the agency or department of government which originally classified the document — or, when the classification was done at the White House, by the department or agency which has primary interest in the subject. About 7 percent of the classified documents in the Johnson Library have gone through this process. . . . In much less than that time — within 5 years — it is our hope and goal to have all the other papers now in the collections at least reviewed, if not totally opened. Because we plan to continue to acquire papers, the overall review process will be open-ended. In terms of priorities, the presidential papers got first attention, then LBJ's Congressional papers. Next in line are his papers from the Senate and vice presidency. After that, we will concentrate on the papers of our other donors.[21]

How do researchers use the finding guides? Assume that one is interested in the question of White House staffing. The White

House Central Files (WHCF) Finding Guide is the place to begin. These Central Files consist of *Subject, Name, Chronological,* and *Confidential* files. The Subject File is for correspondence pertaining to the functions and operations of the White House, the federal government, foreign and other governments, and correspondence from private companies or individuals. Material in the Subject File is segregated into two categories, "Executive" and "General." "Executive" material consists of correspondence and other papers of particular importance because of source or nature of content. These generally include incoming letters and other important documents received from agencies, members of Congress, and other prominent correspondents. It may also include such letters even though no action was taken on them at a high level. It includes copies of outgoing letters, memorandums, and other documents that were acted upon or brought to the attention of the president or a designated top White House official.

"General" material, although important because it is addressed to the president, is not as important in terms of level of handling or subject matter as the "Executive" material. "General" includes all letters and documents that are not classified in the "Executive" category and, for example, may include routine communications from members of Congress, memorandums exchanged among lower-echelon officials, and letters from the public at large. Cross-reference is not made between the "Executive" and "General" categories. A yellow folder label affixed to the left side of the folder designates the "Executive" material. A green folder label affixed to the right side of the folder designates the "General" material. The designation "Executive" or "General" also appears in the upper right-hand corner of each case file.[22]

The WHCF Subject File in the Johnson library lists sixty subjects:[23]

Agriculture	AG	Meetings-Conferences	MC
Arts	AR	Messages	ME
Atomic Energy	AT	National Security-Defense	ND
Business-Economics	BE	Natural Resources	NR
Civil Aviation	CA	Outer Space	OS
Commodities	CM	Parks-Monuments	PA

Countries	CO	Peace	PC
Disasters	DI	Personnel Management	PE
Education	ED	Political Affairs	PL
Federal Aid	FA	Postal Service	PO
Federal Government	FE	President	PP
Federal Government-		Procurement-Disposal	PQ
Organizations	FG	Public Relations	PR
Finance	FI	Publications	PU
Foreign Affairs	FO	Real Property	RA
Gifts	GI	Recreation-Sports	RE
Health	HE	Religious Matters	RM
Highways-Bridges	HI	Reports-Statistics	RS
Holidays	HO	Safety-Accident Prevention	SA
Housing	HS	Science	SC
Human Rights	HU	Social Affairs	SO
Immigration-Naturalization	IM	Speeches	SP
Indian Affairs	IN	States-Territories	ST
Insurance	IS	Tariffs	TA
International Organizations	IT	Transportation	TN
Invitations	IV	Trips	TR
Judicial-Legal Matters	JL	Utilities	UT
Labor Management		Veterans Affairs	VA
Relations	LA	Welfare	WE
Legislation	LE	White House	
Local Governments	LG	Administration	WH
Medals-Awards	MA		

The White House Administration category (WH) would then be consulted (Appendix B) and requests for materials made. From here researchers are on their own.[24]

The Language of Presidential Libraries

In any foreign country, if you speak the language it will be easier in the backroads. The same is true in a presidential library. Nobody wants to be caught saying a linear foot is a shoe size or not knowing the difference between a president's papers and his files. Libraries use the term "linear foot" as a measurement to indicate the size of manuscript and archival holdings. One linear foot is equivalent to approximately 2,000 pages of materials. Less than one linear foot is indicated as (– 1). Do not use the term, however, in regard to microfilm — you might get a frown and be treated like a freshman at orientation week. Microfilm holdings are indicated by number of rolls and oral history interviews by number of pages, not by feet or rolls.

Perhaps the biggest misunderstanding in a library is between "papers" and "files." Papers are materials that are donated directly to the library by an individual or his or her heirs, whereas files are materials that are left in the White House and are part of the president's papers. The Freedom of Information Act does *not* apply to donated materials (papers), only to files. Moreover, files of aides are *not* personal papers; for example, the files of John Smith are those materials accumulated in the White House and left there. The papers of John Smith are those that he gave to the government — with or without restrictions.

Researchers should also understand just how Literary Property Rights (LPR) apply to their research. The library advises all researchers that

> under common law, the author of an unpublished work has the right to first publication. Such rights are perpetual and descend to the author's heirs after his death regardless of the physical ownership of the document itself, unless such rights are explicitly assigned, donated or abandoned to the public domain. This does not apply to documents prepared by officials or employees of the United States Government as part of their official duties. Such documents are in the public domain. Some persons who have given papers to the Library have donated the literary property rights in them to the Government. Permission to reproduce copyrighted materials in the Library's still picture, motion picture, and cartoon collections must be obtained from the copyright holders. Their names, if known to the Library, will be furnished upon request. The Library reserves the right to refuse to accept a copying order if, in its judgment, fulfillment of the order would involve violation of copyright law.[25]

Know Your Rights

THE single most important type of information is readily supplied by the library staff—the legal rights of the researcher. Scholars, whatever their research, are sure to encounter withdrawal sheets placed in front of folders that list unavailable materials. Executive Order 12065 permits researchers to request agencies of the federal government to declassify documents that are currently closed for national security reasons. How does one know its classification? The withdrawal sheet gives the information. If the withdrawal sheet indicates that the document has been removed because of national security classification, the researcher may request declassification. The library provides the following instructions:

1. Fill out a standard mandatory classification review request form, which a member of the library staff will provide.

2. For each document you request you must, so far as possible, provide the following: date of the document and its subject or title, names of the correspondents, type of document (memorandum, letter), and file location (document collection title, box number, folder title). Most of this information should be available on the withdrawal sheet.

After we receive your request:

If the document was created by an agency—

1. Within 20 days we will submit copies of the document to the originating agency, which has authority for declassification decisions.

2. The agency will review the document, advise you of its decision, and send you copies of the declassified documents. This review may take considerable time.

3. When the agency advises us that it has declassified materials and has sent copies to you, we will send you a bill for reproduction costs for each item that was declassified. (Failure to pay these charges will be grounds for denying or suspending action on future mandatory review requests.)

4. If the agency denies your request for declassification, you may

appeal that decision directly to the agency concerned. The agency will inform you of appeal rights. Ask a staff member about this procedure.

If the document was created by the White House —

1. We will submit copies of the document to agencies of primary subject matter interest for advice concerning declassification within 20 days. This review by the agency or agencies may take considerable time.

2. The library director has authority for declassification decisions. He will act after consideration of agency opinions.

3. We will advise you of the final decision on your request and will provide you copies of opened materials immediately after a decision has been reached. You will be billed a reproduction charge for each item that you are furnished.

4. If your request is denied, you may appeal this decision to the Deputy Archivist of the United States through this library. The Deputy Archivist will advise you directly of his decision.

There are four limits on your mandatory review rights:

1. A document must be at least 10 years old to be considered for mandatory review. (Federal records are exempt from this limitation.)

2. A document that has been exempted from declassification in whole or in part within the past 12 months will not be rereviewed.

3. A document that has been submitted for review and exempted from declassification will not be submitted if it is due for review under systematic review procedures within the next 2 years. (Systematic review is a declassification procedure which pertains to documents more than 20 years old.)

4. A single mandatory review request must be limited to 25 items of 100 pages. Should you desire a larger quantity to be reviewed, you may divide your request into several parts. Each part will be acted on separately. We will process the remaining parts of your request as time permits.

The Freedom of Information Act (FOI) provides a legal avenue for access to *federal* records, but most materials in the library are *not* federal but personal papers and therefore are not subject to FOI. Nevertheless, the library does provide guidelines:

If you are denied access to federal records and desire to request access under the Freedom of Information Act, you should follow this procedure:

1. Make a written request to the library, stating explicitly that you are asking for access under the Freedom of Information Act.

2. Describe the records you want as specifically as you can in your request so that we can identify this material with a reasonable effort.

3. We will respond to your request within 10 workdays. During this time we will, in the case of restricted records, consult with the agency that originated the records to determine if the reason for the restriction still exists. If consultation requires more than 10 workdays, we will notify you and will provide a response within 10 additional workdays.

4. You may appeal any denial of access under the Freedom of Information Act to the Deputy Archivist of the United States who will have 20 workdays to respond to your appeal. If your appeal is denied, the Deputy Archivist will advise you of your rights to judicial review.

Finally, those individuals who donated materials to the library may have placed restrictions on access to these materials. You have the right to request a review of such items to determine if the reason for closure still exists:

1. You must make written request to the library director for review of closed items. In this request you must cite specific documents and identify each document as fully as possible. Usually this requirement can be met by providing the date, subject, name of correspondents, type of document (memorandum, letter), and location of the item (collection title, box number, file folder).

2. We will usually act on your request within 10 days. If we cannot respond within that time, we will advise you of the reason for delay.

3. If the donor of the items you want reviewed has reserved the right to determine if the item may be opened, we must forward your request to the donor. If the donor denies your request, you may not appeal that decision.

4. If the library director denies your request, you may appeal that ruling to a three-member Board of Review chaired by the Dep-

uty Archivist of the United States. You must make this appeal in writing to the Deputy Archivist through the library director. The board will usually respond within 30 working days. No further appeal is available.

There are two limits on your right to appeal donor restricted documents:

1. , You may not request review of a document that the Board of Review has considered within the past 2 years.

2. You may not request review of a document in a collection that has been open for research for less than 2 years.

Some "Tips" on Managing One's Economy and One's Life

TRAVEL and accommodations to presidential libraries can be quite an expense — especially if one is engaged in comparative research. Grants-in-aid are available from the Hoover, Roosevelt, Truman, and Johnson libraries. Information and applications can be obtained by writing to each library. Reproduction costs at the library are 15 cents a page; 20 cents by phone order.

Oral history interviews and library books can be checked out of the library overnight (see Appendix C). It is a poor use of time to read them in the reading room when they can be read in one's motel while relaxing in the evening (and in many places that is all there is to do). Hours at the library can be spent more fruitfully by going through the documents. Also, it is not unusual to find former friends of the president or administration officials who now reside nearby, and lunches or interviews with these people are often possible. The credentials of being an established researcher in the library will almost always gain an interview. Finally, the library will rarely be able to fulfill a request for many xeroxes on the same day, but the archivists will sometimes reproduce a handful of important documents for your immediate use. Above all else, however, enjoy the experience of working with historical materials. I hope that this guide enriches that experience.

Appendix A: Presidential Library Fact Sheet

Herbert Hoover Library
West Branch, Iowa 52358
319-643-5301
Dedicated: August 10, 1962
Reading room hours: 8:45 A.M. to 4:45 P.M. on weekdays; 9:00 A.M.
to 12:00 noon on Saturdays
Museum admission: 75 cents, age 16 and over
Grant-in-aid available
Thomas Thalken, director

Franklin D. Roosevelt Library
Hyde Park, New York 12538
914-229-8114
Dedicated: June 30, 1941
Reading room hours: 9:00 A.M. to 4:45 P.M., on weekdays only; July
and August 9:00 A.M. to 4:45 P.M., also on Saturday
Museum admission: 50 cents, age 16 and over
Grant-in-aid available
William Emerson, director

Harry S Truman Library
Independence, Missouri 64050
816-833-1400
Dedicated: May 8, 1954
Reading room hours: 8:45 A.M. to 4:45 P.M., Monday through Fri-
day, and on Saturday by appointment
Museum admission: 75 cents, age 15 and over
Grant-in-aid available
Benedict Zobrist, director

Dwight D. Eisenhower Library
Abilene, Kansas 67410
913-263-4751
Dedicated: May 1, 1962
Reading room hours: 9:00 A.M. to 5:00 P.M., Monday through Friday
Museum admission: 75 cents, age 16 and over
Grant-in-aid not available
John Wickman, director

John F. Kennedy Library
Columbia Point
Dorchester, Massachusetts 02125
617-929-4523
Dedicated: October 20, 1979
Reading room hours: 8:30 A.M. to 4:30 P.M., Monday through
  Saturday
Museum admission: 75 cents, age 17 and over
Grant-in-aid not available
Dan H. Fenn, Jr., director

Lyndon B. Johnson Library
Austin, Texas 78705
512-397-5137
Dedicated: May 22, 1971
Reading room hours: 9:00 A.M. to 5:00 P.M., Monday through
  Saturday
Museum admission: No charge
Grant-in-aid available
Harry Middleton, director

Gerald R. Ford Library
Ann Arbor, Michigan 48109
313-668-2218
Dedicated: April 27, 1981
Reading room hours: 9:00 A.M. to 5:00 P.M., Monday through
  Saturday
Museum: Located in Ford's hometown of Grand Rapids, Michigan;
  now under construction
Grant-in-aid not available
William Stewart, acting director

APPENDIX B

OUTLINE OF WHITE HOUSE ADMINISTRATION CATEGORY FROM THE LYNDON B. JOHNSON LIBRARY

MATERIAL in the White House Administration (WH) category

pertains to the operation, maintenance and administration of the White House, the executive office building, and other temporary offices of the president. Includes material on finances, personnel, procurement, office space, and transportation. 9'5". (1'4" restricted.)

Related material is filed under the following subject categories: transitions to Incoming Administration (FG 11–8), White House Theatre (AR 7).

WH	White House Administration
	Material on White House office procedural matters, including overtime authorizations for the staff and handling of personal mail. Mostly cross references. ¾".
WH 1	Accounting
	Consists of lists of expenditures from Special Projects appropriations; memoranda regarding payment on bills incurred by staff while performing official functions; and possible reduction of expenditures by the White House Office. 1'. (4 items restricted.)
WH 2	Budget
	Material on authorized budgets for the White House office. Mostly cross-references. ½". (3 items restricted.)
WH 3	Buildings, Grounds
	Floor plans for different parts of the White House; thank-you letters for visits with the president at Camp David; memoranda on furnishings and decorations for the White House, upkeep and improvement of the grounds around the White House; memoranda on the design for the new executive office building. 8¾". (9 items restricted.)
WH 3/AR	Art
	This file was not used. See WH 3–1.

WH 3/CM   Furniture
This file was not used. See WH 3-1.

WH 3-1   Furnishings
Material on paintings loaned by museums to the White House, biographical information on artists represented in the White House; requests by staff for paintings and new furnishings for their offices. 2¼". (3 items restricted.)

WH 3-2   Buildings Management
Memoranda on maintenance and operation of the White House; requests for working spaces for the press. [Attached to EX WH 3 11/4/66 is the "White House Operation and Maintenance Agreement between the White House, National Park Service, and the General Services Administration."]

WH 3-2-1   Conference Rooms
Material on the use of the Cabinet and Fish rooms and lighting and furniture in these rooms. Mostly cross references. ¼".

WH 3-2-2   Office Space
Requests from staff members for office space in the White House and Executive Office Building. 3¼". (2 items restricted.)

WH 3-2-3   Parking Space
Contains complaints about the White House parking situation, and requests for parking places. ¾". (1 item restricted.)

WH 3-3   Architecture
Floor plans, memoranda, feasibility studies, and estimated costs for renovations and maintenance of the White House and the Executive Office Building; memoranda on the possibility of turning the fish room or the White House theatre into the television studio. 5½". (6 items restricted.)

WH 4   Contracts
              Consists of orders for pens, platforms for pens,
              and books needed by the White House Office;
              bids from contractors for construction of a com-
              munications enclosure adjacent to the Situation
              Room; costs for providing furniture for staff
              rooms in the White House; list of equipment
              needed by the mail and correspondence sections.
              This file contains a large amount of cross refer-
              ence material. ½". (9 items restricted.)

WH 5   Office Management
              Memoranda outlining procedures to follow in
              preparation of letters for the President's signature,
              drafting statements for the President, sending
              messages of greeting, referring correspondence to
              government agencies; form letter samples; memo-
              randa describing the duties of the correspondence
              section. 2¾". (4 items restricted.)

WH 5-1   Mail (Parts of GEN WH 5-1 were opened 9/73)
              Material concerned with the handling and an-
              swering of mail at the White House including
              streamlining of mail policies, management of
              Presidential mail, replies to critical mail, answer-
              ing of congressional mail; lists of staff and their
              areas of expertise for answering mail requests; let-
              ters expressing views on the Vietnam War; De-
              partment of Defense analysis of mail received
              dealing with Vietnam; tabulations of mail re-
              ceived on various domestic issues; weekly reports
              on the subject and disposition of mail addressed
              to President Johnson. [Filed EX WH 5-1, 2/24/65,
              are two memos on views of a Cabinet meeting
              dealing with the handling of White House Cor-
              respondence. Filed EX WH 5-1, 6/1/65, is a mail
              distribution guide giving chief responsibilities of
              various Presidential and staff assistants.] 2' 5¼".
              (1¾" restricted.)

WH 5–1–1   Mail Reports
Weekly summaries of Presidential mail and its content. (These summaries include mail that was referred to agencies.) The General File was not used. 4″.

WH 5–2   Records
Memoranda on material that should be sent to White House Central Files; records of Presidential foreign policy decisions; movement of Presidential papers from the White House to the Johnson Library; control and disposition of White House Office papers. ¾″. (1 item restricted.)

WH 6   Personnel-Management
Requests for temporary aid for White House Staff Offices, White House passes for new and detailed employees; departure letters from summer and full time employees of the White House Office to staff members or the President; procedural matters in employment of personnel; partial list of staff in the White House Office. This file contains a large amount of cross reference material. 5″. (½″ restricted.)

WH 6–1   Applicants
Memoranda on possible employment at the White House, additional personnel for the White House Office, suggested candidates to be speechwriters for the President. 1″. (3 items restricted.)

WH 6–1/A–Z   Applicants
Material concerned with obtaining jobs at the White House or in government service, including recommendations, resumes, biographic information and sample speeches. 1′ 10¾″. (4″ restricted.)

WH 7   This file was not used.

WH 8   Protection
Presidential itineraries; memoranda on protection

of the President, Vice President and candidates in the 1964 Presidential race, and Department of Defense assistance to the Secret Service.

WH 8-1   Accident-Fire
            Memoranda on defective wiring in the Oval Room, improvement in fire fighting equipment and techniques relating to helicopter flights in and out of the White House grounds. Most of this file is cross reference material. ¾". (2 items restricted.)

WH 8-2   Civil Defense
            One item on testing emergency power for the White House. – ½". (1 item restricted.)

WH 8-3   Physical
            Material on issuance of White House passes to new staff members and members of the press, clearances for workmen at the White House, checking of the White House communications system. 2½". (9 items restricted.)

WH 9   This file was not used.

WH 10   Staff Meetings (Opened (10/24/75)
            Agenda, memoranda and list of topics covered at weekly staff meetings (these meetings reviewed various Presidential directives, as well as discussing policy problems); summaries of these meetings for the President; memoranda on discontinuing and reinstituting these meetings. The General File was not used. 2¼". (7 items restricted.)

WH 11   Supplies, Materials, Services
            Memoranda and correspondence concerned with obtaining supplies or services for the White House Office including stationery, extra copies of *Challenge to Americans,* magazines, teleprompter equipment, public address system, typing equipment,

furniture, and photographic support for the White House Photo Office. 6½". (½" restricted.)

WH 12   Telecommunications
Material concerned with maintenance and improvement of telecommunications equipment at the White House and the LBJ ranch. 3¼". (7 items restricted.)

WH 12–1   White House Communications Agency
Memoranda on White House Communications Agency's responsibilities and audio coverage of the President. This file contains a large amount of cross reference material. 1¾". (5 items restricted.)

WH 13   Travel, Transportation
Material on curtailing the use of the Presidential aircrafts, the propriety of paying travel expenses for White House employees, and transportation billed to the D.N.C. 1". (6 items restricted.)

WH 13/A–Z   Travel, Transportation/A–Z
Requests for travel expenses from staff members to attend foreign meetings and conferences. ¾".

WH 14   Vehicles
Material on the use of aircraft and automobiles by the President; requests from Mrs. Johnson's staff for travel expenses. This file is primarily cross reference material. ½".

WH 14–1   Airplane, Helicopter
Material on the use of Presidential airplanes and helicopters including flight certificates (certificates sent to those who rode on Presidential aircrafts), manifests (list of those who are to ride on the Presidential aircraft); thank you letters to the President from those who were invited to ride on Pres-

idential aircraft; flight forecasts; memoranda on possible magazine articles on the Presidential airplanes and procuring new Presidential helicopters or airplanes. 1'8½". (1" restricted.)

WH 14-2   Automobiles
Memoranda and lists on proper and improper use of White House cars. 2½". (7 items restricted.)

WH 14-3   Yacht
Material on maintenance and usage of Presidential yachts and thank you letters for cruises. 2½". (6 items restricted.)

Appendix C:

Letters Suggested by the Lyndon B. Johnson Library to Request and Grant Access to Restricted Oral History Interviews

SUGGESTED LETTER TO INTERVIEWEE

Interviewee's Name
Address

Dear _____:

Brief paragraph explaining your position and topic.

Suggested paragraph for permission:

The LBJ Library staff has told me that access to your oral history interview(s) is not allowed without your written permission. It will be a great help to me with my research if you are willing to grant that permission to me.

If you agree to do so, please fill out the enclosed form and return it to the Supervisory Archivist, LBJ Library, Austin, Texas 78705.

Thank you very much.

Sincerely,

_____

Researcher

SUGGESTED LETTER FROM INTERVIEWEE

Dear Supervisory Archivist:

I hereby grant permission to _____ to use my oral history interview(s) recorded for the LBJ Library.

This researcher may:

Yes   No

ACCESS

_____ _____ Read the interview(s) at the Library.

_____ _____ Listen to the tape recordings(s) of the interview(s) at the Library.

_____ _____ Receive an interlibrary loan copy of the transcript(s) from the Library.

_____ _____ Purchase a xerox copy of the interview(s) from the Library.

USE

_____ _____ Quote from the interview(s) without restriction.

_____ _____ Quote from the interview(s) governed by copyright restrictions: may publish brief "fair use" quotations from the interview(s) without my consent.

_____   _____   Must clear any direct use or quotation of the material with me.

Signed:

_____

Interviewee

_____

Date

NOTES

1. Larry Berman, "Johnson and the White House Staff," in Robert A. Divine, ed., *Exploring the Johnson Years* (Austin: Univ. of Texas Press, 1981), 187–213.

2. The Ford museum is located in the president's hometown of Grand Rapids, Mich.

3. John C. Fitzpatrick, ed., *The Writings of George Washington from the Original Manuscript Sources, 1745–1799,* 39 vols. (Washington, D.C.: U.S. Government Printing Office, 1931–40), vol. 37, p. 284.

4. Ibid., vol. 1; Herbert B. Adams, ed., *The Life and Writings of Jared Sparks,* 2 vols. (Boston: Houghton Mifflin, 1893).

5. Louise Lovely, "The Evolution of Presidential Libraries," *Government Publications Review*, 6, no. 1 (1979):27–35.

6. U.S., Congress, House, Committee on Government Operations, *To Provide for the Acceptance and Maintenance of Presidential Libraries and other Purposes: Hearings before a Special Sub-Committee, H.J. Resolution 330, 331, 332,* 84th Cong., 1st sess., 1955, p. 394; Helen D. Bullock, "The Robert Todd Lincoln Collection of the Papers of Abraham Lincoln," *Library of Congress Quarterly Journal* 5 (Nov. 1947); Kenneth Duckett and Francis Russell, "The Harding Papers. How Some Were Burned . . . and Some Were Saved," *American Heritage* 16 (Feb. 1965): 24–31.

7. Margaret Truman, *Harry S Truman* (New York: Morrow, 1973).

8. Cited in H. G. Jones, *The Records of a Nation* (New York: Atheneum, 1969), 146. The group included Charles Beard, Samuel

Morison, William Dodd, Randolph Adams, Frederic Passon, Julian Boyd, and Helen Taft Manning.

9. Ibid., 145. An advisory committee was soon established and included Waldo Leland, R.D.W. Conner, Robert Binkley, W.E.B. Dubois, Guy Stanton Ford, Douglas Southall Freeman, Edwin Gay, Monsignor Peter Guilday, Allan Nevins, Bessie Louis Perre, and Walter Prescott Webb. Notes from this meeting can be located in "Minutes, First Meeting of the Executive Committee," Dec. 17, 1938, FDR Library File Box, Roosevelt library.

10. Waldo Leland, "The Creation of the Franklin D. Roosevelt Library: A Personal Narrative," *American Archivist* 18 (Jan. 1955): 11–29; R.D.W. Conner, "The Franklin D. Roosevelt Library," *American Archivist* 3 (Apr. 1940): 81–92; Herman Kahn, "The Presidential Library — A New Institution," *Special Libraries* (Mar. 1959); Herman Kahn, "The long-range implications for historians and archivists of the charges against the Franklin D. Roosevelt Library," *American Archivist* 34 (July 1971): 265–75.

11. J. Frank Cook, "Private Papers of Public Officials." *American Archivist* 38 (July 1975): 314–16.

12. Nixon-Sampson Agreement, Sept. 6, 1974, in *Weekly Compilation of Presidential Documents* 10 (Sept. 16, 1974): 1104–05; Clement Vose, "Presidential Papers as a Political Science Concern," *PS* (Winter 1975): 8–18.

13. J. Frank Cook, "Private Papers of Public Officials," *American Archivist* 38(July 1975): 314.

14. *Presidential Recordings and Materials Preservation Act,* 44 USC 2107 (Supp. V., 1975); Public Law 93–526, 88 Stat. 1695.

15. National Study Commission on Records and Documents of Federal Officials, Sec. 202, Public Law 93–526; final report March 31, 1977, cited in Lovely, "The Evolution of Presidential Libraries," 32. Lester J. Cappon, "Why Presidential Libraries?" *Yale Review* 68 (autumn 1978): 33. Membership on the commission included Herbert Brownell, (chairman and former attorney general of the U.S.), Philip Buchen (special counsel to President Ford), J. Edward Lumbard (federal judiciary), Gaylord Nelson (Senate), Lowell P. Weicker, Jr. (Senate), Allen Ertel (House), Robert Lagomarsino (House), John Thomas (State Department), David Cooke (Defense Department), James Rhoads (Archivist of the U.S.), Elizabeth Hamer Kegan (Library of Congress), William Leuchtenburg (American Historical Association), Ann Morgan Campbell (Society of American Archivists), Frank Freidel, Jr. (Organization of American Historians), Lucius Battle (com-

sat), Ernest May (professor of history at Harvard, representing the public).

16. U.S., Congress, Senate, Committee on Appropriations, Subcommittee Hearings, *Treasury, Postal Service, and General Government Appropriations for Fiscal Year 1979*, 95th Cong., 2d sess. (Washington, D.C.: U.S. Government Printing Office, 1978), 859.

17. See "Historical Materials in the Dwight D. Eisenhower Library," Jan. 1981, available from the library; Fred Greenstein, "Eisenhower as an Activist President," *Political Science Quarterly* 94 (Winter 1979–80): 575–99.

18. The library information package will include a wide range of information: list of holdings, motels, restaurants, travel, and, if available, a grant-in-aid application.

19. "Historical Materials in the Dwight D. Eisenhower Library," plus information sheet.

20. Louise Lovely, "The Evolution of Presidential Libraries," p. 29.

21. Harry J. Middleton, "The LBJ Library," *Discovery* 4 (Dec. 1979): 16–17.

22. This information is provided in the Johnson library finding guides.

23. The WHCF subjects vary from library to library. In the Eisenhower library, for example, "the White House Central Files comprise the largest collection in the Library, totaling approximately 6,000,000 pages. All of the major foreign and domestic issues and policies associated with the Eisenhower Administration, as well as the political events of the period, are documented by the Central Files. To date, approximately 2,000,000 pages of the Central Files comprising, for the most part, the more historically significant segments of the collection have been processed. Available for research at this time are the Official File (OF), 80 percent of the General File (GF), and 50 percent of the President's Personal File (PPF). Only a small portion (less than 5 percent) of the Confidential File (CF) has thus far been processed. The unprocessed portions of the General File and the President's Personal File largely pertain to subjects of marginal historical value such as message requests from organizations, public requests for photographs, birthday congratulations, and invitations. The Confidential File, on the other hand, is largely unprocessed because of the high percentage of security-classified documents in the file. Researchers may request that selected portions of the General File and the President's Personal File be processed and made available for research. Whether such requests can be honored, however, depends upon the size of the request,

when the materials will be needed by the researcher, and the amount of staff time that can be diverted from other projects at the time of the request" ("Historical Materials in the Dwight D. Eisenhower Library," 1981).

24. For substantive examples of research, see, Divine, *Exploring the Johnson Years.*

25. Handouts on Literary Property Rights from all libraries.

10

Interviewing Presidential Aides:

A Journalist's Perspective

DOM BONAFEDE

GOOD JOURNALISTS must apply a medley of techniques in interviewing news sources. They must demonstrate the thorough preparation of a courtroom attorney (without seeming persecutorial or accusatorial); the persuasiveness of a salesman; the charm of a political fund-raiser; the impartiality of a judge; the integrity of a clergyman; the curiosity of a child; and, at opportune times, the audacity of a cat burglar. More than merely possess those characteristics, they must know when to call on any one or a combination of them. Essentially, interviewers are not unlike actors who must subtly project various shadings of their roles.

In its simplest terms, an interview is an intimate inquiry, formal in structure yet generally casual in ambience, whose principal objective is to elicit information. Beyond that primary horizon, it illuminates the personality and philosophical attitude of the interviewee. When conducted artfully, with thorough preparation and an appreciation of mutually recognized concerns, it is, in a large measure, a quasiscientific exercise. Indeed, to Oriana Fallaci, who has won renown as an interviewer of world leaders, the politically powerful comprise a unique species who must be "analyzed coldly, surgically." It was during an interview with Fallaci that Henry Kissinger, then U.S. secretary of state, compared himself to that exemplar of American heroism, "the cowboy who leads the wagon train by riding ahead alone on his horse . . . into the town, the village, with his horse and nothing else." Although the analogy was gratuitously made to Kissinger's everlasting regret, it nonetheless exposed a facet of a complex, compulsive personality, beyond any offered in the volumes of words written about him. As a writer once said of Fallaci, "She has made it her business for quite a few of her 50 years to pin down those in power—persuading them that a date with her and her tape recorder is a date with history—to cajole them to tell her how they got where they are and what they plan to do about it."[1]

The Evolution of the Art of Interviewing

POSING evocative questions in pursuit of reason and knowledge is ideally suited to teaching, reporting, and scholarship, each of which is dedicated to the elusive search for truth. Daniel Defoe, the creator of *Robinson Crusoe* and *Moll Flanders,* is traditionally cited as the father of modern journalism for his use of reportorial techniques in exposing social evils of early-eighteenth-century England. The founder of a pamphlet called *The Review,* Defoe assailed the perniciousness of debtor prisons, religious bigotry, and political hypocrisy. Almost fifty years after the great London plague of 1665, he wrote *Journal of the Plague Year,* based upon research into published accounts, eyewitness reports, and interviews with survivors. Defoe vividly depicted the panic and despair that swept the city, the ominously tolling church bells, and the rumbling through the cobblestone streets of the death cart, preceded by the cry, "Bring out your dead."

It was not until the middle third of the last century, however, that James Gordon Bennett, the Scottish immigrant who became a legend in American journalism, developed the interview as an integral tool of news gathering. Bennett's *New York Herald* created a sensation when it published an interview with Rosina Townsend, the madam of a "fancy house" where a murder had occurred. As a result of the *Herald*'s stories, a young suspect was released by the police.

Shortly afterward, another journalistic giant, Horace Greeley, popularized the interview by using it to disclose intimate details in the lives of celebrities. As part of a historic interview by Greeley in July 1859 at Salt Lake City, Utah, Brigham Young, head of the Mormon church, acknowledged that he had fifteen wives. "I know no one who has more, " Greeley quotes Young as saying, "but some of those sealed to me are old ladies whom I regard rather as mothers than wives, but whom I have taken home to cherish and support."[2] On the basis of the interview, Greeley fashioned an attack against polygamy and came out in defense of women's rights in an era when such a stand was considered highly radical. At the conclusion of the interview, Greeley wrote:

The degradation (or, if you please, the restriction) of woman to the single office of childbearing and its accessories is an inevitable consequence of the system here paramount. I have not observed a sign in the streets, an advertisement in the journals, of this Mormon metropolis, whereby a woman proposes to do anything whatever. No Mormon has ever cited to me his wife's or any woman's opinion on any subject; no Mormon woman has been introduced or has spoken to me; and, though I have been asked to visit Mormons in their homes, no one has spoken of his wife (or wives) desiring to see me, or his desiring me to make her (or their) acquaintance, or voluntarily indicated the existence of such a being or beings."[3]

As the editors of *A Treasury of Great Reporting* noted, "Three years later Congress prohibited polygamy for the future in the territories and ultimately the Mormons bowed to the sentiment of the country."[4]

A reporter from Bennett's *Herald* was present when John Brown, the fiery abolitionist was captured at Harpers Ferry by federal troops under Col. Robert E. Lee. Wounded in the assault,

Brown was interviewed by authorities and the *Herald* reporter, whose story presented a verbatim account of the questions and answers in accordance with the common practice of the period. Included was the following colloquy, underscoring the prescience of "God's angry man":

> Reporter of the *Herald* — "I do not wish to annoy you; but if you have anything further you would like to say I will report it."
>
> Mr. Brown — "I have nothing to say, only that I claim to be here in carrying out a measure I believe perfectly justifiable, and not to act the part of an incendiary or ruffian, but to aid those suffering great wrong. I wish to say, furthermore, that you had better — all you people at the South — prepare yourselves for a settlement of that question that must come up for settlement sooner than you are prepared for it. The sooner you are prepared, the better. You may dispose of me very easily. I am nearly disposed of now; but this question is still to be settled — this Negro question, I mean; the end of that is not yet."

The reporter additionally recorded that in response to being called "fanatical" by a bystander, Brown declared, "And I think you are fanatical. 'Whom the gods would destroy they first make mad,' and you are mad."[5] With a remarkable paucity of words, Brown, by suggesting that the South was as possessed by the question of slavery as he and his followers, thus forecast the conflagration that was to come.

In mid-nineteenth-century America, however, interviewing as a journalistic technique was scorned and denounced by critics, one of whom declared it was "the most perfect contrivance yet devised to make journalism an offense, a thing of ill savor in all decent nostrils." *The Nation,* a magazine that appealed to intellectual liberals, maintained, "The interview is generally the joint product of some humbug of a hack politician and another humbug of a newspaper reporter."[6]

Nevertheless, the style initiated by Defoe, Bennett, Greeley, and their journalistic brethren was adopted and refined by generations of reporters and writers as an invaluable vehicle in the eternal quest for information about ourselves and our global environment. Speaking before the American Society of Newspaper Editors in 1927, the *Chicago Daily News* foreign correspondent Edward Price Bell asserted that the interview ably served in "bridging the gulf between genius and the common understanding."[7]

The contemporary interviewer, whether from the journalistic or academic community, is considerably abetted by several factors. Foremost among these are the public's demand for information; universal acceptance of the interview as an effective instrument in reporting and researching; and widespread recognition that communications is a vital element in the political process, notably in educating the electorate, gaining public support, and mobilizing coalitions. There is also a keener awareness today of the need for "openness" in both government and business and of the public's right to know.

On a more humanistic level, people like to talk, expound, offer their opinions, and provide a rationale for their actions and decisions. This applies particularly to those in official positions, few of whom are entirely free of the sin of self-pride. Pragmatists as well, they recognize that in expressing their views they are, in effect, not only performing a public service function but also propagating their political goals. Often, an invisible line separates the two, and it is incumbent upon the interviewer to delineate one from the other.

Lastly, a symbiotic relationship exists between the interviewer and the interviewee. Although their objectives differ, they rely on each other: the interviewee wants his positions and policies ventilated; the interviewer seeks information to write a story or add to research. It is, in a sense, a marriage of mutual convenience. The interviewer, however, must be without passion or bias. The interviewee, in contrast, suffers no such constraints.

PRESIDENTIAL AIDES AS SUBJECTS

THE essential mission of journalists and academics is to explore and analyze the subject at hand, and to write about it coherently, and from an illuminating perspective. In this instance, the subject is the White House organizational and decision-making structure, including the people around the president and their respective roles and functions and how they interact with the federal bureaucracy, other government components, and outside groups.

The public should know as much about presidential aides and advisers as about elected representatives. The concept that White House staff members should be imbued with "a passion for anonymity" as proposed by the Brownlow Commission in 1939 is no longer viable in an age of instant communications, sophisticated public relations, and magnified presidential visibility. The idea may well have been too idealistic and impractical from the start.

Presidents have the right to select virtually anyone they want as their personal assistants; it is about the only area in which they have unchecked authority. On the other hand, the public has a right to know the members of the White House staff, who, unelected, unconfirmed, and, for the most part, unknown, are paid with taxpayers' funds. They have become so much a part of the White House infrastructure and so influential in presidential decision making that it would be impossible fully to appreciate the modern presidency without knowing something about the people surrounding the president. Hence, students of government should seek to ascertain how they fit into the White House hierarchical scheme.

Presidential aides in the post-Watergate era are generally aware of their moral and constitutional obligations yet are keenly conscious that their primary allegiance is to the president who appointed them and at whose pleasure they serve. Mainly for political reasons, but out of personal vanity in some cases, they participate in public forums as presidential surrogates.

David R. Gergen, President Reagan's director of communications, once remarked, "My concept is that the power of the presidency becomes a wasted asset if he comments upon every issue in the passing scene. It is better for him to speak out on the really important issues and let his lieutenants speak on a daily basis."[8] That being so, the notion of anonymous presidential aides is truly a relic of the past. More and more, they perform as presidential spokesmen and willingly, sometimes eagerly, agree to interviews. Media relations, in fact, have become one of their major functions. Consequently, many senior White House aides have become household names, better known than most cabinet secretaries and members of Congress.

It should correspondingly be noted that Washington journalism is fundamentally verbal in nature, as opposed to visual reporting, of, say, a fire, or a demonstration by protesters, or a baseball game. Some experts contend that in the broad range of journalism "more than half of all news stories are directly or indirectly derived from spoken words."[9] That would especially apply to Washington. In the nation's capital what is important and newsworthy, even if admittedly trivial at times, is what political celebrities say, whether orally or in writing. Debates, speeches, statements, reports, news releases, messages, White Papers, declarations, press "leaks," critiques, gossip, and so on, are the stuff that makes news in Washington and contributes to the political climate. Metaphorically, Washington is a vast echo chamber resounding to the cries, boasts, plaints, and demands of thousands of political creatures. Dispassionate observers must have an ear for the salient and significant and not be deafened by bombastic rhetoric or lulled by soothing exhortations. In essence, they become participants in the process, since they must discern what is valid from what is counterfeit, what is political propaganda as opposed to what is in the public interest. That can be more demanding and require greater skill and judgment than the visual reporting of an action-filled drama. Analytical observers must further bear in mind that politicians and bureaucratic officials are genetically inured to compromising, even in the choice of language.

INTERVIEWING TECHNIQUES

INTERVIEWS basically fall into two categories. The routine or informal interview is aimed at obtaining information to be used in support of or as part of a story or article. It is not intended to stand alone, and the source may or may not be identified. The second type is the stylized, personal interview that is focused almost entirely on the individual, his or her personality, achievements, ambitions, views, and comments. It may be the basis for a profile. A professional interviewer would additionally study the individual's record; talk to his or her family, friends, associates, and rivals; and consult with specialists in the area. The distinction between the two types is important in setting up and making plans for an interview, since the in-depth, personal inquiry is obviously more elaborate and time consuming.

Decisions regarding whom to interview are extremely pertinent. Most sought after in Washington are those who occupy prominent positions and are currently in the news because of ongoing news events. Although the inclusion of illustrious officials give an article credibility and name value, it is a mistake to ignore the unknowns in the outer reaches of government. Even the lowest-ranked White House aides have eyes and ears, sit in on meetings, see memorandums, and hear what is going on from associates. They often have less of a political axe to grind and are less concerned about their jurisdictional status and therefore can be fertile sources of information.

Personal relationships are a crucial ingredient in gathering information, but the outside observer should avoid forging close friendships with those in positions of authority. An adversary relationship must be maintained when one seeks objective information, and the source of that information invariably has a prejudicial view. That does not preclude the two sides from establishing a relationship based on trust and confidence; yet favoritism by either or both distorts the informational product. All this bespeaks a delicate situation, but it can be kept within ethical bounds if both sides recognize their institutional responsibilities.

The information gatherer should also try to cultivate his or her own independent sources, persons readily accessible and forthright in their assessments, aside from popular spokesmen whose business it is to disseminate the administration "line." Usually, the interviewer and the source meet as near-strangers but are promptly thrust into a position wherein inquiries of the most familiar kind are pursued. Following a common scenario, the interviewer at first comes across as an aggressive inquisitionist, and the source, wary of the other's motives, takes refuge in guarded replies. As they take each other's measure, they feint and parry and generally engage in parlor-room diplomacy. It is therefore essential that the interviewer, through tact, sincerity, and show of knowledge, break down the barriers and put the source at ease. The best interviews are more like a discussion between two learned friends than an interrogation.

The interviewer, while respectful, must never appear awed by the source's rank, title, and position but should take the attitude that the source has agreed to the interview and that they are meeting on equal ground. The chances are that the source would not have agreed unless he or she felt it would be of potential benefit. Besides the exposure, the interviewee as often as not picks up information from the questioner. Nor should the interviewer disclose any sense of shock or surprise at anything. I recall that during an interview with the late Haitian president François ("Papa Doc") Duvalier, the dour, owlish-looking dictator sat behind a desk that prominently displayed a Bible and a huge revolver. Discretion required that I make no mention of the items, which seemed magnified by their juxtaposition.

Currently, the interview is a fundamental tool of modern journalism, so much so that in the opinion of some critics there is an overreliance on it to the neglect of documentary research and other investigatory techniques. To some extent, the Washington interview encourages a clubby kinship between the principals. Few in political Washington are alien to the ways and wiles of the press. They know the respected and widely read reporters and columnists and the prestigious publications and are selective in granting interviews. Especially are they cognizant of the universal exposure of television. Like the crusaders in search of the Holy Grail, Washington politicians yearn for an appearance on a network evening news program or Sunday talk show. It might be said that while politics is the machinery that makes Washington run, the media provides the grease.

Interviewing leaves room for imagination and creativity. Prior to President John F. Kennedy's burial at Arlington National Cemetery, columnist Jimmy Breslin, then with the *New York Herald Tribune,* drew a Shakespearean motif by interviewing the gravediggers. Immediately before the 1964 presidential election, Breslin visited a poor Chicano neighborhood in Phoenix, Arizona, and talked with the residents, most of whom were unconcerned and uninvolved, about the candidacy of Republican senator Barry Goldwater, who lived in the fashionable suburb of Scottsdale.

In 1960 while a reporter with the *Washington Post,* long before he became famous as an author and commentator on American society, Tom Wolfe wrote a series about Haiti in which he sketched a social portrait of the impoverished country by interviewing its intellectuals, artists, and Sorbonne-educated elite rather than its political and business leaders, as was customary with most newsmen.

Numerous other front-rank journalists and television commentators, including Fallaci, Walter Cronkite, David Frost, Barbara Walters, Studs Terkel, Mike Wallace, and the legendary Edward R. Murrow, gained fame and wealth by adapting interviewing techniques to their personal style. There are memorable scenes of Wallace confronting sources head-on, of the ingratiating Walters interviewing Anwar Sadat and Menachem Begin in the dawning hours of the Mideast peace agreement, of Cronkite scoring a coup by revealing in an interview with former president Gerald R. Ford at the 1980 Republican National Convention that candidate Ronald Reagan had offered to make Ford "assistant President" if he agreed to go on the ticket as his runningmate.

During an interview with the Ayatollah Khomeini in 1979, the indomitable Fallaci complained to the Iranian leader about the face veil she was required to wear in his presence and finally, her patience exhausted, declared, "I'm going to take off this stupid, medieval rag right now." And the 1980 presidential race had barely gotten under way when Senator Edward M. Kennedy, in a televised interview with Roger Mudd, appeared to be uncertain in his responses and unconvincing as to why he would make a good president, getting his campaign off to a rocky start from which it never really recovered.

Every interviewer cannot be like the *New York Times*'s James Reston, meeting on equal terms with the famous and powerful in an atmosphere of total rapport, but there are guidelines that journalists and academics can follow to refine their approach.

Above all, the art is in knowing the individual being interviewed and the subject being discussed and in having a mental compass to keep the interview on course. The interviewer must never go to an interview without being equipped with a list of questions, either memorized or, preferably, in writing. The questions should be in sequential order so that one leads easily and conversationally into another. The interview should not be composed of unconnected bits and pieces but developed as a whole.

The interviewer requesting a meeting with a White House aide or any other administration official should remember that nothing obligates the person to consent to an interview. Accordingly, the interviewer is a guest liable to normal rules of social protocol and, conversely, should be treated with the deference and consideration that any gracious host shows a guest.

Dos and Don'ts

Here is a list of suggestions that an interviewer may follow, some of which may not suit everyone and a few of which may be challenged. Yet, each contains an element of merit.

Do Not

Represent yourself as someone other than who you are.

Conduct an interview over a meal or drinks; there are inevitably distractions, and it becomes difficult to take notes and keep the discussion on track.

Start off with tough questions. Rather, ease into the interview with simple questions to allow time for each of the participants to become accustomed to the other.

Couch questions in a hostile or accusatory manner; it will cause the source to become suspicious of your motives and tend to be uncommunicative.

Act startled at any of the interviewee's replies or show any reaction except genuine interest. A surprised look on the part of the interviewer could indicate to the source that the replies are too revealing, and they will probably become more restrained.

Persist in continuing a line of questioning if the source insists on dropping it. Instead, try to persuade him of the advantages of disclosure or return to it later.

Shut off a source who goes into a lengthy discourse. More may be revealed than you expect, and your question will eventually get answered.

Try to upstage the interviewee. The interviewer is there to gain information, not exhibit his expertise or fount of knowledge. In this connection, while you may want to correct the source on a factual matter, never argue or engage in a heated debate with him.

Use gimmicks. It is considered unprofessional. While interviewing White House aides, one political science professor laid out several cards marked with prospective answers. In response to each question the aides were instructed to turn over the appropriate card. "I thought he was playing some sort of game," an interviewee remarked.

Waste time asking perfunctory questions regarding age, education, family, and so on. Such information can be found in official biographies and other background references.

Become irritated when the interviewee strays from the subject or seems vague. Patiently repeat or reword your question.

Encourage the presence of witnesses or monitors. It is a reflection on the interviewer's integrity and is a disruptive presence.

Violate the ground rules established at the start of the interview. If you do, your chances of ever returning are considerably diminished.

Overstay the time allotted without the expressed consent of the interviewee.

Allow the source to control and have veto power over the finished text. This is apart from returning after the interview to check quotes or points of information.

Talk more than the interviewee. You should not allow him to dominate the direction of the interview or arbitrarily decide the issues to be discussed, but, remember, you are mainly there to listen.

Some of the positive suggestions listed below may overlap the preceding precautionary guidelines but nonetheless will serve to underscore an intended point.

Do

Attempt to obtain an appointment with the top official in the agency or office; if you succeed, subordinates will fall in line.

Learn who in the source's office makes appointments and drafts schedules and request an appointment through them if you do not know the source personally. Also, carefully explain the purpose of the proposed interview. Make the request by telephone, rather than by mail, which usually delays the process.

Set the ground rules at the start of the interview, as to whether parts or all of it will be on the record, on background, or off the record. Make certain each side understands the agreement to avoid confusion and possible complaints afterward.

Discourage off-the-record interviews, since information you cannot use except in an advisory way is of limited value.

Use a tape recorder if the source agrees and it does not inhibit him. Most Washington officials are accustomed to such devices. They are particularly useful in a discussion entailing complex issues and further serve to confirm what was said.

Complete your homework prior to the interview so that you are acquainted with the character and political position of the interviewee and can ask the relevant questions. That is vital to a successful interview. The interviewee quickly knows whether the questioner is familiar with the subject and if not, is likely to lose interest in carrying on the conversation.

List your questions so that one naturally flows into the next one and allows the issue under discussion to expand gradually. This sets the groundwork for the more difficult or tough questions. Despite what some journalism textbooks propose, ask general questions early in the interview and get into specifics later.

Have a central focus and some idea of where the interview is likely to lead, but be flexible if it should veer off on an unexpected path. You may reap an unanticipated dividend.

Try to create a relaxed, congenial air by being pleasant but not excessively friendly. An interview, after all, is conducted for business purposes.

Phrase your questions so that they are simple, brief, and easily understood. Academics, too often, are guilty of posing long-winded questions. Washington officials are experienced in such situations and do not need to be lectured; in fact, they resent it. Also, time is of the essence.

Make certain you understand the exact meaning of a response. If in doubt, ask for a clarification.

Follow up immediately when you think that further explanation is required. Otherwise, you may forget or not have time to return to the question.

Be candid rather than conspiratorial in your choice of words and never ask a "loaded" question or one designed primarily to embarrass the interviewee. Veteran Washington officials instinctively spot such questions and are likely to take umbrage.

Make arrangements to get back to the source after you have reviewed your notes to fill in any gaps and clear up possible misunderstandings.

Leave the interview on good terms, even if it was not as helpful as you had hoped. You have, at least, established a contact and may want to return.

In many respects, the interview is just a starting point, albeit an essential one. Research and additional interviews are almost always necessary to give body and meaning to any article or other work of scholarship. Journalists mostly agree that the source should not see the finished text before it is published. They are split, however, on whether the source should be allowed to see the transcript of a tape-recorded interview. That is a personal decision that the interviewer must make. My experience has been that when shown a verbatim transcript of the questions and answers, the source rarely if ever asks that particular comments be radically changed or deleted but is more likely to suggest that some points be clarified or embellished. That can be highly beneficial to the writer. With no exceptions, the finished product must be controlled by the writer.

Finally, it should be kept in mind that a productive interview is contingent on the same ingredients that contribute to any compatible human relationship, namely honesty, candor, intelligence, and respect, as well as the avoidance of arrogance and duplicity. The interviewer's passport to Washington's inner offices is his or her reputation for integrity and competence.

NOTES

1. Jane Howard, "A Woman," *Quest* 81 (Apr. 1981): 14.
2. Louis L. Snyder and Richard B. Morris, eds., *A Treasury of Great Reporting* (New York: Simon & Schuster, 1949), 108.

3. Ibid., 109.

4. Ibid.

5. Ibid., 123.

6. Mitchell V. Charnley, *Reporting,* 2d ed. (New York: Holt, Rinehart & Winston, 1966), 212.

7. Ibid.

8. Dick Kirschten, "In Reagan's White House, It's Gergen Who's Taken Control of Communications," *National Journal* 13 (July 25, 1981): 1331.

9. Charnley, *Reporting,* 188.

11

Interviewing
Presidential Aides:
A Political Scientist's
Perspective

JOSEPH A. PIKA

PERSONAL INTERVIEWS have played a central role in the development of several social science disciplines; within political science they have been especially important in congressional studies and are likely to prove equally and perhaps even more so in studying the presidency. Because executive-branch processes are less accessible to public observation and lack behavioral indicators comparable to those of the legislature, presidential researchers are likely to depend heavily on participants' accounts of activity. Nonetheless, it is important to emphasize that investigators planning to employ interviewing techniques not only face numerous hurdles (particularly winning access and gaining confidence) but must also be sensitive to limitations of their data.

One's interviewing abilities, no less than those for other methods of data collection, increase with experience. Many of the observations in this chapter are drawn from a series of interviews, principally with current and former members of White House staffs, that I conducted in Washington during 1976–77. Most subjects had served in the White House Office of Congressional Relations, although I also spoke with assistants in the Office of Public Liaison, National Security Council (NSC), Office of Management and Budget (OMB), and Domestic Council and with congressional staff assistants and departmental bureaucrats.

Interviews were especially critical for my longitudinal study of the White House Office of Congressional Relations across four administrations. My financial resources were too limited to support visits to several presidential libraries, and the papers from two administrations included in the study, those of Nixon and Ford, were unavailable at the time. In addition, written records were unlikely to capture the central features of a presidential lobbyist's job: interpersonal interaction. To understand this important White House staff specialization, I asked the actors themselves to describe their activities. Similarly, any analyst working with interview data is seeking insight into the behavior of elite actors by drawing on their specialized knowledge; the interview should emphasize the subject's definition of the situation, interpretations of his or her own behavior, notions of relevance, and cognitive frameworks.[1]

There is no single formula for effective interviewing. Each encounter is potentially unique, since it involves the interaction of personal attributes, attitudes, and situational behaviors of interviewer and respondent. As a result, most commentaries recommend that interviewers adjust their techniques to subject characteristics and responses, although some researchers prefer to follow a more standardized format. As a research technique, interviewing is unusual in that investigator and subject unavoidably become involved in a social relationship. For some social scientists, such as Eugene J. Webb and his colleagues, this interpersonal dynamic undermines the method's reliability. "Interviews and questionnaires intrude as a foreign element into the social setting they would describe, they create as well as measure attitudes, they elicit atypical roles and responses, they are limited to those who are accessible and will cooperate, and the responses obtained are produced in part by dimensions of individual differences irrelevant to the topic at hand."[2] At a minimum, such criticisms highlight the importance of judicious use and careful analysis of interview data. Even the most experienced academic interviewers recognize that not all questions are susceptible to study through interviews. As Lewis A. Dexter has stated, "there are many times and circumstances when the elite interview is emphatically *not* the technique of choice." Rather, "interviewing is the preferred tactic of data collection when in fact it appears likely it will get *better* data or *more* data or data *at less cost* than other tactics!"[3]

Preinterview Preparation

In deciding whether to undertake interviews as part of a study, researchers must consider both the type of data they hope to gather as well as the feasibility of the project. Interviewing is most appropriate as a means to study people, events, and settings that are not directly observable or otherwise represented by some definable set of data.[4] Lacking alternative sources, researchers can rely upon the accounts of those who were present, although Dexter has questioned "simply using interviews as substitutes for direct observation."[5] A critical factor to consider in designing research is *accessibility of data* to the prospective subjects. In this connection, Robert L. Kahn and Charles F. Cannell have suggested that data sought by the interviewer may be *forgotten, repressed,* or *unfamiliar* in terms of the academic's concepts and terminology.[6]

Forgotten information may simply be no longer available at the level of conscious recollection that is tapped by most interviews. The passage of time dims the vibrancy and detail of memory, and researchers need to recognize that the person being interviewed today about a position or event from the past has undergone substantial life changes resulting in different perceptions of his or her previous activities. Forgetfulness, however, may be less of a problem than embellishment. Daniel Aaron included this problem among the effects of time on the recollections and motives of respondents. "The living relic is his own ancestor; and feeling a deep familial piety for his defunct historical self, he indulges in ancestor worship, tidies up embarrassing disorders of his dead past, reverently conceals his old skeleton in a hidden closet."[7] My interview subjects sometimes commented on the tendency to project themselves as more important than they really were. Another pattern was more worrisome, however; accounts of previous service, remembered fondly and with considerable personal pride, occasionally seemed almost rehearsed given the number of times they had probably been told and retold. Retrospective interviewing, therefore, is a difficult task. Perceptual frameworks have altered, sharp corners have become rounded, whole portions of experience have receded from conscious memory.

Interviewers must also prevent their analytic aspirations from exceeding subjects' capacities. For example, in seeking to disaggregate the influences that combined to shape a group of respondents' role definitions, I asked them, "Which jobs that you've held or political activities do you think best prepared you for the job?" I discovered that from the subject's perspective, a personal history is cumulative and indivisible; consequently, the question resulted in somewhat embarrassed and confused responses, an outcome that is not surprising in retrospect but had been wholly unanticipated during the design stages.

There are certain times when interviews are likely to be most productive. Some of the literature on roles, for example, suggests that the best time to explore a position occupant's role definition is just after completion of the apprentice period; at this point, the occupant is most conscious of his or her behavior and enjoys demonstrating knowledge and mastery of the position to others.[8] At this point, however, subjects are least likely to have time for interviews, and in expectation of continuing job responsibilities, they may not be fully candid. A more propitious time to conduct interviews is shortly following or preceding departure from government service. Members of an out-going administration have fewer time demands and are ready, willing, and able to discuss their experiences; there is a nostalgic cast to such interviews but also a high degree of candor and a firm grasp of detail, since many have recently reviewed office files and their own responsibilities in order to prepare archival records and complete job résumés.

Repression of data is sometimes linked to emotional stress, but students of politics will probably be more concerned about intentional repression to avoid exposure or personal damage. While serving in White House or departmental positions, subjects are likely to fear political repercussions arising from their remarks. Once returned to private life as lobbyists, lawyers, legislative aides, journalists, or consultants of various sorts, they are likely to fear professional damage. Although concern about these possibilities varies substantially among subjects, it was a persistent undertone throughout the interviews I conducted; even figures of prominence, with lucrative and secure positions, display a surprising degree of concern. As one White House staff veteran earnestly said while escorting me to the door of his office, "I hope you don't hurt me with anything I've said!"

Putting such fears to rest is an essential step in conducting a successful interview. Executive actors no doubt resemble congressmen in their ability to verbalize experiences at distinct levels of personal revelation. Richard F. Fenno suggests three operative levels: a readily available, "reflexive" set of remarks for the public record; a nonroutine, nonreflexive level for private consumption; a third level of great intimacy and no consumption.[9] The interviewer seeks to elicit the second level, a goal likely to be frustrated unless the subject's confidence is won.

From the outset, interviewers must establish a clear-cut set of rules that will govern the use of interview materials, and they must also attempt to convince the subject of their professionalism. Both are difficult tasks for young, inexperienced academics who are likely to be unfamiliar with the range of possible rules and who lack a publication track record or network of contacts that might attest to their professionalism. A particularly vexing problem is that subjects often are far more familiar with journalistic procedures and purposes than they are with those of the academic world. Thus, the first time a subject suggested that our interview would be on a "deep background" basis, I floundered until it was clear that he meant complete anonymity. The subject should also clearly understand that the academic's general purpose is considerably different from the journalist's: publication, if it comes, will be in an academic journal of limited circulation or in book form, rather than in a current, mass readership publication, and it will come later, after many political issues have lost their saliency.

There are no iron-clad rules regarding use of interview materials; what is important is that the researcher resolve these issues prior to the actual session, make them known to the subject, and then abide by the agreement. Anonymity ensures that there will be no direct attribution of any comments. If one plans to use illustrative quotations, care must be exercised to ensure that the subject is not inadvertently identified through an awkward lead-in, such as, "A former Ford administration speech writer who is now doing the same thing for the current Senate majority leader. . . ." Anonymity may reduce the clout and dramatic appeal of findings, since pseudonyms or unattributed quotations depersonalize an account. One alternative is prior clearance or attribution after clearing materials with the person involved, a procedure that may reassure the subject and has the further advantage of encouraging respondents to provide clarifying remarks on early drafts. This arrangement, for example, was adopted by historian Henry F. Graff in his study of the Johnson administration's Vietnam decision making.[10] Of course, one must deal with the inevitable questions concerning prior censorship and anticipate the possibility of a "messy" exchange with subjects who feel misquoted or misunderstood.

Concerns about data repression may be exaggerated. Because many executive-branch officials have had extensive experience in dealing with journalists and possess exceptional communication skills, they have little need to fear self-inflicted damage during interviews. Thus, confidence in the ability to avoid damage may be just as widespread as fear. There may also be a correlation between confidence and respondent status; top-echelon White House staffers and "secure" professionals evidenced less overt concern than lower-level staffers and career builders. Nonetheless, even more secure figures were often cautious at the outset of an interview, since they were presumably less concerned with hurting themselves than having this unknown questioner commit some subsequent blunder.

Unfamiliarity is a two-way problem: subjects may require a certain amount of "schooling" in areas of the researcher's concern, but academics may also find it difficult to become fluent in the colloquialisms and nuances of the subject's world. Conversation, after all, requires a shared set of mutually intelligible terms and frameworks in order to proceed with any semblance of meaning. Subjects unfamiliar with the terms of reference employed by the researcher or unable to understand the logic of a question are unlikely to provide useful information, and elite groups will probably be most disturbed by this awkwardness.

Subjects who have had previous contacts with academics may be more attuned to a researcher's purposes. Fenno partially explores this in his discussion of respondent "receptivity."[11] At one level, receptivity deals with the subject's ability to be responsive based on knowledge of the academic enterprise, concerns, terminology, and so on. It also, however, deals with general attitudes that subjects may hold toward academics — particularly hostility to intellectuals in general or to academic approaches. Difficulty on either dimension could seriously damage interviews.

Although several of my own subjects indicated familiarity with my milieu by asking whether I knew an academic acquaintance, recalling some previous interview experience, or mentioning terms from graduate course work, more of them seemed unfamiliar with academics and occasionally confused my interview purposes with those of journalists, a group with whom they had had much greater contact. For example, at the conclusion of one session the subject unexpectedly asked, "OK, what's your angle in all this?" and was persistently skeptical when assured that it was as innocuous as the description indicated. The association with journalists also illustrates the need for researchers to "instruct" their subjects in what they are seeking. Otherwise, the interviewee may be responding to the researcher on the basis of a faulty perception, as in the case of one subject, who started off our session saying, "A lot of my journalist friends have asked me about _____ and I guess you could, too."

Happily, I encountered overt hostility very seldom, but I often noted a rejection of academic "distance," "perspective," and "objectivity," mixed with a sense of superiority in having survived the school of hard knocks. One Nixon staffer near the close of a surprisingly open and candid session that emphasized the personal difficulties of service during such a tumultuous time argued, "As an academic, you can't grasp what I'm saying. Perhaps you have a glimpse of understanding but you have to *be* there and get hit in the gut a few times."

The subject's familiarity with the academic enterprise is not, however, an unalloyed benefit; it could be detrimental to one's research purposes if subjects merely mirror the interviewer's concerns and terminology rather than respond authentically in terms of their own perceptual frameworks. In this regard, however, it is reassuring to see how willing elite subjects are to challenge the researcher's interpretations and the general thrust of questions.

Conversely, academics may find it difficult to move from the concerns of a scholarly community to those of the subjects' world in order to translate research questions into a set of queries that will effectively tap the respondents' knowledge and concerns. This perhaps explains why "in and outers," persons who move between government and academia, have proved especially successful in the field of executive studies. I found that despite an extensive review of the public record, including journalistic, academic, and participant-observer accounts, it took me considerable time to feel sufficiently conversant with the subjects' experience to understand readily the nuances and shades of meaning contained in responses. This proved a particularly important factor in my study which concentrated on specialists in verbal communication, persons who were unusually sensitive to subtle differences in phrasing. Researchers concentrating on elite groups with less verbal facility may find the gap between subject and academic experiences to be a less serious hurdle.

By developing a thorough grasp of the subject's context, one is also less likely unwittingly to employ a loaded expression that could have negative effects on the interview. This was brought home to me early in a series of interviews with White House liaison specialists, when I asked whether they could be described as lobbyists. Two replies proved especially revealing: "What the hell else are they?" "Yes, and I don't think that's a bad word." In the first case, the respondent's impatience indicated that he felt this was a senseless question, one which was so self-evident as to require no response. The second was a more defensive response, quite possibly reflecting the subject's expectation that this young, bearded academic harbored stereotypical good-government attitudes.

Identifying the universe of subjects to be included in a study and locating them for the purpose of conducting interviews can be a difficult but certainly not an insurmountable task. Because of this, cross-sectional studies, explicitly focused on a highly identifiable group, are more readily undertaken than longitudinal, multiadministration studies or those encompassing subjects from several organizations. Attempts to push research back in time to include subjects from previous administrations must deal with the hurdles of death, dispersion, and disability. Nonetheless, given the proclivity of former administration officials to profit from their experience and contacts, it may be possible to conduct more extensive comparative administration studies on the basis of personal interviews than have thus far been undertaken.

Published information concerning White House staffers tends to be limited in scope, often ambiguous regarding responsibilities, and inconsistently presented across administrations. Names of numerous officials in the Executive Office of the President (EOP) and in departmental positions can be obtained from the *U.S. Government Organization Manual,* which also employs fairly standard organizational distinctions to indicate responsibilities. A more extensive listing of possible contacts including telephone numbers can be found in Brownson's *Congressional Staff Directory,* and the *National Journal* includes a White House telephone directory in one issue each year. Perhaps the most useful directory, however, is the *Federal Executive Telephone Directory,* which is published quarterly and therefore is likely to be the most up-to-date source. The *Washington Post, National Journal,* and Congressional

Quarterly *Weekly Report* are useful sources of information on roster changes as well as for reports on the operation of specific White House and EOP staff units.

Tracking down former staffers is a more difficult task. Before 1970 only the most senior and visible White House personnel received journalistic attention. Thus, a variety of sources are needed to piece together staff rosters: government, journalistic, academic, and popular accounts of administrations. The Kennedy library has compiled a partial staff roster for the use of researchers, but this assistance is not available for all administrations.

The amount of difficulty in identifying actors depends on how far down in the organizational hierarchy one wishes to go. For some studies, senior actors may prove sufficient and most informative; for others, however, it may be necessary to tap lower-level actors, if only as a cross-check for the data collected from superiors.

Once names have been accumulated, public telephone directories are a readily available research tool. Operating on the assumption that elite actors will be able to draw on their experience in obtaining future positions, one can profitably examine directories for most East Coast urban areas starting with Washington, D.C. Some of the *Who's Who* directories also may be helpful. Finally, many of the best leads can be obtained from members of the "old boy" network; members of former administrations keep track of each other's whereabouts, and many unproductive hours can be saved by asking other interview subjects about the current address and position of former coworkers.

THE INTERVIEW SCHEDULE

MANY of the data problems discussed above can be addressed through a carefully crafted interview schedule.[12] Very few academic interviews appear to be truly "unstructured" to the extent that subjects talk randomly of motives, intentions, and experiences. A researcher's determination of the interview's general subject and guidance of the session constitute a form of minimal structure. "Semistructured" interviews, often of an exploratory nature and emphasizing subject perceptions, may follow a format in which questions have no set wording or sequence. This stands in marked contrast to a highly structured interview that follows a carefully planned set of standard questions asked in a fixed order. Such a session proceeds in a manner comparable to a survey type of interview in which the researcher imposes relatively restrictive structures on the respondent's thinking and may employ fixed-response questions in which the subject is asked to select from a set of alternatives.[13] To my knowledge, John Kessel's study of the Domestic Council made the most extensive use to date of structured techniques in dealing with executive subjects.[14]

The intermediate format, and that which has been most widely used, is the semistructured interview, also termed the "focused interview." In this case the interviewer has a set of topics to be explored but does not seek to follow identical wording or a set order. Thus, the form and timing of questions is discretionary, though control of the interaction and the initiative remain firmly with the interviewer throughout the exchange. This type of interview subtly blends interviewer guidance of the conversation with greater opportunity for subject elaboration and probing follow-up questions than is generally the case in more structured formats.

Each format presents an array of analytic costs and benefits, and interviewers generally strike a balance between more or less structure that is personally comfortable as well as analytically justifiable. Thus, approaches may range from Stephen J. Wayne's semistructured interview to Aberbach, Chesney, and Rockman's use of a standardized schedule that had to be made more flexible in the field.[15] In general, a more highly structured format is most appropriate for examining questions that are already clearly defined and on which the researcher has "highly precise expectations,"[16] while a less structured format is relatively exploratory and stresses subject rather than researcher definitions of a problem.

Fenno suggests that the principal trade-off among formats

is between analytical range and analytical depth, with less structured exchanges being potentially more revealing owing to their intensity.[17] On the other hand, more structured encounters may provide "a greater density of relevant data" as opposed to the "low-grade ore" of less structured sessions. Webb and his colleagues term this an interview's "dross rate," the proportion that is irrelevant to the researcher's purposes.[18] In fact, one seductive aspect of less structured interviews is the ease with which tangential ideas and perspectives can be pursued. Fenno and Lewis Dexter have both suggested that this tendency to stray from a narrow topic may result from the fact that data collection and analysis proceed simultaneously in elite interviews rather than seriatim; interviewers process responses, adjust the wording and order of questions during the session itself, and in the process are often reformulating their basic research concerns.[19]

It has often been assumed that elites would be resistant to standardized techniques. Kessel argues that this assumption was certainly not borne out by his Domestic Council subjects, although my own experience accords more with that of Aberbach, Chesney, and Rockman, who note how important it was for them to be flexible in their interviews. The critical variable may be the degree of "subject sophistication"; Congressional Relations specialists were perhaps more accustomed to being interviewed than staff in the Domestic Council. In any event, I found that a structured format worked quite poorly and interview quality improved markedly after I switched to a focused format in which the same general areas were explored with each respondent although the topics arose in a more conversational manner.

We may well discover that the customary distinction drawn between elite and nonelite subjects is far too simplistic; respondents in the so-called elite category are likely to vary substantially, and interview techniques may thus require adjustment. "Receptivity," verbal communication skills, and interview fatigue are three important factors. Dexter notes in connection with the last item that "like strains of bacteria that have learned to be resistant to antibiotics, interviewees in certain social groups in the U.S. have learned to be interviewed."[20] He terms this "resistance" and emphasizes its prevalence among legislative actors, although he suggests that it may arise from fatigue in being besieged by requests for academic interviews.

Regardless of the format adopted, one way to determine whether you are tapping the intended dimensions and employing language meaningful to subjects is to pretest the interview schedule with individuals in analogous positions or with ones who have held similar positions in other administrations. For example, before interviewing White House legislative staffers, I scheduled several sessions with their departmental counterparts. Although I had to modify the schedule to reflect substantially different activities and pressures, the experience was valuable.

Two other design suggestions might be helpful: delay any potentially conflictual questions until the end of the session, and do not ask subjects to "name names," that is, implicate others in any way. By the conclusion of an interview one has usually established a pattern of exchange with the subject that allows a "ticklish" question to be broached comfortably. Similarly, the subject should have built up enough confidence in the interviewer to answer even more revealing questions. Subjects are quite willing to speak in general terms about themselves and their activities, and although many employ specific examples on their own during the interview session, it is better left to the subject's discretion to do so.

Gaining Access

Because of busy schedules and fears of subsequent damage to themselves, elites confront all researchers with the hurdle of gaining access. This may prove a particularly difficult task for graduate students and young academics, who lack the advantages of professional standing and, often, personal contacts. Nonetheless, many factors work in the researcher's favor, and other avenues may be consciously pursued to improve chances of winning access. My own experience was that the vast majority of subjects approached for an interview eventually agreed, although not always on the first request. Response rates reported for a number of studies vary substantially but seem generally high. (See Table II.I.)

Since there are few instrumental gains that a subject can expect from such an experience, intrinsic satisfaction seems to be the predominant motivation in responding to a request for an interview. Many respondents seem to take genuine pleasure in providing assistance to an academic (perhaps the more struggling the better) and in being given the opportunity to teach someone else about their own life experiences. An element of flattery may be involved as well. Dexter argues that the interview experience provides an unusual occasion for self-analysis, an "opportunity to talk to an understanding stranger . . . who will presumably make no claims, no use of the remarks, which will affect the speaker in the future."[21] Thus, it is not unusual to have subjects say at the conclusion of a session that they enjoyed it, at least in part, it seems, because they were able to recall a period seen as the pinnacle of their careers. As one put it nostalgically, "I know how proud I'll be the rest of my life to say I worked for Jerry Ford. . . . I recognize the rest of my life will probably be a come down because I'll never sit behind another desk as powerful as that one." Pride in past accomplishments is also often translated into a sense of obligation borne by people in public life to provide access to researchers.

Only two instrumental values could be readily served by participating in a study. Remote as it may seem, some subjects may seek to assume a heroic dimension in publications, which would enhance their own role from the past. I also found at least three subjects who indicated some interest in writing about their White House experiences and mentioned a diary or journal that had been maintained during their service. Speaking with an academic could have provided a different perspective or theme for their future works. Although there is no way to determine how widespread such motives may be, all evidence points overwhelmingly to the dominance of intrinsic satisfactions, a factor which perhaps explains the high response rates reported in Table II.I; access may be more readily available than is often assumed. Nonetheless, goodwill is expressed only after an interview, and the research-

TABLE 11.1

RECENT SUCCESS IN GAINING ACCESS TO EXECUTIVE-BRANCH SUBJECTS

RESEARCHERS	SUBJECTS	INTERVIEWS SOUGHT	INTERVIEWS HELD	RESPONSE RATE (%)
Aberbach, Chesney, and Rockman	Supergrade civil servants	68	65	96
Covington	Past and present staff members of EOP units:			
	OMB	11	10	91
	CEQ*	12	10	83
	NSC	12	8	75
Kessel	Nixon's Domestic Council staff	28	16	57
Light	Past and present members of White House staffs: legislative liaison, domestic policy, economic policy, personal staff	172	126	70
Pika	Past and present members of White House staffs:			
	Legislative liaison	34	31	91
	Public liaison (Ford)	11	9	82
	OMB/NSC	8	8	100

*Council on Environmental Quality.

SOURCES: Joel D. Aberbach, James D. Chesney, and Bert A. Rockman, "Exploring Elite Political Attitudes: Some Methodological Lessons," *Political Methodology* 2 (Winter 1975); Cary R. Covington, "The Presidency as a Learning Organization: The Development of Organizational Memory within Presidential Agencies" (Ph.D. diss., Univ. of Illinois, Urbana-Champaign, 1981); John Kessel, *The Domestic Presidency* (Belmont, Calif.: Duxbury Press, 1975); Paul Charles Light, *The President's Agenda: Domestic Policy Choice from Kennedy to Carter (with Notes on Ronald Reagan)* (Baltimore: Johns Hopkins Univ. Press, 1982).

er's initial task is to overcome barriers that might prevent the experience from ever taking place.

Initial interview requests may be made through a formal letter or a direct telephone inquiry. Obviously, if the researcher can only be on site for a limited period of time, a premium must be placed on prior scheduling. This may present a major difficulty, since interviews must be sandwiched among more pressing appointments, out-of-town trips, and unexpected demands on time. The availability of subjects varies significantly by "seasons": it is virtually impossible to schedule sessions in the midst of a presidential election campaign, but members of a just-defeated administration often have an abbreviated work schedule with job-hunting as the major contending demand on their time; former staffers engaged in private business in the D.C. area seem heavily influenced by the congressional calendar. I found it absolutely essential to be in the Washington vicinity for a prolonged period of time and relied primarily on telephone requests made late Thursday afternoon, Friday, or early Monday, since appointment calendars are maintained on a week-to-week basis.

In either case, the content of the request is largely the same: the researcher introduces himself or herself, presents formal affiliation, describes the project briefly, and suggests possible meeting times as well as the amount of time needed. The project description should be adequate to explain why this person is being contracted but not so detailed that the subject will feel unqualified to answer specific concerns. The length of time requested should be the absolute minimum, since in my experience the subjects often scheduled longer periods and frequently continued past the agreed-upon limit.

Some subjects personally screen requests, whereas others merely decide on the basis of information supplied by a receptionist or personal assistant. Since I primarily relied on telephone contacts, it was not uncommon suddenly to be speaking directly with the intended subject. Thus, it was important to be primed with an efficient introduction and project description as well as a convincing set of responses to counter any signs of discomfort or uncooperativeness. In some cases, however, dealing with the boss may be preferable to confronting an unseen, highly efficient, and often imposing "gatekeeper" whose transmitted message could prove vital in having the interview granted.

Persistence is absolutely essential. Refusals to grant interviews usually come in the form of polite excuses regarding time constraints. Repeat requests are tolerated, and one generally learns a lot from how the second request is handled. Repeated refusals obviously indicate the need for a different approach or an improved set of personal references.

Being a doctoral candidate from the University of Wisconsin proved to mean little in Washington; clearly this is not the case if one is fortunate enough to find alumni among potential subjects or one has a recognizable D.C.-based sponsor, such as the Brookings Institution. I never used the letter of introduction from my home university, which I had carefully obtained before entering the field. Instead, subjects were far more likely to ask about personal references. Thus, any contact that a faculty member or colleague might have in D.C. is a potential character reference, even if two or three times removed. Lacking any contacts whatsoever, the researcher may resort to an incremental strategy: success in interviewing several subjects can provide the means to convince subsequent interviewees that you are a legitimate researcher who asks reasonable questions, verifiable by a simple telephone call.

Success in any interview-based endeavor hinges at least partly on a researcher's ingenuity in using "influence and knowledge of channels to secure access to needed data."[22] For example, in the midst of my dissertation research, I faced closed doors from a number of key assistants in the Nixon administration. Part of this response, I learned later, was simply a "rule of thumb" that several had adopted in refusing journalistic interviews. To overcome the problem, I pursued several strategies. Requests were periodically renewed (in one case three telephone calls and two letters), and an effort was made to upgrade the attractiveness of each one. A faculty member provided me with a letter of introduction to a well-known, respected D.C. figure who was willing to attest to my professional integrity after a personal interview. In addition, I used as references interviews conducted with other staff members, and in one case of persistent refusals I asked a particularly helpful interview subject if he could intervene in my behalf with his former boss (and patron). Unfortunately, it is impossible to know which of these tactics was most effective, since several were pursued simultaneously.

In terms of interview time and location, the researcher must generally accommodate the schedules and convenience of the subjects. Most of my interviews were conducted during working hours in the subject's office. Those conducted at home were informal and productive, primarily because no other family members were present to distract attention. Lunch-time sessions proved a poor idea; it is difficult to eat, take notes (or find an electrical outlet), maintain eye contact, and keep the conversation focused on "business."

Overscheduling can be a major logistical problem. Researchers operating under serious time constraints or facing the dilemma of either scheduling an interview or possibly losing it tend to arrange too many sessions for one day. Physical demands on the researcher, such as finding offices and arranging transportation, are thus multiplied, as is the risk of having a carefully designed schedule fall apart because of unanticipated changes by the subjects. Overscheduling can also produce psychological stress, arising from the complex array of personal, situational, and substantive variables encountered in a series of interview sessions.

If the research will include a number of people from the same office, department, or administration, should the interviews start with the big or little fish? The advantage of starting lower in the hierarchy is that the researcher can become familiar with many details before confronting the most important actor. The researcher will then often be in a better position to evaluate data collected from the more authoritative figure. On the other hand, a more accomplished interviewer, confident of his or her skills and completely familiar with the subject matter, may find dealing with the top figures a more efficient use of time. In addition, a successful interview could lead the way to more productive sessions with subordinates who would then feel free to talk. A third option is to deal with second-echelon staffers first (lieutenants) and then move up and down in the hierarchy. Having been screened by loyal assistants in fact may prove helpful in gaining access to the most senior figures.

The Interview Session

ALL interviews proceed on two tracks: informational and inter-personal.[23] Researchers, therefore, must be acutely conscious of the ways in which their physical and verbal behaviors might influence the data being collected. Developing rapport with the subject is an important task, yet there is very little time in which this can be accomplished, and one hopes to avoid missteps that might hinder the process.[24]

In following a semistructured format, the researcher will find it beneficial to review quite carefully the areas to be explored with each subject before arriving at the arranged location. In most cases, it is helpful to write reminders on five-by-seven-inch cards, which can easily be consulted during the session. One method of proceeding with the interview is to begin with direct factual questions and develop a conversational tone in order to build the subject's confidence; the researcher can then gradually shift to more complex and even challenging questions. Dexter, describing more exploratory sessions, recommends starting with a multi-interpretable question that enables the subject to express his or her own perceptual framework.

Probably the most valuable quality an interviewer can possess is being a good listener. This requires being able to generate and maintain an unusually high level of intensity over a sustained period, which makes a good interview draining for both conver-sationalists. The supportive cues one normally provides in con-versation, both verbal and nonverbal, are an important part of the listener's task. At the outset, interviewers may feel that their major task is merely to get subjects talking, so they adopt a less intrusive manner to avoid disrupting the flow. Well-timed inter-jections, however, not only provide focus (thereby minimizing the dross rate), but also maintain the subject's interest by helping the exchange to develop.

Facial cues are one means to guide the subject, although they are more difficult to provide while taking notes, since less eye contact can be maintained than is the case in most conversations. Cue-giving may also seem exaggerated: nodding too vigorously or laughing a bit too heartily are probably useful even if they seem unnatural. One trick an interviewer may wish to cultivate is taking maximum advantage of the closing moments of a session when subject-interviewer rapport is at its height and the momentum can be sustained just a bit longer. After pen and paper have been put away or the tape recorder stopped and thanks have been offered, subjects sometimes provide the most revealing statements; these can be committed to memory and quickly recorded after leaving the office. Frequently they deal with the interview experience itself or they are highly personal reflections upon the topics discussed.

Each interview is a potential adventure. However carefully one prepares by reviewing published accounts, gathering biographical data on the subjects, and anticipating the exchange, the personal dynamics to be encountered are unknown and the challenges are substantial in having quickly to establish credentials and rapport with a new and influential person. Despite the immense variability of these sessions, however, interviewers may find themselves adopting typical roles during the interviews. Most often these are variants of student orientations adopted as a means to thrust subjects into the position of teacher, a role that most subjects adopt quite willingly. Initially, I assumed the role of a "naive sponge," consciously attempting to soak up every vestige of information from subjects. This orientation, however, carries with it an unwillingness to broach touchy subjects, a reluctance that diminished as my confidence increased both with the method and the material. Gradually, I found a more knowledgeable role comfortable, that of the "informed student," which I suspect gives the interviewer greater credibility in the eyes of the subjects. Dexter briefly touches on yet a third orientation, which rests on "bullying" subjects as a means to elicit responses, but adoption of such a technique requires a highly combative personality and always runs the risk of damaging the present interview, one's future reputation, and access of scholars to the same subject in the future. Such a style also violates the informal norms that proscribe aggressive behavior on the part of interviewers and recognize the favor that subjects are doing in providing time and access.

A vexing problem that all neophyte interviewers are likely to encounter is the choice between note taking and tape recording as a means to keep records of interview sessions. Neither method is self-evidently preferable, and experienced interviewers differ over their relative merits. Taping is likely to provide greater sensitivity to nuance and the nature of subject-interviewer interaction.[25] It also allows the interviewer to devote more attention to cue-giving and formulating the next question. There can also be no doubt of a quotation's accuracy if one has it on record in verbatim form. Fenno, however, suggests that this may be a disadvantage, since it forecloses the option available in non-taped sessions of a subject's denying that such statements had ever been uttered.[26] Implicitly, therefore, Fenno is suggesting that subjects might react differently in a taped exchange.

Note taking can be made both more accurate and less onerous than it may first appear. Nearly everyone who discusses interview procedure refers to a personalized short hand that allows them to keep a complete record. In my own experience, few subjects spoke so rapidly that it caused a problem, and even these people could be slowed down with carefully given signals. It is important, however, to review notes as soon as possible after the session has concluded in order to fill in abbreviated exchanges and ensure maximum accuracy. Although this is a time-consuming task, it may result in researchers' developing greater familiarity with their materials while in the field, thereby enabling them to formulate new questions and reformulate others while conducting the research. One acquaintance comes to mind who repeatedly told me of the great data he had been able to record on tape but who could never describe exactly *what* he had. Transcribing tapes, of course, is prohibitively expensive, yet the data are more cumbersome if left in raw form.

Perhaps the most important question in the notes versus tape controversy is whether the choice will have an impact on the interview data. If either the subject or interviewer is uncomfortable with tape recording, behavior could be altered during the sessions. Young researchers are probably more susceptible to "mike fright" than their elite subjects, who have had numerous opportunities to use microphones.[27] Subject ease with taping is indicated by Aberbach, Chesney, and Rockman's report that only 8 of 203 subjects refused to have their sessions taped.[28] Fenno suggests another concern: if one's purpose is to obtain "qualitatively interesting comments, the tape recorder can only be inhibitory," since it makes interaction less spontaneous.[29] Finally, the researcher may be reluctant to inject an additional source of unpredictability into the interview sessions; this is a particularly relevant concern in elite interviews where, by definition, the universe of subjects is small and possesses specialized knowledge, which makes subjects less easily replaced than participants in survey studies.

OTHER POTENTIAL INTERVIEW PROBLEMS

RESPONDENT HOSTILITY

THIS situation, judging from research reports and my own experience, does not arise frequently, since hostility or contempt would lead subjects to reject initial requests for interviews. Nonetheless, such situations may arise from an initial misunderstanding or an unexpected response to an apparently innocuous question. For example, I conducted a brief interview with one subject who had initially begged off owing to the political sensitivity of his position during an election year; in response to a second request, however, he agreed through his secretary to schedule an "interview." He must have been extremely surprised when after the initial exchange of pleasantries I opened my notes to begin the session, because he had expected a candidate for a *job* interview. Given this sudden turn of events, I decided to barge ahead noting sample questions, citing coworkers who had been interviewed, and "forcing" the exchange, which was relatively brief. In any conflictual situation one needs to make measured comments, restrain the impulse to verbalize anger, and limit losses.

MAINTAINING THE INITIATIVE

Some subjects simply defy control, particularly raconteurs who revel in telling tales from the past or in pontificating on a subject near and dear to their hearts. The difficulty here is to maintain reasonable contact with one's original research questions. One pontificator, for example, announced at the interview's outset, "Before we start I'd like to make a general observation." After twenty minutes of my trying to interject different ideas and topics, a more conversational interaction developed. It was not unusual, however, for subjects to launch into rather detailed recollections of how they had first met the president or had campaigned for his election. It is important to develop the capacity to listen respectfully but also to redirect the conversation gracefully into other channels.

A similar problem confronted Henry Graff in interviewing Lyndon Johnson. How does one manage to interrupt the president? LBJ, in particular, must have been a forceful, dominating subject. Young academics face the same problem if overcome by the status differential between themselves and their subjects. One must guard consciously against such tendencies, particularly during the early stages of a career.

MULTISUBJECT INTERVIEWS

Since interpersonal dynamics are complicated by the group setting, multisubject interviews are usually difficult to conduct. One must be concerned with rivalries and status differences that may impinge on the subjects' comments. In addition, each subject is likely to be formulating ideas within a somewhat different framework or sequence, thus making the conversational flow more difficult to follow. If such a session is unavoidable, a follow-up interview with one subject, who could be asked about hidden dynamics, may be profitable.

TELEPHONE INTERVIEWS

IT was my experience that the absence of visual cues and the greater speed at which a telephone conversation proceeds make this type of interview difficult to conduct also. Silences, necessary in order to take notes or formulate the next question, are especially anxiety-producing and place great pressure on the parties to move on. In part, this is because the subject does not observe note taking (a cue to slow down). Relying on auditory stimulation may also make it difficult for the interviewer to concentrate intently on *what* is being said, a possible explanation for why responses seem considerably briefer over the telephone. On the other hand, Paul C. Light concluded after completing sixty-nine telephone interviews and fifty-seven in person that "there was virtually no difference between the two methods in terms of the length of the interviews, or, more important, in terms of the quality of the interviews." Significantly, telephone interviews were far less expensive, averaging approximately half the cost of personal interviews.[30]

SCHEDULE FOUL-UPS

NEEDLESS to say, it is important to be prompt for appointments, allowing ample time for locating the interview site. Early arrival permits a review of questions and sometimes useful observation of the outer office. On the other hand, cancellations, reschedulings, or short delays occasioned by the subject (not at all uncommon) prove to be almost welcome inconveniences, since respondents seem eager to compensate through increased cooperation. Once, after waiting two hours in the reception room of the West Wing of the White House, I finally headed down the drive only to be called back just before reaching the guard-house. The tardy staffer had been unavoidably delayed on Capitol Hill, several times had called to let me know of the difficulty and then seemed to feel exceedingly guilty that he had kept me waiting, so much so in fact that he delayed a dinner appointment. The interview was long, perceptive, and quite candid, a treasure earned through patience. Although not all delays are quite so fruitful, several were.

Data Analysis

The mechanics of analyzing interview data will differ according to the format enployed. Standardized formats facilitate analysis insofar as responses are more comparable in form and content. In less structured formats, "analysis" often accompanies data collection, which makes it doubly important that researchers re-examine conclusions drawn during the field portion of their projects and trace inferences drawn from materials in order to avoid unwarranted conclusions.

Aberbach, Chesney, and Rockman describe one of the most ambitious efforts to provide rigorous analysis of open-ended interviews. Developing valuable data, they argue, does not necessarily require reliance on structured interviewing techniques, which elites might find objectionable: "Even if the interview situation and instrument are not highly structured, structure may be gained during the coding process. The fundamental methodological issue is not whether the questions should be structured, but when in the research procedure the investigator should impose a structure on, or derive a structure from, the respondent's opinions."[31] Thus, the data were coded for manifest items (direct responses to particular questions), latent items (mode or style of response), and global items (general traits and styles characterizing the entire interview). On the whole, the discussion illustrates the difficulties attending an effort to develop qualitative observations into data susceptible to quantitative analysis. What is most laudable, however, is the authors' willingness "to detail and to justify as explicitly as possible the transformation procedures and rules" that underlay analysis.[32]

Beyond such basic mechanics, several more fundamental issues must be considered in using interview data: subject truthfulness, interviewer effects, data contamination, and impact of the subject's current context. Both internal and external checks are available to help evaluate the accuracy and truthfulness of subject responses. Internal checks can involve attempts to evaluate a subject's reputation, including ulterior motives that might affect the interview, and efforts to evaluate the plausibility of a subject's views. Biographical data, available for many executive-branch subjects, provide one means to gauge the experience that lies behind attitudes. Still, it is virtually impossible to divine ulterior motives unless one seeks to become an investigative reporter. Evaluating the logic and internal consistency of data, on the other hand, is an easier task, although care must be taken not to discount data that are internally inconsistent; researchers must remember that the subject's perceptual framework is being analyzed, not evaluated.

External checks generally are a more productive means to evaluate data. Journalistic and academic accounts constitute one type of perspective, but collecting data from several subjects provides an even stronger basis for cross-checks. It is often advisable, in fact, to tell subjects at the time of an interview that it is merely one in a series, thereby making it clear that the materials will be subjected to an accuracy test. Again, it is important to recognize that inconsistencies across interviews may represent differing perceptions rather than an attempt to be misleading.

In addition to the dilemmas of retrospective interviewing noted earlier, there is the problem of determining whether a subject's accounts are drawn from first- or second-hand experience, and if the latter, whether they are accurate. The sharing of stories among co-workers and acquaintances in the Washington community raises the possibility that a subject's views do not emerge from his or her own experience. In this case, data may be suggestive but certainly should not be taken as authoritative.

Because interpersonal interaction is an inherent feature of

297

interviewing, researchers have an unavoidable effect on their subjects. In particular, one must be sensitive to the intrusive nature of questions and ways in which interactions may influence content. In general, more structured formats increase the risk of creating attitudes and eliciting nonauthentic responses from a subject. Interpersonal effects emerging in more informal sessions, however, may be no less influential. On the whole, elites may be more resistant to "suggestion" than nonelite subjects, although their reactions are possibly more complex and sophisticated.

It is also worth noting that interviewer effects may result from changes in the interviewer rather than the subject. Over the course of a project, interviewers improve skills, develop familiarity with the subjects' world, and may come thoroughly to empathize with the actors being studied. Thus, data collected early in a project may differ in content as well as quality from those collected later. The interviewer, therefore, is a variable filter through which respondents' data are processed.[33]

Concerns about data contamination focus on influences other than those associated with subject or researcher that might reduce the reliability of interview materials. Subjects' responses could be heavily shaped by previous contacts with other academics, popularly held and therefore conveniently available journalistic accounts of an activity or decision, and interaction with co-workers. Dexter suggests that some subject populations may have received so much attention that when questioned, "they may no longer reply with information from experience, but with the kind of information which previous interviews have taught them is desired."[34]

My own concern about these influences arose as a result of comments made during interviews. Several subjects explicitly referred to Larry O'Brien's account of congressional lobbying under Kennedy and Johnson, while others made it clear that they closely followed current press accounts of the staff as well as those that had dealt with themselves and their predecessors. Since press accounts rested heavily on office occupants as informants, in which direction should one draw the causal arrow? It also became apparent that I was not the only person interviewing these subjects. Two other academics had recently held sessions with several of them, and the Carter transition team had also been contacting many of them prior to taking office. Fortunately, my academic counterparts were most forthcoming in discussing their contacts and even made some interview materials available for my use (provided I observe the same rules of confidentiality). I also was able to consult some of the transition-team materials. Nonetheless, there was no way to determine the effect that such contacts might have had on subjects' discussions with me.

Another source of possible contamination is informal communications among the subjects themselves. Such communications may be useful if they aid the researcher in gaining access, but they could be damaging if they serve to preshape responses or result in any form of collusion. This problem is particularly relevant in research focusing on several members of the same organization or cohesive group. In such cases, the interviewer might ask subjects not to discuss specific features of the interview.

Finally, personal interviews may be conditioned by the current context. Members of the Washington community closely follow the daily press, which serves as a medium of communication as well as a source of valuable information. To what extent do interview data reflect such transitory phenomena rather than established attitudes, orientations, and cognitions? This danger is an unavoidable feature of research that is necessarily cross-sectional, that is, research that consists of views expressed at a single point in time. Respondents are likely to focus on recent issues, patterns, and examples, and unless the researcher has the luxuries of time and wealth, it is virtually impossible to undertake subsequent interviews that might reveal attitude stability.

CONCLUSION

INTERVIEWING has played a central role in the development of presidential studies, and it promises to be a useful means to pursue many questions in the future. As a data-gathering method, it requires considerable sensitivity and sophistication on the part of the researcher; it should not be regarded as the "residual method" that requires little preparation or aptitude. In particular, the method is unique in the demands it makes of personal interaction skills; researchers must be able to develop rapport with subjects in order to draw maximum benefit from their unique perspectives and from opportunities for participation in elite processes.

In comparison with legislative actors, current and former executive-branch officials may constitute a relatively unspoiled universe of subjects, and academics may thus encounter less resistance and fatigue. They are, however, likely to face other problems, particularly the need to establish subject familiarity with academic purposes and procedures and overcome fears of damage. As one subject phrased it, "They can see nothing to gain but imagine plenty to lose" in giving an interview.

Interviewing also has limitations as a method. In addition to those noted earlier, we must remember that elite interviews limit one's knowledge of the presidency to perceptions and experiences of the Washington community, a decidedly elite perspective which has been subjected to increased criticism in recent years.[35]

NOTES

1. Lewis A. Dexter, *Elite and Specialized Interviewing* (Evanston, Ill.: Northwestern University Press, 1970), 1–5.

2. Eugene J. Webb, Donald T. Campbell, Richard D. Schwartz, and Lee Sechrest, *Unobtrusive Measures: Nonreactive Research in the Social Sciences,* (Skokie, Ill.: Rand McNally, 1966), 1.

3. Dexter, *Elite and Specialized Interviewing,* 4, 11.

4. Robert Bogdan and Steven J. Taylor, *Introduction to Qualitative Research Methods: A Phenomenological Approach to the Social Sciences,* (New York: Wiley, 1975), 1–7.

5. Dexter, *Elite and Specialized Interviewing,* 132.

6. Robert L. Kahn and Charles F. Cannel, "Interviewing: Social Research," in *International Encyclopedia of the Social Sciences,* vol. 8 (New York: Macmillan 1968), 152.

7. Daniel Aaron, "The Treachery of Recollection: The Inner and Outer History," in R.H. Bremner, ed., *Essays on History and Literature,* (Columbus: Ohio State Univ. Press, 1966), 10.

8. Theodore Sarbin and Vernon L. Allen, "Role Theory," in Gardner Lindzey and Elliot Aronson, eds., *The Handbook of Social Psychology,* 2d ed., vol. 1 (Reading, Mass.: Addison-Wesley, 1968), 549.

9. Richard F. Fenno, Jr., *Home Style: House Members in Their Districts* (Boston: Little, Brown, 1978), 280.

10. Henry F. Graff, *The Tuesday Cabinet,* (Englewood Cliffs, N.J.: Prentice-Hall, 1970).

11. Fenno, *Home Style,* 254–55.

12. Dexter prefers the term "guide" to "plan," since he feels techniques should be flexible. "Schedule," much like "plan," connotes a high degree of structure, but as the text makes clear, even the most exploratory session is shaped by the interviewer's determination of subject and direction of the discussion. Thus, at a minimum, there is an implicit schedule that can be more or less rigorously followed.

13. This discussion adopts Robert Peabody's descriptions of structured and semistructured formats but differs with respect to unstructured interviews. See Robert L. Peabody, "Research on Congress: A Coming of Age, in Ralph K. Huitt and Robert L. Peabody, *Congress: Two Decades of Analysis* (New York: Harper & Row, 1969), 28–34.

14. John Kessel, *The Domestic Presidency* (Belmont, Calif.: Duxbury Press, 1975); see Appendix B, 139–44, in Kessel's work for the questionnaire including card sort and relatively fixed-response questions.

15. Stephen J. Wayne, *The Legislative Presidency* (New York: Harper & Row, 1978); Joel D. Aberbach, James D. Chesney, and Bert A. Rockman, "Exploring Elite Political Attitudes: Some Methodological Lessons," *Political Methodology* 2 (Winter 1975): 1–27 (this is a detailed description of the procedures followed in conducting and coding the interviews).

16. Ibid., 4.

17. Fenno, *Home Style,* 255.

18. Webb et al., *Unobtrusive Measures,* 33.

19. See especially Fenno, *Home Style,* 283.

20. Dexter, *Elite and Specialized Interviewing,* 137.

21. Ibid., 37.

22. Ibid., 35.

23. Dexter refers to these as "games" (Ibid., p. 136).

24. Brevity of the typical session stands in marked contrast to the extensive "soaking" in his subjects' experience described by Fenno.

25. Dexter, *Elite and Specialized Interviewing*, 60.

26. Fenno, *Home Style*, 260.

27. Charles Morrissey, "On Oral History Interviewing," in Dexter, *Elite and Specialized Interviewing*, 114.

28. Aberbach, Chesney, and Rockman, "Exploring Elite Political Attitudes," 10.

29. Fenno, *Home Style*, 280.

30. Paul Charles Light, *The President's Agenda: Domestic Policy Choice from Kennedy to Carter (with notes on Ronald Reagan)* (Baltimore: Johns Hopkins Univ. Press, 1982), Appendix A, 235.

31. Aberbach, Chesney, and Rockman, "Exploring Elite Political Attitudes," 13.

32. Ibid., 19.

33. Webb et al., *Unobtrusive Measures*, 22.

34. Dexter, *Elite and Specialized Interviewing*, 137.

35. In particular, see Bruce Miroff, "Beyond the 'Washington Community': A Broader Theory of the Presidency" (paper presented at the Annual Meeting of the American Political Science Association, Washington, D.C., Aug. 31–Sept. 3, 1979); and Valerie Bunce, "Policy Cycles and the American Presidency" (paper presented at the Annual Meeting of the Midwest Political Science Association, Cincinnati, Ohio, April 16–19, 1981).

CONTRIBUTORS

LARRY BERMAN, associate professor of political science, University of California at Davis, is the author of *The Office of Management and Budget, 1921–1979* (Princeton, N.J.: Princeton University Press, 1979) and *Planning a Tragedy* (New York: Norton, 1982).

DOM BONAFEDE is chief political correspondent for the *National Journal* and worked for more than ten years as a White House reporter. He is a frequent contributor to national magazines and is a senior writer for the *Washington Journalism Review.*

JENNIFER DETORO, director of information services, *National Journal,* was formerly director of the White House Library and chief reference librarian of the Office of Management and Budget.

GEORGE C. EDWARDS III, professor of political science, Texas A&M University, is the author of *The Policy Predicament* (with Ira Sharkansky) (San Francisco: Freeman, 1978), *Presidential Influence in Congress* (San Francisco: Freeman, 1980), *Implementing Public Policy* (Washington, D.C.: Congressional Quarterly Press, 1980), *The Public Presidency* (New York: St. Martin's, 1983), numerous articles, and several edited volumes.

LOUIS FISHER, an analyst in the Congressional Research Service, is the author of *President and Congress* (New York: Free Press, 1972), *Presidential Spending Power* (Princeton, N.J.: Princeton University Press, 1975), *The Constitution Between Friends* (New York: St. Martin's, 1978; 2nd ed. to be published by Princeton Univ. Press in 1983), *The Politics of Shared Power* (Washington, D.C.: Congressional Quarterly Press, 1981), and numerous articles.

JOHN H. KESSEL, professor of political science, Ohio State University, is the author of *The Goldwater Coalition* (Indianapolis: Bobbs-Merrill, 1968), *The Domestic Presidency* (Belmont, Calif.: Wadsworth, 1975), *Presidential Campaign Politics* (Homewood, Ill.: Dorsey, 1980), and numerous articles.

Martha Joynt Kumar, professor of political science, Towson State University, is the coauthor, with Michael Grossman, of *Portraying the Presidency* (Baltimore: Johns Hopkins University Press, 1980) and is a frequent contributor to professional meetings and journals.

G. Calvin Mackenzie, associate professor of political science, Colby College, is author of *The Politics of Presidential Appointments* (New York: Free Press, 1981), coeditor with Joseph Cooper of *The House at Work* (Austin: University of Texas Press, 1981), and numerous articles.

Joseph A. Pika, assistant professor of political science, University of Delaware, is a frequent contributor to professional meetings and journals.

Norman C. Thomas, Charles Phelps Taft Professor of Political Science, University of Cincinnati, is the author of *Education in National Politics* (New York: McKay, 1975), *Rule 9* (New York: Random House, 1966), numerous articles, and two edited volumes.

Stephen J. Wayne, professor of political science, George Washington University, is the author of *The Legislative Presidency* (New York: Harper & Row, 1978), *The Road to the White House* (New York: St. Martin's, 1980), numerous articles, and one edited volume.

INDEX

Studying the Presidency is set in eleven point Baskerville type with one point spacing between the lines. Bulmer was selected for display. The book was designed by Guy Fleming, composed by Metricomp, Inc., Grundy Center, Iowa, printed by Thomson-Shore, Inc., Dexter, Michigan, and bound by John H. Dekker & Sons, Grand Rapids, Michigan. The paper on which the book is printed bears the watermark of S.D. Warren and is designed for an effective life of at least three hundred years.

THE UNIVERSITY OF TENNESSEE PRESS : KNOXVILLE